14 ROOMS

PRESENTED BY
FONDATION BEYELER
ART BASEL
THEATER BASEL

CURATED BY
KLAUS BIESENBACH
HANS ULRICH OBRIST

ARCHITECTURE BY
HERZOG & DE MEURON

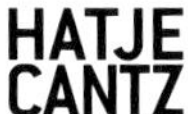

TABLE OF CONTENTS

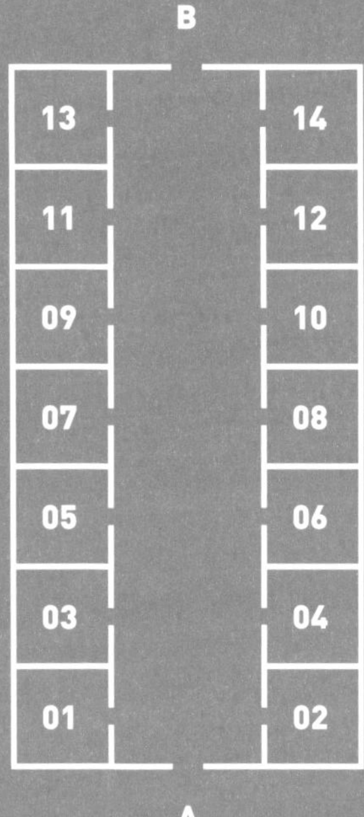

B
13
11
09
07
05
03
01
14
12
10
08
06
04
02
A

FOREWORD

SAM KELLER
MARC SPIEGLER
GEORGES DELNON

For all three producers of <u>14 Rooms</u>—Fondation Beyeler, Art Basel, and Theater Basel—this ten-day exhibition represents the latest step in a redefinition of their cultural terrain. By bringing to Basel this singular project—curated by Klaus Biesenbach, Director of MoMA PS1 and Chief Curator at Large at the Museum of Modern Art in New York, and Hans Ulrich Obrist, Co-Director and Director of International Projects at the Serpentine Gallery in London—we reflect the blurring of the line between audience and artwork, while embracing the belief that visual artists can just as well create their artworks by working with human beings as by deploying bronze, canvas, inkjets, oil paints, video, or any other method of physical production.

This marks our second collaboration with the Manchester International Festival. In 2009, the same three organizations produced the Basel edition of <u>Il Tempo del Postino</u>, co-curated by Hans Ulrich Obrist and Philippe Parreno. Originally commissioned by Alex Poots of the Manchester International Festival, it proved to be a highlight of the year within the international art scene. We expect the same reception for <u>14 Rooms</u>, which has followed a similar path. Co-commissioned by Alex Poots and Heiner Goebbels of Essen's RUHRTRIENNALE, it debuted in Manchester in 2011 as <u>11 Rooms</u>, then was staged with <u>12 Rooms</u> as part of the RUHRTRIENNALE 2012–14. In 2013, the Australian patron John Kaldor produced <u>13 Rooms</u> as part of Sydney's long-running Kaldor Public Art Projects series. And now, by bringing the latest, largely expanded version to Basel during the week of the world's most important art fair, we place <u>14 Rooms</u> squarely in the spotlight of the global art world.

For each edition the curators revised their list of artists with a view towards the context of its staging. Of the fourteen pieces in Basel, four are entirely new commissions, five are included for the first time, and five are truly historical pieces dating as far back as 1963. Given Art Basel's internationalism and the massive quantities of stellar work on view in Basel during Art Basel, the lineup naturally features a fascinatingly diverse array of talents, spanning three generations and four continents: Marina Abramović, Allora & Calzadilla, Ed Atkins, Dominique Gonzalez-Foerster, Damien Hirst, Joan Jonas, Laura Lima, Bruce Nauman, Otobong Nkanga, Roman Ondák, Yoko Ono, Tino Sehgal, Santiago Sierra, and Xu Zhen. In addition, there will be two special projects surrounding <u>14 Rooms</u>, an installation by Jordan Wolfson in the form of an epilogue and a historical documentation of an unrealized project by John Baldessari from 1970. We wish to thank each and all of the participating artists for their enthusiasm in collaborating on this unique and ambitious project, and offer our most sincere gratitude towards the curators for giving us the opportunity to stage this show in Basel. More than seventy performers worked in this production and we likewise thank them for their essential contributions.

The list of supporters who have made this singular event possible is equally long, with representatives from many different sectors. The government of Basel contributed generously to the project, allowing us to amplify its public components, and our special thanks go out to Mayor Guy Morin and to Philippe Bischof, head of the city's cultural department. From the corporate sector significant support came both from UBS and MCH Group, Art Basel's parent company. The private patrons supporting the project represent the upper echelon of major international collectors and philanthropists: Cristina Bechtler, Denise and Rolando Benedick, Joop van Caldenborgh, Ulla Dreyfus-Best, Nicoletta Fiorucci, Wendy Fisher, Francesca von Habsburg, Maja Hoffmann, Guillaume Houzé, Pierre de Labouchere, Michael Ringier, Tony Salamé, Gerd Schepers, Franz Wassmer, and Dasha Zhukova.

Designed with a high level of direct personal commitment from both of its founding partners, Herzog & de Meuron's purpose-built architecture plays a crucial role in shaping the exhibition, serving as the interstitial structure tying together a series of intimate experiences in a public space. We also thank the hardworking 14 Rooms team, under the project management of Ann-Christin Rommen, Marc Bättig, and Associate Curator Samuel Leuenberger and composed of staff from the three organizing institutions, as well experts drawn from all over the world.

Finally, we thank you, the visitors, who activate this singular project by transforming the instructions of fourteen artists into a milestone moment in the history of performance art.

Sam Keller, Director Fondation Beyeler
Marc Spiegler, Director Art Basel
Georges Delnon, Director Theater Basel

CURATORS IN CONVERSATION
SYDNEY, 2013

KLAUS BIESENBACH
HANS ULRICH OBRIST

KLAUS BIESENBACH (KB) Imagine you are with your colleagues when somebody says, "Please come to my office and close the door behind you." The mood of the situation completely changes. Or imagine you are in a high-rise building and you use the elevator. The doors close. The elevator moves to the next floor, the doors open and somebody comes in. That person is naked. The elevator doors close again. You are left alone with this naked person for several minutes. Or imagine you arrive late to a theater performance and you are ushered to walk down to the left and then enter through the door on the right. You follow the directions and end up on the stage with the actors.

Leading up to Marina Abramović's solo exhibition in 2010 at the Museum of Modern Art, there were two years of workshop sessions called The Performance Workshop, which was about performance art, live art, interpretations of scores, and how museums should preserve, collect, and exhibit this kind of art. We all sat around a huge table and the table became a stage around which everybody was equal. Nobody was on the podium, nobody was put on a pedestal; we were all participants, as we are in 13 Rooms.

So what is very important for 13 Rooms is in the title. It's not called 13 Performances because it's not thirteen performances. It's not called 13 Artists because that would be irritating. It's not called 13 Sculptures because that could be misunderstood. Instead, it's called 13 Rooms: when you enter Pier 2/3 at Sydney's Walsh Bay you discover a very large, generous warehouse space divided into thirteen rooms with doors that you can open and enter.

HANS ULRICH OBRIST (HUO) A lot of the inspiration for this show has come from the idea that live art can also be sculpture and have a duration similar to a physical object; that is, from morning to night, throughout the opening hours of a gallery. But when the last visitors leave, and the gallery closes its doors for the evening, the sculptures will all walk out as well.

One key inspiration is Gilbert & George. They, more than any other artists, have really explored this idea. Whenever they enter a room, they're living sculpture, and they did some amazing early pieces using this idea. For example, for Christmas 1969 they proposed to the Tate their idea to do a sculpture—a living sculpture—where you have, not Jesus, but Gilbert & George for the entire Christmas season during the gallery's opening hours. Or there's The Singing Sculpture, which John Kaldor brought to Australia in 1973, where they stood on a table inside the gallery and sang "Underneath the Arches" for hours at a time.

This leads us to Tino Sehgal, who draws primarily from his background in dance rather than from the traditional plastic arts. As Tino told me in conversation:

"While visual art proposes that we can extract material from natural resources to then transform it and have a product that is there to endure, dance transforms actions to obtain a product or artwork and produces and de-produces this product at the same time."

As such—and unlike natural resources—Tino's works can never be exhausted or depleted. I always remember a conversation with Eugène Ionesco, the great playwright and pioneer of the theater of the absurd. When we met in Switzerland in the 1980s, he told me that even as we spoke his play <u>La Cantatrice Chauve</u> was being performed in Paris. It had been performed in Paris every single night for more than forty years. I was a kid at that time and I was really impressed, because this piece was as permanent as all the public artworks in bronze, marble, or stone; it had been on for thousands and thousands of days.

KB The original <u>11 Rooms</u> exhibition was first commissioned by Manchester International Festival in 2011. The festival organizers are very progressive; they commissioned Björk to do her first performance piece when she normally does concerts, they commissioned Antony to perform his album <u>Swanlights</u> and they asked Hans Ulrich, Philippe Parreno, and a group of artists to present <u>Il Tempo del Postino</u> in 2010. <u>Il Tempo del Postino</u> was an exhibition in which contemporary artists Doug Aitken, Matthew Barney, Jonathan Bepler, Tacita Dean, Trisha Donnelly, Olafur Eliasson, Liam Gillick, Dominique Gonzalez-Foerster, Douglas Gordon, Carsten Höller, Pierre Huyghe, Koo Jeong-A, Arto Lindsay, Philippe Parreno, Anri Sala, Tino Sehgal, and Rirkrit Tiravanija all did exhibition pieces that were presented onstage instead of inside a museum space. Every artist had a time slot in the theater.

Dominique Gonzalez-Foerster did this beautiful piece in which an orchestra was playing music and then, one after the other, each member of the orchestra left. Doug Aitken did this piece where he initiated a live auction. I don't know what he was auctioning off, but there were auctioneers all over the theater, it was incredible. Douglas Gordon made the whole theater dark, it was completely pitch black and then Joy Division's song "Love Will Tear Us Apart" was sung a cappella. Then when the festival asked Hans Ulrich and I to do something the next year we were pretty clueless as to how we could follow that.

Then came the rules of the game. I was visiting Villa Borghese, and I'm not so much a curator who puts things in frames or on pedestals, but I was walking and I saw a sculpture here and a sculpture there and I turned around, walking in front of them, backwards and forwards to look at them. When you're in this state of heightened attention you are aware of your own time, your own volume, your own pace in that space, your proportions. You question, is that sculpture actually life-sized or is it larger than life? Is that person depicted in the sculpture older than myself or is that a younger person? So I remember that I called Hans Ulrich and said: "I'm in the Villa Borghese. Perhaps we should do an exhibition where you have one room and you just look at one sculpture, and then another room where you look at another sculpture, and then another room and another sculpture." In front of the Villa Borghese was one of these acrobats who stands still as a sculpture while being painted all silver.

As Hans Ulrich and I were on the phone, this one-word idea became a sentence, and we came to the conclusion that yes, we would do a sculpture gallery, one room after the other, but in each room it would be a "living sculpture," always a human being or more than one person, but not the artist him- or herself.

HUO We also liked the possibility of creating an exhibition that could be restaged later. We were interested in this idea because, like music, it could become part of a catalogue of works that can be performed again in different contexts. This idea of repeatability—the idea that an exhibition can be opened up and restaged like Duchamp's <u>Boîte-en-valise</u>—is something that Philippe Parreno and I certainly sought to achieve with <u>Il Tempo del Postino</u> at the Manchester International Festival in 2007. There we sought to reconceive the idea of the exhibition as a way of occupying time rather than simply occupying space. There was a conscious effort on our part to push against the constricting space and time frame of the traditional exhibition. We wanted to rethink the exhibition and all of its elements as something like a generative, evolving open score. As a curator, one often does these exhibitions where one gathers some objects or quasi-objects or non-objects for a limited amount of time and then the show is over. Exhibitions are not usually collected by museums. Selected works from exhibitions are, but not entire exhibitions. So this idea really appealed to us, particularly as there are so many artists who work with the idea of instructions and with time-based art, which allows you to curate shows according to a score.

A lot of artists are creating work in which they basically delegate to or instruct other people. We didn't invent this idea; we observed it in the world. It's something that we can reproduce endlessly and we think that quality is extremely interesting for exhibitions. Art can travel over time, not just through objects and not just through documentation. Painting has always been a lasting, valued art form. Then you have the quasi-object, which can also travel to some extent over time. Or you have ephemeral performances by artists that can't be replicated but can be documented in film, photographs, and so on. Then there's the option we're exploring here, the idea of instructional art, which creates a valid possibility for art to travel and endure. <u>13 Rooms</u> is like this: from the basic texts we can restage it in different places all over the world, and it can also happen again in 50 years' time, or when we're all dead in 100 years. It can happen somewhere completely different in the world and can be revised for different locations.

From the moment we decided on this concept it was easy, but it still didn't all click together immediately. I think curating is a slow process; you need time to research lots of different geographies. As you can see in this exhibition, the artists are from many different continents. We really wanted to find out if there is work in Latin America that relates to this idea. Is there work in Asia? Is there work in Australia? Is there work in Africa? It's still not finished, and that's why it's great that this exhibition can tour over many, many years, because we can continue to learn and build up an archive. In Australia, for example, the young artists Clark Beaumont have joined the project and John Baldessari will create a work; he'll unearth a forgotten project with a living sculpture that he first did in the late 1970s.

Slowness is not only important for the curatorial process but also for the experience of the <u>13 Rooms</u> exhibition. It's surprising, but normally people don't actually spend much time in front of artworks in museums. The Louvre once analyzed it. Even in front of the <u>Mona Lisa</u>, visitors only spend a few seconds on average—it's quite shocking. And the same thing is true for videos or time-based work in a museum. Very often, people just run through it. However, the experience of <u>13 Rooms</u> creates the opposite of this acceleration: it's deceleration. Movement is slowed down by the fact that you have to open the door—it's like entering somebody's house. It's an intimate encounter.

It can be an encounter in dark space or light space. With Marina Abramović it's painfully light. With Xavier Le Roy it's almost completely pitch black. With an artist like Tino Sehgal it's a conversation. With Santiago Sierra it's the opposite: it's total silence. With Roman Ondák it's the basic experience of exchange. With Lucy Raven, whose work was presented in <u>11 Rooms</u> and <u>12 Rooms</u>, it was an interaction mediated by technology. So there are all kinds of different interactions that can happen; they take time and slow things down. Exhibitions are fundamentally a medium of social encounter. This is why, as Roman has told me, his work is in fact "quite media-specific to the exhibition." As he says: "The exhibition has always been about individuals also seeing each other . . . It's much more related to people than to things."

KB When we started laying out the exhibition, we looked at the many different concepts. Allora & Calzadilla had a slightly different concept with their circular space for <u>Revolving Door</u>. You have Santiago Sierra who focuses on the corners of the room. With Marina it was clear that if you made the room a perfect cube then it would be a bit too intimate. Most of the rooms are actually 5 by 5 by 3.5 meters and these dimensions retain the domestic sense of the rooms. It's very important to us that it feels like entering a domestic room with a door and not a gallery. It created a more human scale, the scale of the body, and that was exactly what we needed for the performances. I think these dimensions really allow both an intimate, human scale and also the flow of the pieces. By opening the door

you step over a threshold and you overstep into somebody's privacy—like I mentioned in the beginning in the elevator scene.

HUO It's important to say that <u>13 Rooms</u> is very different in the setting of Pier 2/3 at Walsh Bay in Sydney from how it was as <u>11 Rooms</u> in Manchester and <u>12 Rooms</u> in Essen. For <u>13 Rooms</u>, the architecture within this heritage pier has been designed by Harry Seidler and Associates Architects and we're extremely pleased with how the exhibition has made a quantum leap.

The rooms remain the same dimensions and, as Klaus says, their intimacy is certainly important. So inside Pier 2/3 we've built the rooms of a house, almost as if you were to have a salon-sized room transferred into an exhibition context. Obviously, as the exhibition is restaged in different locations, the house is going to grow and we're going to have more and more rooms. In the end, it might be a big Winchester widow's house with hundreds of rooms. It might become the biggest group show in history if it continues to travel for the next fifty years! Who knows? We're very optimistic.

KB I think that exhibitions are sometimes like plots, like recurrent stories. You have an idea of the story, you have the draft of a story, you have a summary of a story, you have the long version of a story, you have the version with added chapters. I think that an exhibition is always a combination of certain stories and plots. For example, Hans Ulrich is well known for the exhibition <u>Do It</u>, which is a show that's only instructions. It's very conceptual; it's not objects, it's just instructions, which I think in today's market-driven economy is very important. Then there are other exhibitions that are considered "live art" exhibitions or "live exhibitions" or "performance exhibitions" or whatever you want to call them.

We observed that there are many artists
working with instruction pieces that involve
labor, performance, reinterpretation, dance,
or acting. Then we thought we could propose
the idea of art as an instruction even to artists
who hadn't worked that way, because it's an
important artistic practice. So you bring the
motif of the instruction exhibition together
with the motif of the performance exhibition
and there you have, together with the domestic scale and the doors, the exhibition experience of 13 Rooms. The exhibition provides
situations for experience and participation
and the possibility of direct involvement,
however you define this.

First published in the exhibition catalogue 13 Rooms, the
27th Kaldor Public Art Project in Australia, presented in
Sydney, April 2013.

CURATORS IN CONVERSATION
BASEL, 2014

KLAUS BIESENBACH
HANS ULRICH OBRIST

HANS ULRICH OBRIST (HUO) One year after Sydney and three years after the first project in Manchester, we are presenting <u>14 Rooms</u> here in Basel! At the same time, it still feels as if everything has only just begun!

KLAUS BIESENBACH (KB) Although it might look as if we have only just started with our work, it's also important to note that we learned and took a lot away from each of the three previous projects. From the example of Sydney we learned how it is possible for an exhibition to spread out in the urban context: we were at a pier in the harbor, near the museum and the opera. A long line formed in front of the exhibition every day. As a result of this line, the exhibition spread out toward the city in an organic way and got people talking about it. Wherever large crowds of people gather a new public and urban space is created, initiating new levels of dialogue. This idea of public space in connection with the exhibition is something that we want to take with us to Basel.

HUO For <u>14 Rooms</u> it's not only the exhibition architecture that is important, but also the particular urban architectural environment where the exhibition takes place.

In the first edition of the project in Manchester, we built simple, almost Spartan rooms in the Manchester City Gallery. In Essen, the exhibition was housed in David Chipperfield's Museum Folkwang, which gave the project a special atmosphere. In Sydney with Harry Seidler, it was the first time that an architect designed the concept for the exhibition himself. In his version, the design resembled a small village. The idea for Basel, which we came up with in dialogue with Marc Spiegler and Sam Keller, was to have architects develop an concept.

We invited Herzog & de Meuron to create yet again that, importantly, not only focuses on what happens in the exhibition, but also how what occurs around an exhibition is interwoven with the urban fabric. Even though Herzog & de Meuron built the amazing new exhibition hall with the oculus for Messe Basel, they proposed that the project take place in one of the old exhibition halls which is a bit removed from the big art and fair hubbub and is therefore also inscribed in the urban context in a very different way.

KB For us it was important that Herzog & de Meuron, who have indeed built such outstanding museums all around the world, here suddenly went into an old existing structure, offering a type of public urban space for regular civilians—in contrast to the new hall at Messe Basel, where the space is only meant for potential buyers and potential business.

It is interesting that THE global museum architects are local in one place of the world.

I find this a beautiful metaphor, as well as the fact that the local strength, what the city is best known for, is the art market. Basel is the mother of art fairs, and it became clear to us that we had to incorporate this fact into our deliberations. It is now the case that, although 14 Rooms is taking place during the time of the biggest art market week, the architectural situation sets it quite deliberately apart, as an independent exhibition organized and situated separately.

HUO In our cities there are fewer and fewer public spaces where people don't have to justify their presence through consumption. This is exactly the reason why Herzog & de Meuron came up with idea of making the exhibition hall a public space. The hall will be open on all sides and entry will be free of charge.

KB It will be a public space where nothing will be sold, but instead—inspired by Tony Bennett—it will be place that is simply social, where people go, where they don't have to buy anything, but deal with in verbal matters. At our exhibition people can, on the one hand, see a seriously curated art exhibition, and on the other there is also a social space where people can talk and exchange ideas about the exhibition. In Manchester, Essen, and Sydney this took place where people were waiting in front of the exhibition. Douglas Gordon once said that art is often an excuse to have a dialogue about essential topics like loneliness, cyborgs or "selfies," fear, shame or vanity. I believe that our exhibition presents art that's about life and not art about art.

HUO The concept comes not only from Tony Bennett but also from Richard Sennett, who discusses the disappearance of public space in his books. What interests us as well is this idea of opening toward the outside, the creation of public spaces, and how it is possible to create such spaces. The new concept of the mirrored walking hall also contributes to this: visitors stroll between the rooms and through their reflected images become part of 14 Rooms themselves. Around the actual exhibition there will be other attractions that are freely accessible for anyone interested. Besides offering food and drink and places to sit, we are also showing the Baldessari archive. This work consists of the documentation of an early work by John Baldessari, which he proposed to MoMA in 1970. In Unrealized Proposal for Cadaver Piece, Baldessari wanted to exhibit a cadaver in order to address how death is dealt with in art and in society. It's not surprising that it still hasn't been possible to realize this project, although we attempted to do so in Manchester. The archive presents our endless communication with local and global bureaucracy and authorities.

KB With Otobong Nkanga's work, the theme of opening up public space takes on a further dimension. Her work Diaspore deals with migration, exile, and uprooting, looking back at the home left behind and forward at a new country. Uprooted exiles appear with the same plant, the Queen of the Night, a plant that originally comes from South Asia and has itself experienced the process of migration. Public space today has to be available to a colorfully intermixed population and to open up more and more. The work by Santiago Sierra also alludes to this. He places war veterans in the corner and confronts visitors with the question of how society should deal with such people and how far it needs to open up to them.

HUO The digital age is indirectly present in 14 Rooms in the need to once again produce live experience: the fact that so many artists today want to have this live experience, like the fact that live concerts are once again important in music, can be interpreted as a reaction to digitization. Perhaps this can even be interpreted as a form of resistance. But up to now the digital age has not been directly visible. This is why we are now presenting Ed Atkins's avatar project. Atkins projects a digital figure that is quite similar to him and in front of this projection has a doppelganger. With Ed Atkins, the idea of the avatar comes into 14 Rooms for the first time. Furthermore, in dialogue with Tino Sehgal we decided to present his work from 2004, This is competition. The work deals with a form of reciprocity, two people attempting to talk about one and the same work and constantly complementing each other through the condition of always taking turns in the sequence of words. Based on an algorithm, it analyzes the inner workings of the market and its processes. The two people are forced to interact with one another, have to work together. What develops from this is a feedback loop that never comes to an end. This idea broaches the topic of cybernetics, which already played an integral role for the British architect Cedric Price with his visionary idea for the Fun Palace: to create a place that remains participatory and open and can always be altered.

Which leads us to the idea with Jordan Wolfson, whose robot will inhabit one of the rooms.

KB Jordan Wolfson presents an animatronic robot that stands in front of a mirror and reacts to each individual visitor by means of motion control. The visitor too stands in front of the mirror, and sees the robot and her reflection as well as him- or herself reflected. The robot and her reflection stares visitors directly in the eyes via a motion sensor. This is quite concretely an extension into the twenty-first century, even though we say that 14 Rooms goes back to communication, to direct unmediated experience—where a person comes to a real place where a real person begins to act in front of him or presents a performance that is choreographed extremely strenuously or with great concentration. That is a huge luxury! Being one-to-one on an equal footing with a performer, interpretor, or actor . . . in contrast, here is this robot that blurs the distinction between the real performer and mediation in a disconcerting way. Something similar occurs in the work of Ed Atkins: the image of the artist recorded on video appears on a flat screen before which it is simultaneously re-produced by a live performance, a live experience, something that is actually the reverse of digitization. Jordan Wolfson's cyborg, this loner in its isolation, shows us what will become of us in reality if we sit in front of a digital device: we will isolate ourselves completely.

Another interesting aspect in the work of Jordan Wolfson is the obsession with portraying ourselves. Another work on this topic has been part of the exhibition for years—Joan Jonas's Mirror Check, in which a young woman looks at her body with a hand mirror. Today you would inspect yourself using an iPhone, you'd turn the camera around and look at yourself with the iPhone. It's very important that we address this idea of the "selfie," of self-perception.

Works like Yoko Ono's provide a very different allusion to the digitized, isolated role of the individual in the twenty-first century. She wrote Grapefruit, a book full of instructions, in the 1960s. You could describe it as a prototype for Twitter. Yoko Ono today has 4.7 million Twitter followers, probably because she, as an artist, already did something like Twitter forty years ago. These succinct little truths consisting of 140 characters that get under one's skin, this is something that Yoko Ono has been doing for forty years.

But let's go back again to Ed Atkins: the image of the artist recorded on video appears on a flat screen next to which a live performance is presented—the video is reproduced backwards, so to speak, the reverse of recording takes place. It's not like when someone experiences something in real time, like people singing on stage at the Metropolitan Opera, and it is recorded digitally and projected simultaneously everywhere in the world. No, here the live performer, in a type of karaoke, attempts to reproduce, act, and speak the narration captured in the video in real time right next to the video. People in Milwaukee or India go to the cinema at the same time as the Met Opera performance takes place and watch the Met Opera. This is the reverse, someone reproducing the recorded performance and incarnating it, in the truest sense of the word, once again simultaneously. But it's not only about the performer, it's ultimately about the visitor, because here the visitor as a living person also enters the exhibition space in real time, in real space: it is real! Here and now!

HUO Exactly, and that's why the importance of instructions for this exhibition now has to be emphasized. The reader of the catalogue has a manual with instructions for visiting the exhibition, and the interpreters too have instructions for how they have to realize the individual works. Since these instructions exist, the same exhibition can be realized again and again in the future, just like theater pieces or operas. Two of the participants in the exhibition, Yoko Ono and Bruce Nauman, structure their works based on such instructions and the corresponding participation of the observer. Yoko Ono wrote instructions during her childhood in Japan and created her visionary Grapefruit book as a young artist. Grapefruit was a really big inspiration for Do It and in turn also for 11 Rooms.

Such instructions, which can be repeated in a type of loop, also appear in the work by Bruce Nauman, Wall-Floor Positions, a video work from 1968 showing the artist in his studio. For nearly an hour, Nauman performs a sequence of movements that take place in dialogue with wall and floor. For 14 Rooms he stipulated that the performers repeat his actions. When a performer has gone through the selection of twenty-eight positions, that performer leaves the room and the next comes in to repeat the same loop. It is specifically this concept of loops that was important to us from the very beginning. In this respect, the participation of Bruce Nauman is a dream come true!

If one speaks about instructions, one automatically comes to speak about the participatory aspect of a work. Dominique Gonzalez-Foerster always says that the viewer constitutes at least half of the work. This is by all means true in her work. But we are not allowed to say here what Dominique Gonzalez-Foerster's work for 14 Rooms is, since visitors have to find out by observation what the instructions could be.

KB If an instruction has to remain secret, but the viewer, nonetheless, constitutes at least half the work, this leads to the interesting question of who the other half of the work is. Yoko Ono will install her work Touch in a completely darkened room. The instruction "Touch" implies that visitors are supposed to touch one another. With this, Yoko Ono breaks the last taboo in our society, namely, not only that we can no longer look at each other directly, but Touch goes even farther: we should even touch each other. There is a break with physical distance, with integrity, with the untouchability of strangers. Yoko Ono plays with the interaction of one visitor with another, and what will actually take place in this dark room is the question. What happens when it is full? What happens when it is almost empty? When it is almost empty the touch of a stranger is a more intimate transgression than when the room is full and undesired bodily contact between many people happens unintentionally, as in public transportation, where it is a given.

HUO This reminds me of Yves Klein's Le Vide and Arman's Le Plein. Arman responded to Yves Klein's empty exhibition Le Vide in 1958 at the Galerie Iris Clert in Paris with his exhibition Le Plein in 1960, for which he stuffed the same gallery full of garbage.

Normally exhibitions have a very limited lifespan. They come, they go, there is a tour, it is arranged logically and pragmatically, it goes to two or three cities and costs are reduced as a result. Normally exhibitions are disbanded, it would be highly complex and very costly to reconstruct them at a later point in time. For instance, it would be nearly impossible to put together again the first Berlin Biennale. It would no longer be possible to get particular works because they no longer exist.

Our exhibition, however, functions according to another logic. Just like Do It, this exhibition is a type of loop in time. It will never die because it continues to exist in the form of instructions. It may well be the case that a curator-student or a museum director will bring this exhibition back to life again in a hundred years. That's why it's important for us to pass on lots of information by means of this conversation and the catalogue. Pierre Boulez once told Philippe Parreno and me when we worked on Il Tempo del Postino: "That's the score of the score!"—that is the additional information that, beyond the notes, is there so that people in the future know how a musical piece by Xenakis, Pierre Boulez, or Stockhausen should be played.

After three years from 11 Rooms to 14 Rooms, it's possible to gauge whether it's slowly coming to an end or not. During the preparations for this exhibition, Klaus and I had many ideas for who might take the fourteenth room here in Basel. We would have liked to invite ten to twenty artists, but the Fondation Beyeler and Art Basel told us that forty rooms would be a bit too much . . . although it was painful, we had to limit ourselves. However, as already in Sydney, we are certain that we could continue our project for years, if not for decades. What optimistic prospects!

THE ARTISTS

MARINA ABRAMOVIĆ
ALLORA & CALZADILLA
ED ATKINS
DOMINIQUE GONZALEZ-FOERSTER
DAMIEN HIRST
JOAN JONAS
LAURA LIMA
BRUCE NAUMAN
OTOBONG NKANGA
ROMAN ONDÁK
YOKO ONO
TINO SEHGAL
SANTIAGO SIERRA
XU ZHEN

MARINA ABRAMOVIĆ
LUMINOSITY, 1997

THE PERFORMER, EXPOSED, NUDE, AND WITH HER ARMS EXTENDED, SITS ON A BICYCLE SEAT PLACED HIGH UP ON THE WALL. SHE IS ILLUMINATED IN BRIGHT LIGHT AND APPEARS BEFORE THE VIEWER TO BE FLOATING IN SUSPENDED ANIMATION.

Since the beginning of her career in Belgrade in the early 1970s, Marina Abramović has pioneered performance as a visual art form. The body has always been both her subject and her medium. Exploring her physical and mental limits in works that ritualize simple actions, Abramović has withstood pain, exhaustion, and danger in her quest for emotional and spiritual transformation.

As a student at the Academy of Art, Belgrade, Abramović created texts, drawings, and conceptual works. In the early 1970s she began her work with the medium of performance, using her body as a medium and exploring the interaction between artist and audience. In the early Rhythm series (1973–75) she carried out difficult, sometimes violent, gestures that tested the capabilities and limitations of the audience as a witness.

Between 1975 and 1988 Abramović worked in collaboration with the German artist Ulay. Their shared work over this period negotiated duality and togetherness, gender-specific roles, and the polarity of male and female bodies.

After returning to a solo career in 1989 Abramović continued to pursue new terrain with performances that explored, among other things, her biography—including the history and mythology of the Balkans, her homeland. She continued to travel around the world to places such as Brazil, India, and Japan, learning from different cultural practices.

In 2005 she undertook a revolutionary series called Seven Easy Pieces at the Guggenheim Museum in New York. In it, she re-performed seminal early performance artworks of the 1960s and 1970s by Joseph Beuys, Bruce Nauman, Vito Acconci, Valie Export, Gina Pane, and herself. In 2010 her major retrospective at the Museum of Modern Art in New York included The Artist

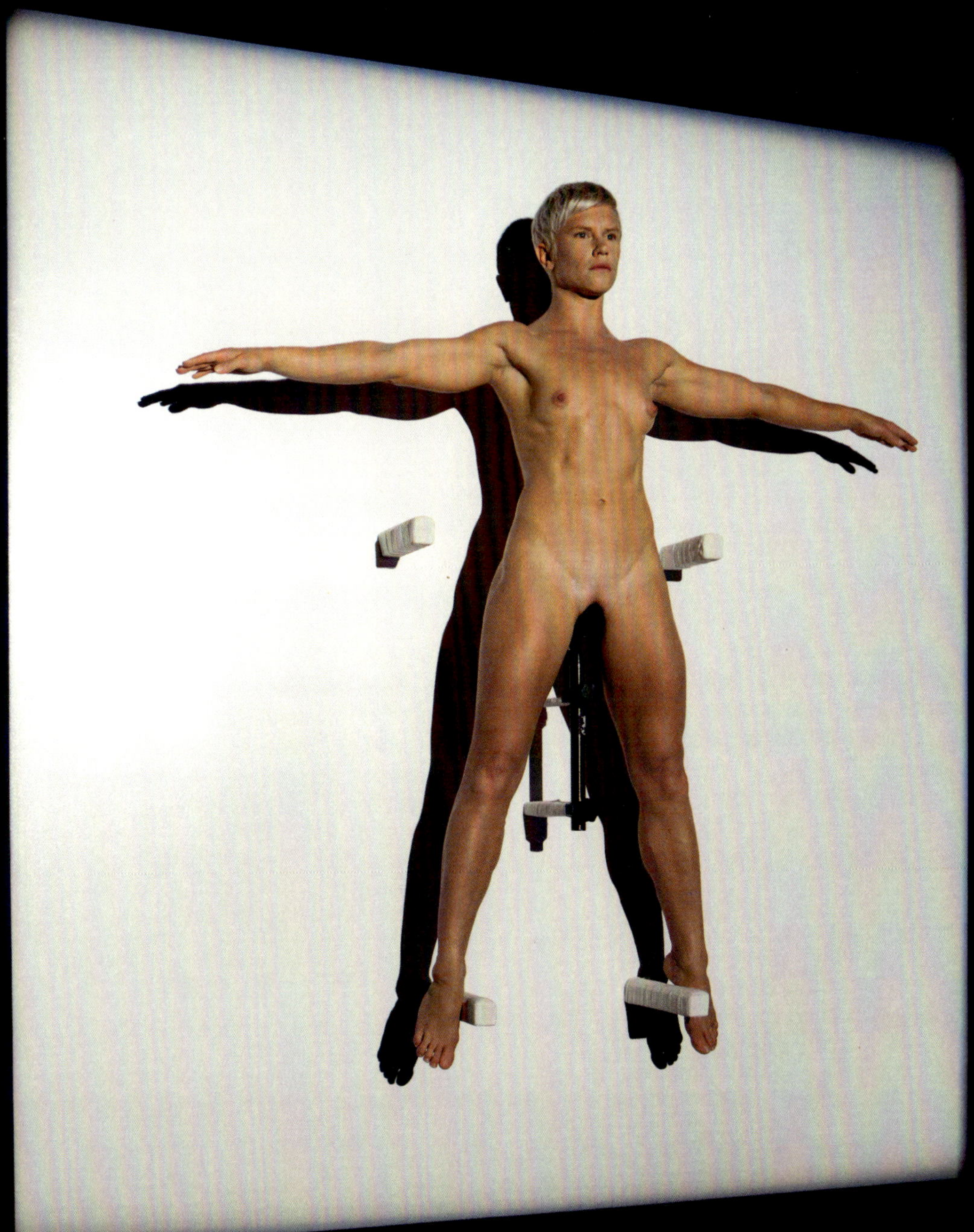

is Present, a new piece in which Abramović spent 736 hours and 30 minutes inside the museum, silently seated at a table across from which over 1000 visitors took up an empty seat one at a time.

In Luminosity, first performed by Abramović in 1997, the artist sat on a bicycle seat placed high up on the wall, bathed in light. She appeared to float in suspended animation before the viewer. This extraordinarily demanding piece, both physically and mentally, in which the performer is positioned precariously for thirty minutes at a time, requires intense focus and discipline. Abramović's spot-lit nakedness gives the audience a voyeuristic sensation but the performer seems at once vulnerable and strong.

Abramović performed Luminosity only three times—in Amsterdam (1997) with a duration of sixty minutes, then later at Sean Kelly Gallery New York (1997) and Grosse Halle, Reitschule, Bern (1998), each time for ninety minutes. The piece is re-performed for 14 Rooms.[1] As Abramović explains: "It's really a work about loneliness, about pain, and about spiritual elevation. About luminosity and about the transcendental quality of the human being in general."[2] (TL)

[1] Performed previously in these contexts: 11 Rooms at the Manchester Art Gallery during the Manchester International Festival in 2011; 12 Rooms at the Museum Folkwang during the RUHRTRIENNALE International Arts Festival 2012–14 in 2012; 13 Rooms at Kaldor Public Art Projects during the 27th Kaldor Public Art Project in 2013.
[2] Artist's audio statement, www.moma.org/explore/multimedia/audios/190/1994 (accessed May 2014).

—

p. 27 Marina Abramović, Luminosity, 1997.
Performed for 13 Rooms at Kaldor Public Art Projects during the 27th Kaldor Public Art Project in 2013.
p. 29 (detail) Marina Abramović, Luminosity, 1997.
Performed for 12 Rooms at the Museum Folkwang during the RUHRTRIENNALE International Arts Festival 2012–14 in 2012.

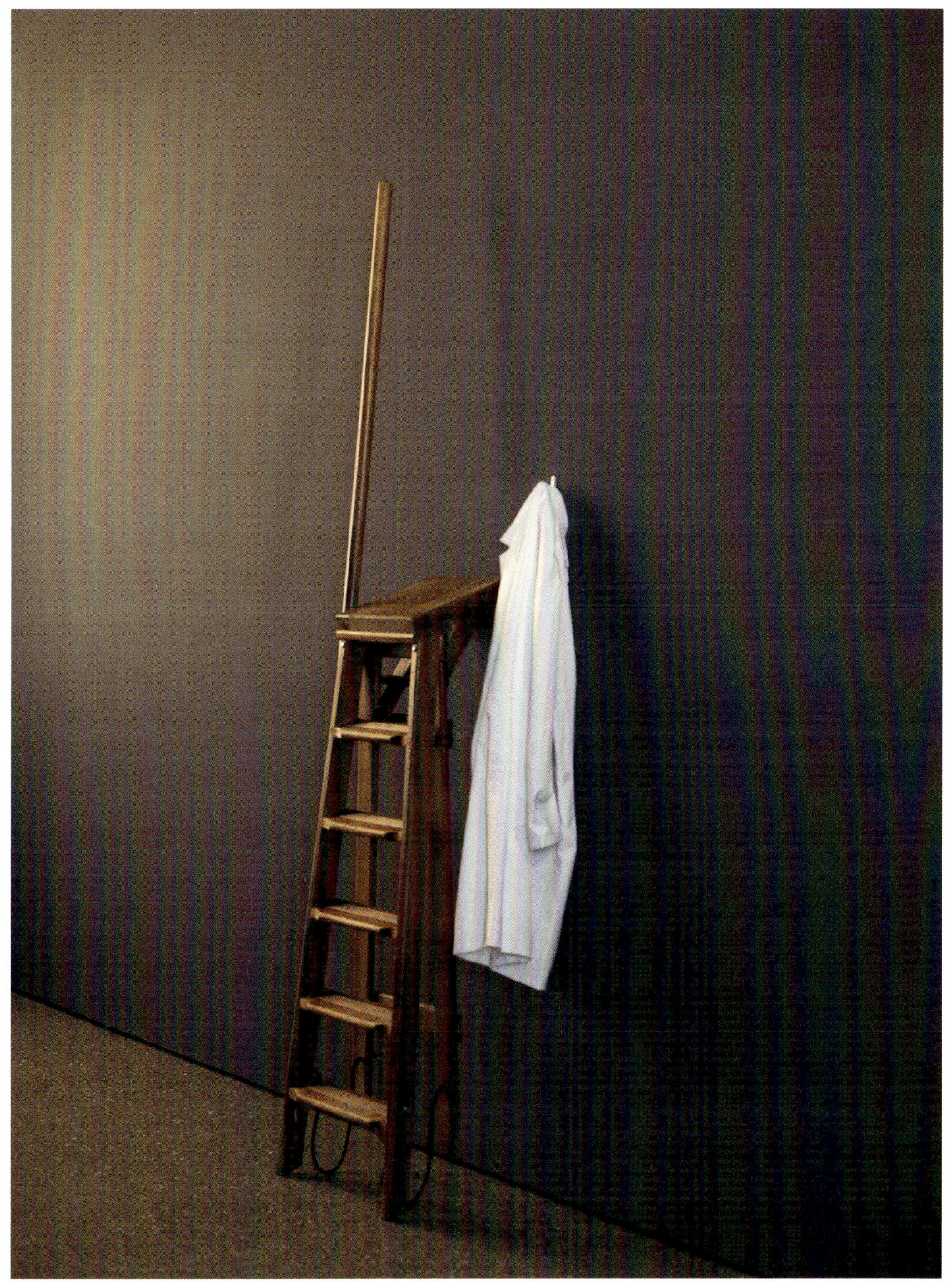

ALLORA & CALZADILLA
REVOLVING DOOR, 2011

A GROUP OF DANCERS IS LINED UP FROM WALL TO WALL, BLOCKING THE VISITOR'S WAY. THEIR MOVEMENTS ARE BASED ON POLITICAL PROTESTS, MILITARY MARCHES, AND CHORUS LINES, AMONG OTHERS. THE LINE WILL SLOWLY ROTATE, OBLIGING THE PUBLIC TO MOVE FROM ONE SIDE OF THE ROOM TO THE OTHER AS IF PASSING THROUGH A REVOLVING DOOR.

Jennifer Allora and Guillermo Calzadilla have been collaborating as an artist duo for fifteen years. Through their experimental combination of performance, sculpture, video, and sound they explore the histories and meanings embedded in culture, reconfiguring and recontextualizing various elements—from architecture and objects to music and bodily movement—to create their poetic artworks.

One of their most famous works, Stop, Repair, Prepare: Variations on "Ode to Joy" for a Prepared Piano, was first performed in 2008 at Haus der Kunst in Munich before acclaimed presentations at the Museum of Modern Art, New York (2010) and as Kaldor Public Art Project 26 at the State Library of Victoria, Melbourne (2012). To produce the work the artists cut a large hole from the center of a Bechstein grand piano and made adjustments to the pedals to allow the performer to enter the piano and play it from within—effectively upside down and backwards. The composition performed is the fourth movement of Beethoven's Ninth Symphony, known as "Ode to Joy" and understood as a testament to human fraternity. The hole in the piano renders two full octaves inoperative, creating variations on the corporeal as well as the sonic dimension of the player/instrument dynamic, the signature melody being played, and its pre-established connotations.

Allora & Calzadilla represented the United States at the 2011 Venice Biennale with their exhibition Gloria. Included in this exhibition was Track and Field, an upside-down military tank transformed into a treadmill for a series of athletic performances by the American Olympic track and field team. In the artists' words: "As artists, we are interested in practices that foreground the material nature of sense and that place the body

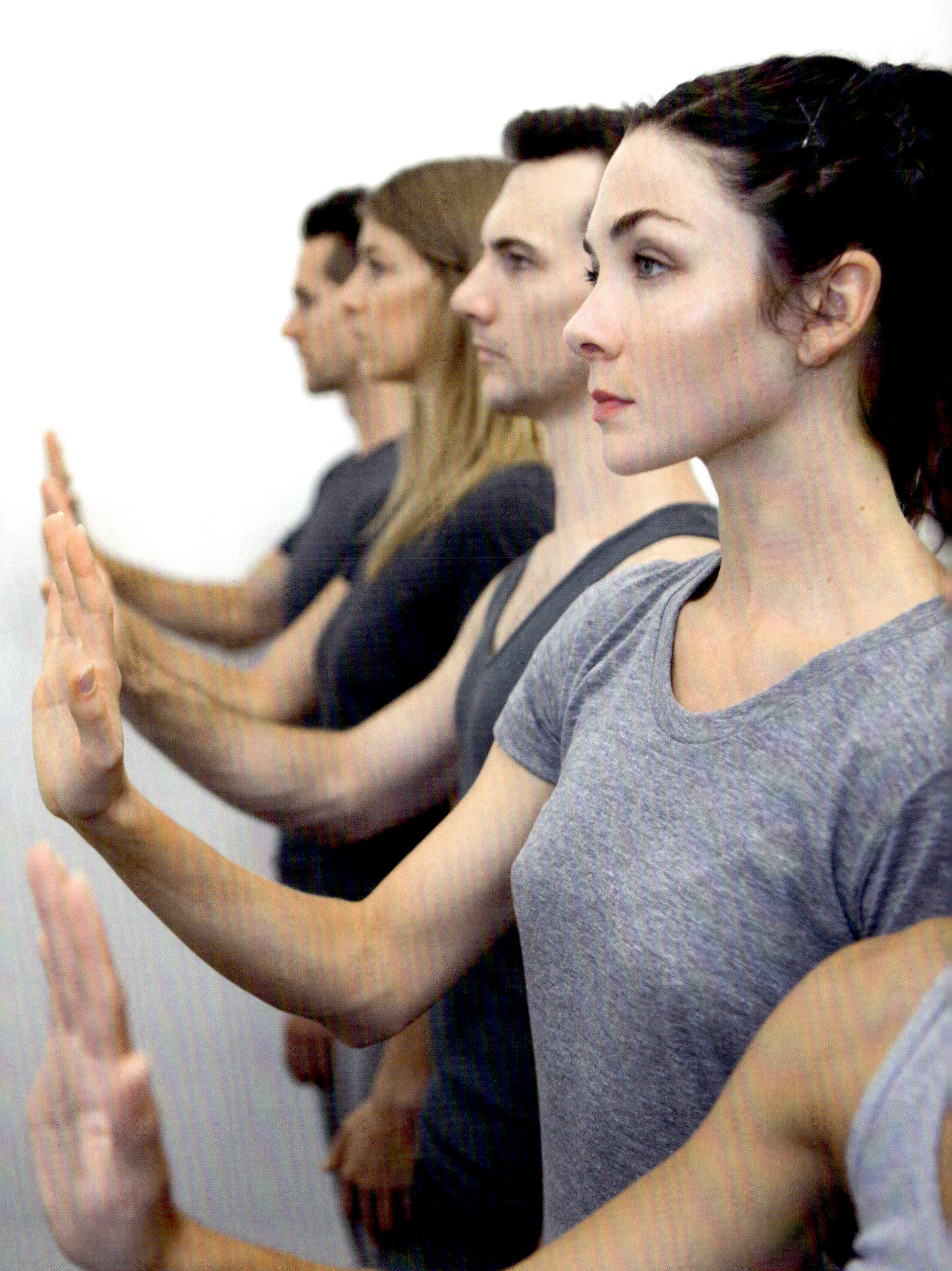

in the center of public forms of subjectivity linked to the organization of power."[1]

In their recent work for documenta 13, Raptor's Rapture (2012), a performer plays the oldest musical instrument found to date—a flute carved by homo sapiens 35,000 years ago from the wing bone of a griffon vulture—in the presence of a living griffon vulture, an evolutionary descendant of one of the oldest creatures to have inhabited the earth and currently threatened with extinction.

In their work for 14 Rooms,[2] titled Revolving Door (2011), a group of dancers spontaneously form a line, or human barricade, that extends from one end of a wall to the other. The line slowly rotates in a circular motion, allowing the public to move from one side of the room to the other as if passing through a revolving door and, paradoxically, making the barricade formation permeable. They circle the space in formation, delivering choreographed movements drawn from political protests, military marches, and chorus lines, among others. A poetic reflection on the many different gestures we create in unison, Revolving Door creates a complex dynamic between the group and the individual. (SF)

[1] Calzadilla quoted in Carlos Motta, "Allora & Calzadilla" (interview with the artists), BOMB, vol. 109, Fall 2009.
[2] Performed previously in these contexts: 11 Rooms at the Manchester Art Gallery during the Manchester International Festival in 2011; 12 Rooms at the Museum Folkwang during the RUHRTRIENNALE International Arts Festival 2012–14 in 2012; 13 Rooms at Kaldor Public Art Projects during the 27th Kaldor Public Art Project in 2013.

—

p. 31 (detail), p. 33 (bottom) Allora & Calzadilla, Revolving Door, 2011.
Performed for 13 Rooms at Kaldor Public Art Projects during the 27th Kaldor Public Art Project in 2013.
p. 33 (top) Allora & Calzadilla, Revolving Door, 2011.
Performed for 11 Rooms at the Manchester Art Gallery during the Manchester International Festival in 2011.

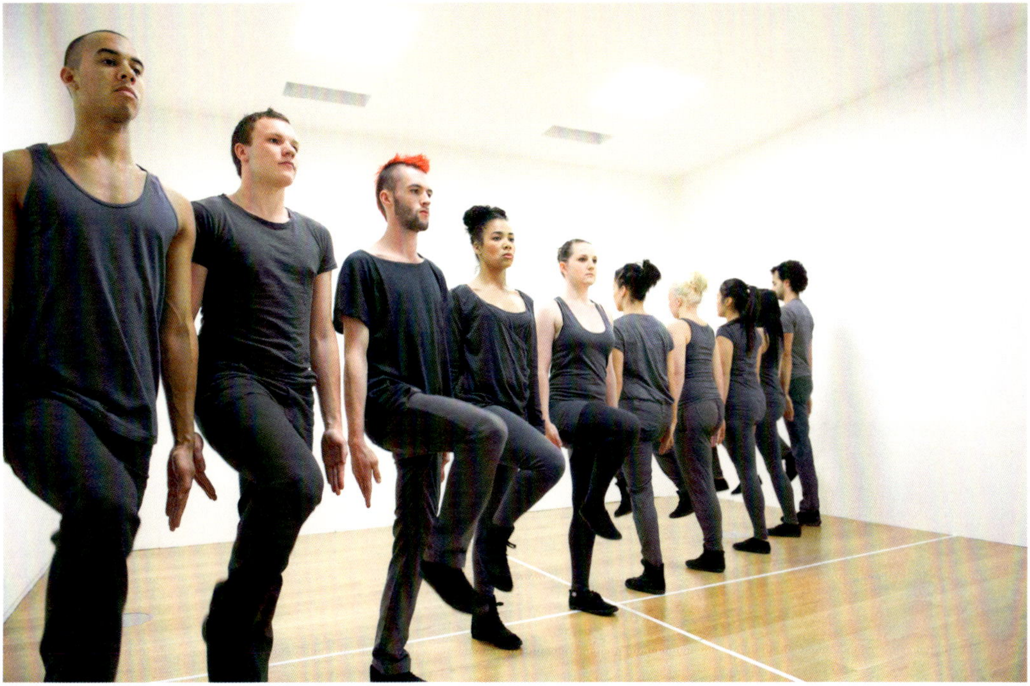

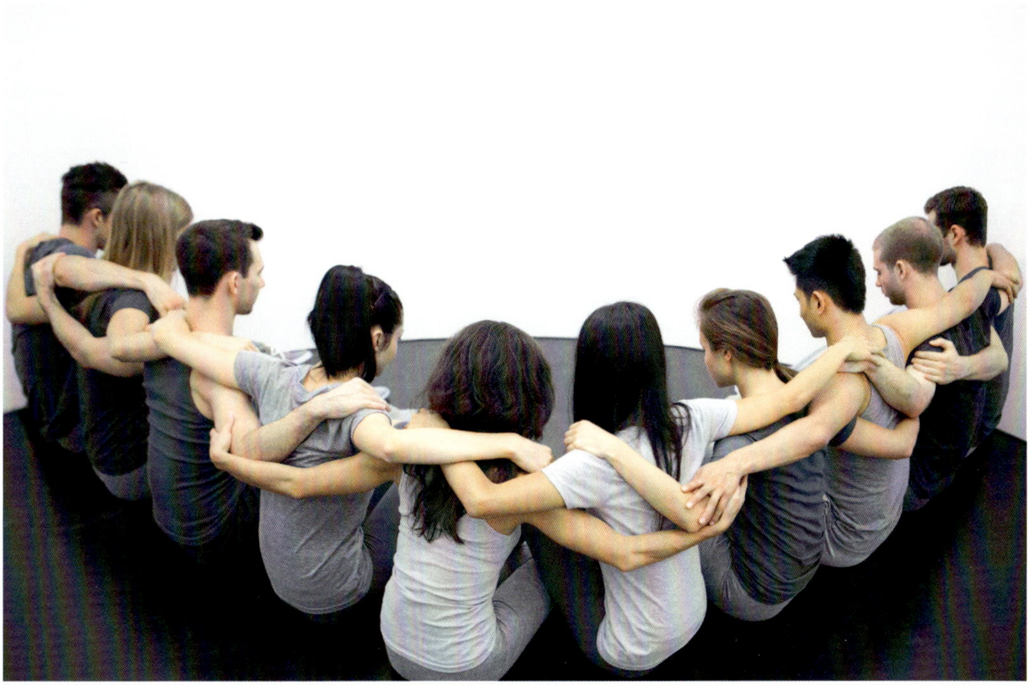

ED ATKINS
NO-ONE IS MORE "WORK" THAN ME, 2014

ON A LARGE UNADORNED FLAT SCREEN A 1:1 SCALE 3-D HEAD, SHAVED AND TATTOOED, BIDS FOR HIS HUMANITY. A REAL-LIFE PERSON IS PRESENT, PERFORMING ACCORDING TO THE DIRECTIVE TO "BEAR WITNESS TO" THE AVATAR'S SIX-HOUR PITCH AT BEING A CONVINCING PERSON.

Ed Atkins makes work in the process of life's mediation through contemporary digital technologies: where and how bodies and beings are represented, to themselves and to others, and in what way our experiences are more or less verifiable, fed back to an embodied and immanent self. Using CGI, HD video, and audio he explores these possibilities by explicitly generating life-like imagery and effects to underscore the mortal and irrecoverable aspects of experience, resisting the material deferral innate to digital technique.

Atkins works alone, generating much of the animation, the writing, the sound, and the performance himself. The precise digital arrangements of his videos simulate such a precise skewering of the humanesque that seduction and repulsiveness are frequently simultaneous responses, as empathy segues cheaply into misrecognition and alienation.

One of the most extreme ways in which the Internet has changed our lives is in the ways in which we relate to one another, get close to one another, become intimate with one another.

No-one is more "work" than me (2014), a new work developed by Atkins for 14 Rooms, originates from the paradoxical cinch of anonymity and extreme intimacy that has become so ubiquitous in online relations, so fundamentally the movement of digitized likenesses and emotions. This six-hour surrogate performance via a stock, decapitated shaven-headed male avatar explores its fundamentally elsewhere corporeality—the complications of his humanity or lack thereof—feelings, a sensitive body, coursing desires—and the ambivalent politics at the heart of its very subject. In the same room, a more conventionally manifest human will be present, improvising, responding to the avatar's six-hour pitch; both figures ambiguous in their state and their possible relation. (EA)

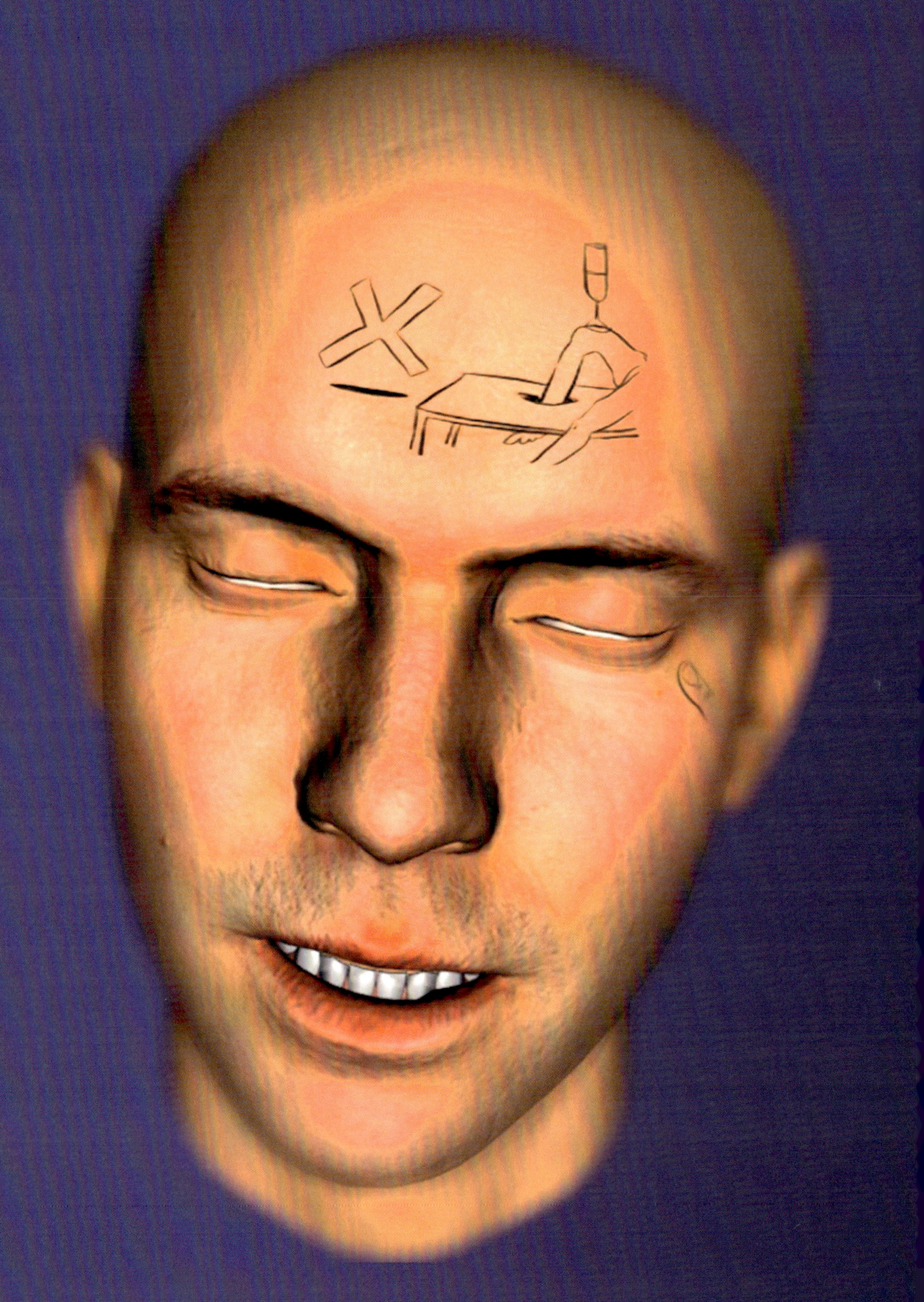

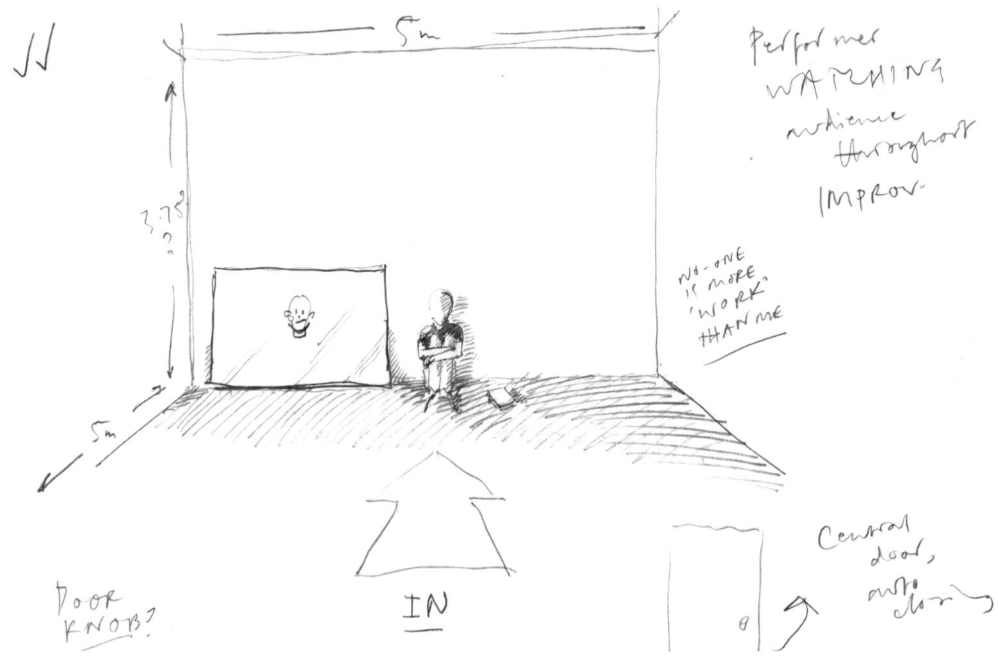

pp. 35, 37 (both) Ed Atkins, Production images for <u>No-one is more "work" than me</u>, 2014
p. 36 Ed Atkins, Sketch for <u>No-one is more "work" than me</u>, 2014

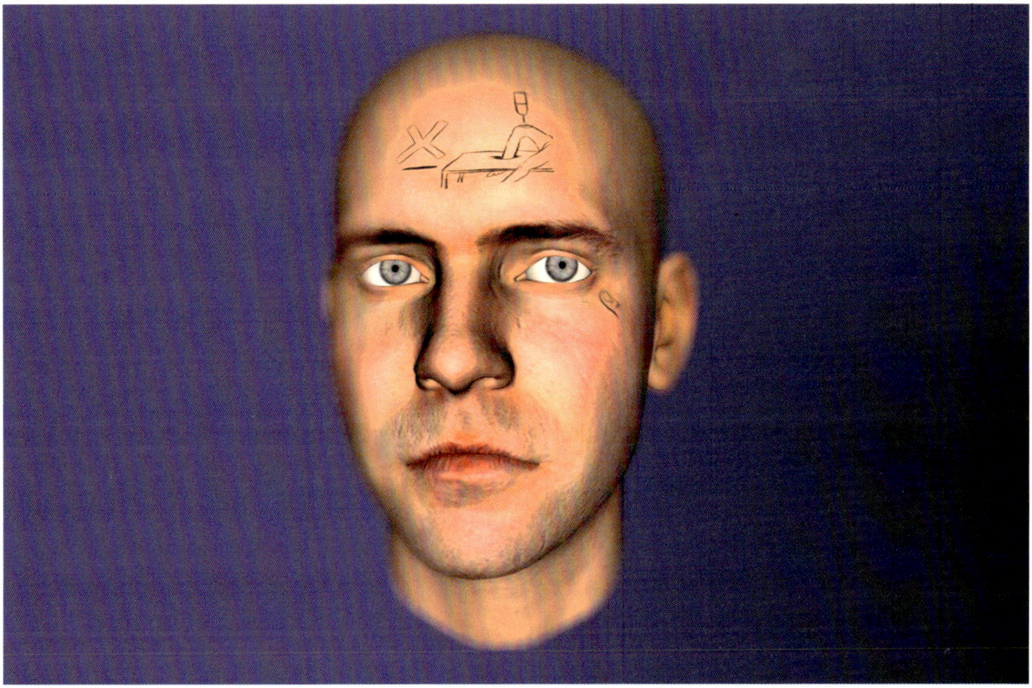

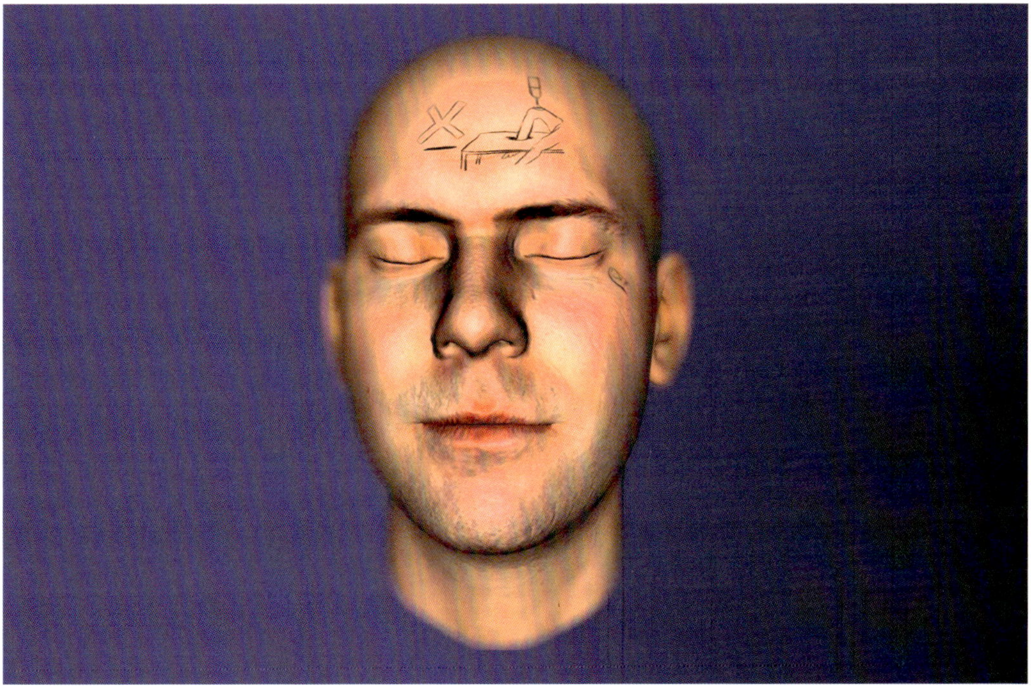

DOMINIQUE GONZALEZ-FOERSTER
R.145, 2014

THE VISITOR'S PERCEPTION OF THE SPACE AND HIS OR HER EMOTIONAL STATE WILL BE CHALLENGED THROUGH MEANS CHARACTERIZED BY AN INCREDIBLY CONVINCING BUT SUBTLE MINIMALISM, ACTIVATED ONLY THROUGH THE AUDIENCE'S PARTICIPATION. THE CONTENT OF THE PRESENTATION IS KEPT A SECRET.

Since the late 1980s, Dominique Gonzalez-Foerster has created a wonderfully subtle yet complex oeuvre including films, installations, and performances which often discuss the dimensions of space and time. She focuses on urban structures and the world of architecture and theater and, with the eye of a scenographer, creates mise-en-scène-like installations that portray multidimensional narratives. For the artist, "the most powerful moment in art is that of heterogeneity. It's not characterized by one style, one signature, or one idea."[1]

In 2007, Gonzalez-Foerster was part of the large scale group exhibition Il Tempo del Postino. The exhibition aimed at redefining how the visual arts can be experienced by determining the "appropriate" time an audience must spend with one particular piece to grasp it. A series of performances was staged in a classical theater with an auditorium where one piece followed the other. Gonzalez-Foerster presented Sol is going home, which consisted of a full orchestra playing a segment of Beethoven's Sixth Symphony. After a few measures were played, the first musician left the orchestra pit. One after the other followed, until only one was left behind to finish the piece alone. To create a natural atmosphere, the artist provided only a few staging elements such as the music, the light, and the scenography and left it to the musicians to leave the room in whichever way they wanted.

Between 2008 and 2012 Dominique Gonzalez-Foerster staged a number of performances in collaboration with Ari Benjamin Meyers. These included such works as NY.2022 at the Solomon R. Guggenheim Museum in New York, K.62/K85 at Performa in New York, and T.451 in Tensta Konstall in Stockholm. Driven to emulate an audience-based experience, the two melted musical scores and architectural bibliography

The Trial
The Castle
Franz Kafka

Today i wrote nothing
Daniil Kharms

7 Stories
Sigzmund Krzhizhanovsky

Plan de Evasion
Adolfo Bioy Casares

El viaje vertical
Enrique Vila-Matas

structures to create a performed narrative. Inspired by specific films, music, and literature, the spectator is drawn into a shared experience of dispersal. Gonzalez-Foerster takes joy in the process of fragmentation, and continued her collaboration with Tristan Bera. Together they developed the piece <u>M.2062</u>, an opera consisting of different lecture performances in which fictional and historical characters like Ludwig II, Scarlett O'Hara, Edgar Allan Poe, and Lola Montez appear; they wander, type words into machines, and exchange ideas of poetry and imagination.

The concept of her presentation for <u>14 Rooms</u> is kept a secret. The visitor's perception of the space and his or her emotional state will be challenged by means characterized by the incredibly convincing but subtle minimalism that is found in Dominique Gonzalez-Foerster's work. (SL)

[1] Artist statement, taken from an interview with Hans Ulrich Obrist, http://www.dgf5.com/info/t3/Texts (accessed May 2014)

—

pp. 39, 41 Notes by the artist: a bibliography to be read and a quote by Frankz Kafka as a reminder.

"You do not need to leave your room,
just sit at your table and listen.
Do not even listen, simply wait.
Do not even wait, simply be quiet, and
the world will reveal itself to you to be unmasked;
it has no other choice.
It will roll in ecstasy at your feet."
Franz Kafka

DAMIEN HIRST
HOLLY, GRETEL, 1992

THE INSTALLATION CONSISTS OF IDENTICAL TWINS, SEATED IN FRONT OF A PAIR OF SPOT PAINTINGS, APPLIED DIRECTLY ONTO THE WALL BEHIND. THE WORK'S TITLE CHANGES ACCORDING TO THE NAMES OF THE PARTICIPATING TWINS: WHEN FIRST EXHIBITED IN 1992 IT WAS VARIOUSLY SUBTITLED <u>MARIANNE, HILDEGARD</u> AND <u>INGO, TORSTEN</u>.

Since graduating from Goldsmiths College, London in 1989, Damien Hirst has developed a large and ambitious body of work that looks broadly at the themes of life, death, and decay, while also parodying and taking advantage of the art system as a capitalist market. He is renowned for works featuring diamond-studded skulls, sharks floating in formaldehyde, simulated autopsies, and live maggots. In keeping with his reputation for astonishing bravado.

<u>The Physical Impossibility of Death in the Mind of Someone Living</u> (1991) is undoubtedly an iconic image of twentieth-century contemporary art and one of Hirst's most famous works. Consisting of a thirteen-foot tiger shark preserved in a long tank of formaldehyde, it generated colossal press attention when exhibited at the Saatchi Gallery's survey of Young British Art in 1992. Another legendary piece, <u>For the Love of God</u> (2007), consists of a cast of an eighteenth-century human skull set with 8601 diamonds. This audacious work was initially displayed at London's White Cube Gallery and combines Aztec and Mexican-inspired decorative patterning on the classic memento mori image of the skull, which has been used by artists for centuries to reference the transient nature of human existence.

First presented in 1992 at Jay Jopling's stall at the inaugural Unfair in Cologne in 1992, Hirst's work for <u>14 Rooms</u>[1] consists of a rotating cast of identical twins positioned in front of two of his iconic spot paintings, which are applied directly onto the wall behind. Rather than a fixed shape, the work shifts continually throughout the duration of the exhibition with the inclusion of different sets of twins, its title changing to reflect the participants' names. In 2009 the piece was exhibited for the second time, employing more than

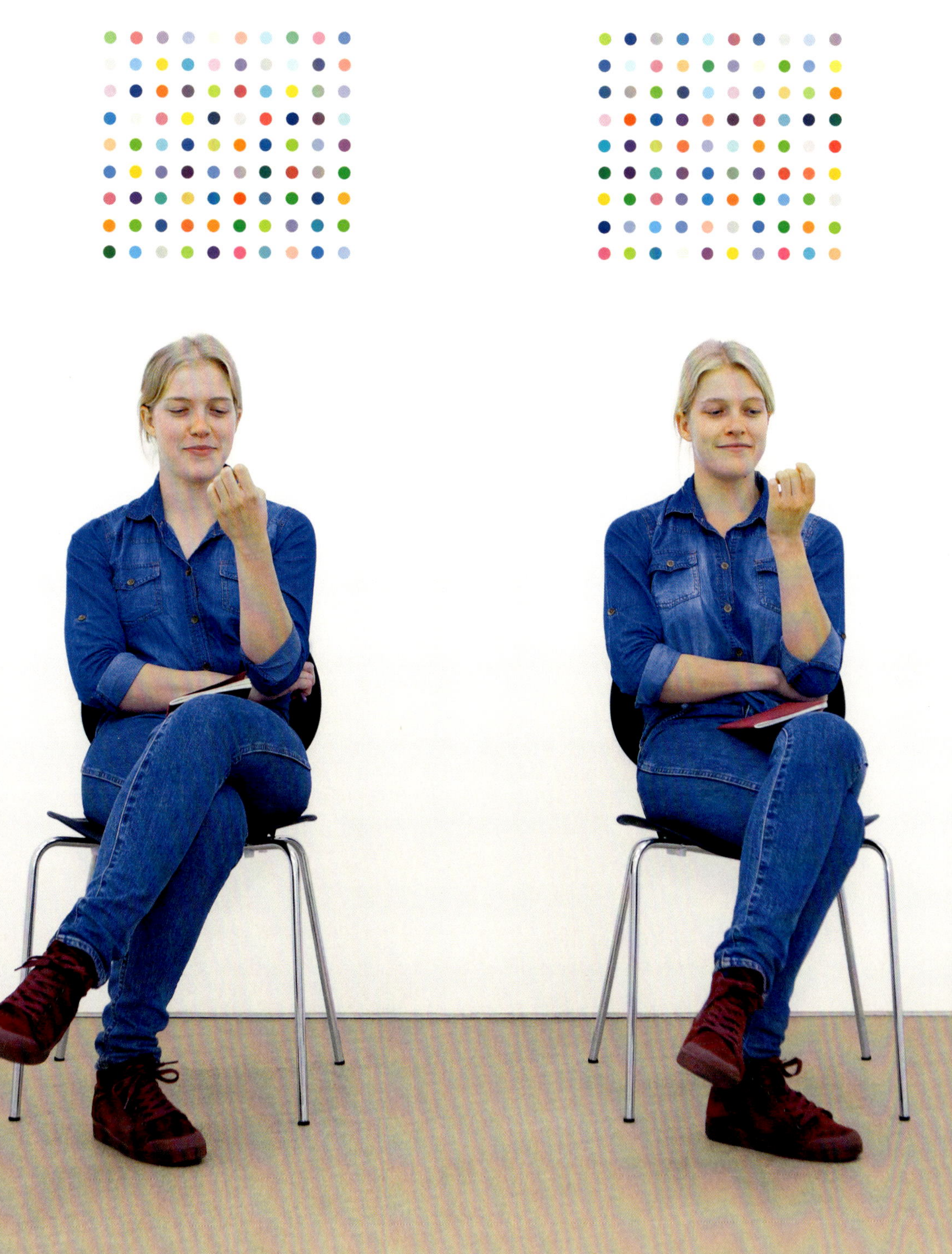

forty sets of twins at the Tate Modern's group exhibition Pop Life: Art in a Material World.

Hirst began making spot paintings in 1986 with the intention of creating an endless series with infinite combinations of colors. The works have a machine-made quality and, much like the principles of Andy Warhol's Factory, challenge ideas of authenticity and authorship, a central theme of pop art that continues to influence contemporary practitioners today. The idea of being at once the same but unique extends to the twins Hirst engages for the work, as he has explained: "I had that dream—which was terrifying—of meeting myself. I know I'm unique. But I think of it as bookends. I think everybody's two. You cut yourself down the fucking middle. You are two. It undermines this idea of being unique. There's a comfort I get from it that I love. Each part of a pair has its own life, independent of the other, but they live together."[2] (TL)

[1] Performed previously in these contexts: 12 Rooms at the Museum Folkwang during the RUHRTRIENNALE International Arts Festival 2012–14 in 2012; 13 Rooms at Kaldor Public Art Projects during the 27th Kaldor Public Art Project in 2013.
[2] Damien Hirst and Gordon Burn, On the Way to Work (London, 2001), p. 131; quoted at http://www.damienhirst.com/holly-gretel (accessed May 2014).

—

p. 43 Damien Hirst, Holly, Gretel, 1992.
Performed for 13 Rooms at Kaldor Public Art Projects during the 27th Kaldor Public Art Project in 2013.
p. 45 (top) Damien Hirst, Curtis, Jeffrey, 1992.
Performed for 13 Rooms at Kaldor Public Art Projects during the 27th Kaldor Public Art Project in 2013.
p. 45 (bottom) Damien Hirst, Marian, Julian, 1992.
Performed for 12 Rooms at the Museum Folkwang during the RUHRTRIENNALE International Arts Festival 2012–14 in 2012.

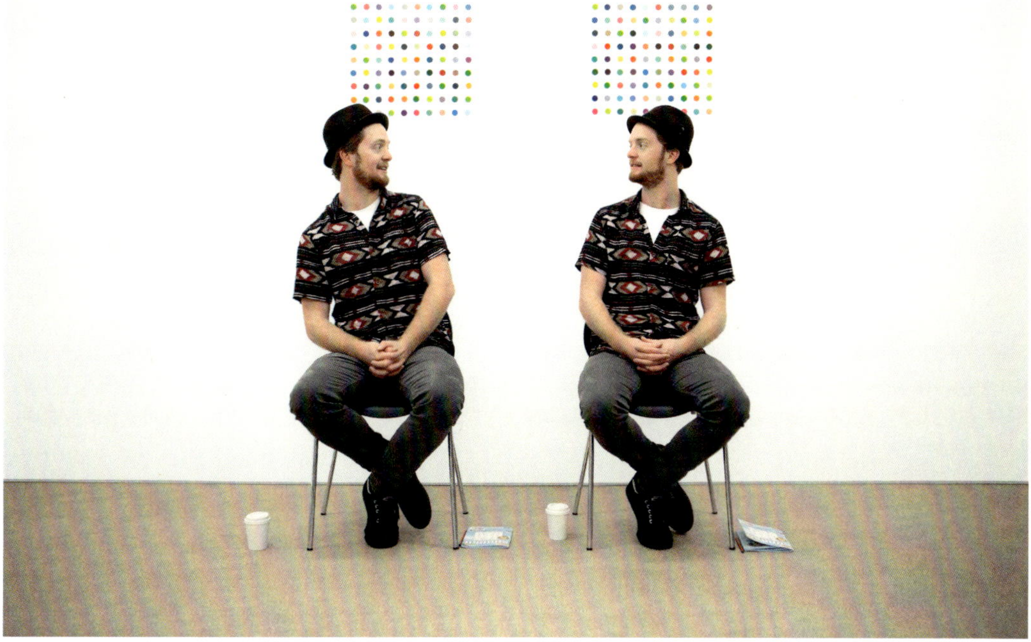

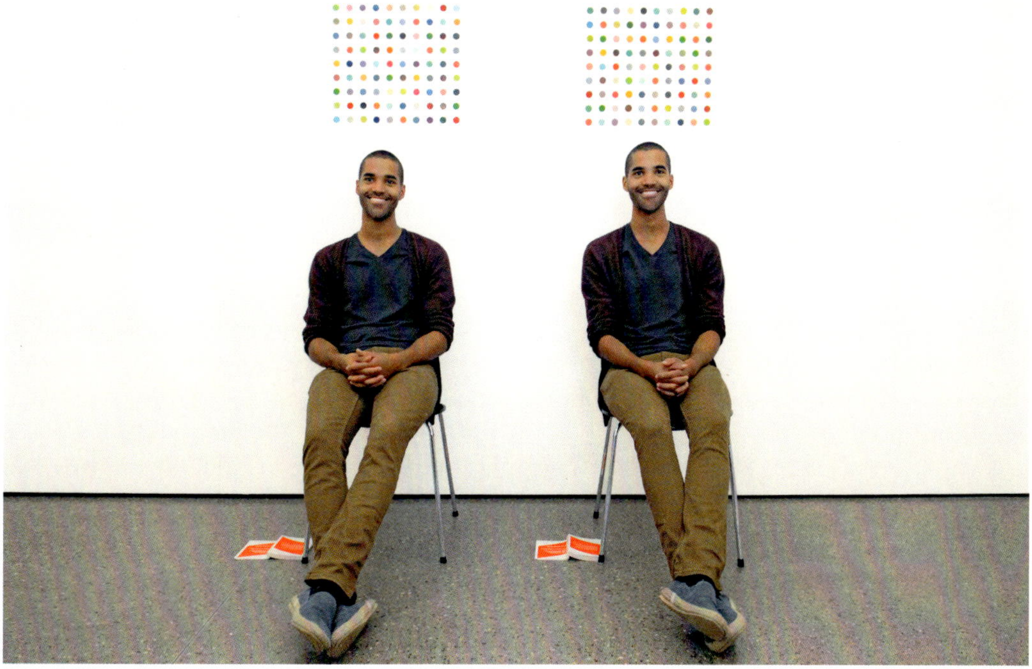

JOAN JONAS
MIRROR CHECK, 1970

THE PERFORMER OBSERVES AND EXAMINES HER OWN NAKED BODY WITH A SMALL, ROUND HAND-HELD MIRROR. THE MIRROR SERVES AS A SYMBOL OF SELF-PORTRAITURE BUT ALSO AS A DEVICE OF FRAGMENTATION, REFLECTING PARTS OF THE BODY BUT NOT THE WHOLE.

Joan Jonas is an acclaimed and influential multimedia artist working with performance, video, drawing, and sculptural installation. After studying art history and sculpture she continued to work with the medium of sculpture while exploring performative actions with the body in relation to film, video, and space in the late 1960s. Jonas found that performance and movement allowed her greater scope to represent image and gesture. Her pioneering works draw inspiration from the fields of film, literature, visual art, contemporary theater, dance, and traditional Japanese theater.

In her early performances Jonas used mirrors as props, creating a distance between performer and viewer in order to explore issues of spectatorship, gender, identity, and the fragmented female image. In her series Mirror Pieces (1968–2004) as well as in her video performances (1972–2013) she ex-plores how awareness shifts when viewing an object or the body from different perspectives. The series also draws attention to the differences between self-perception and the perception of others. In the Mirror Pieces viewers are reflected in full-size mirrors as part of a choreographed performance, forcing them to encounter their self-image within a public setting.

Jonas's Mirror Check, first performed by the artist in 1970 and presented in 14 Rooms,[1] is perhaps one of the most intimate and poignant of this series. We watch as a woman examines her own naked body in a small, round hand-held mirror. Carefully and thoughtfully observing reflections across her entire body, she explores each different angle and perspective. The mirror here serves as a symbol of self-portraiture, but also as a device of fragmentation, reflecting parts of the body but never the whole. There is a discrep-

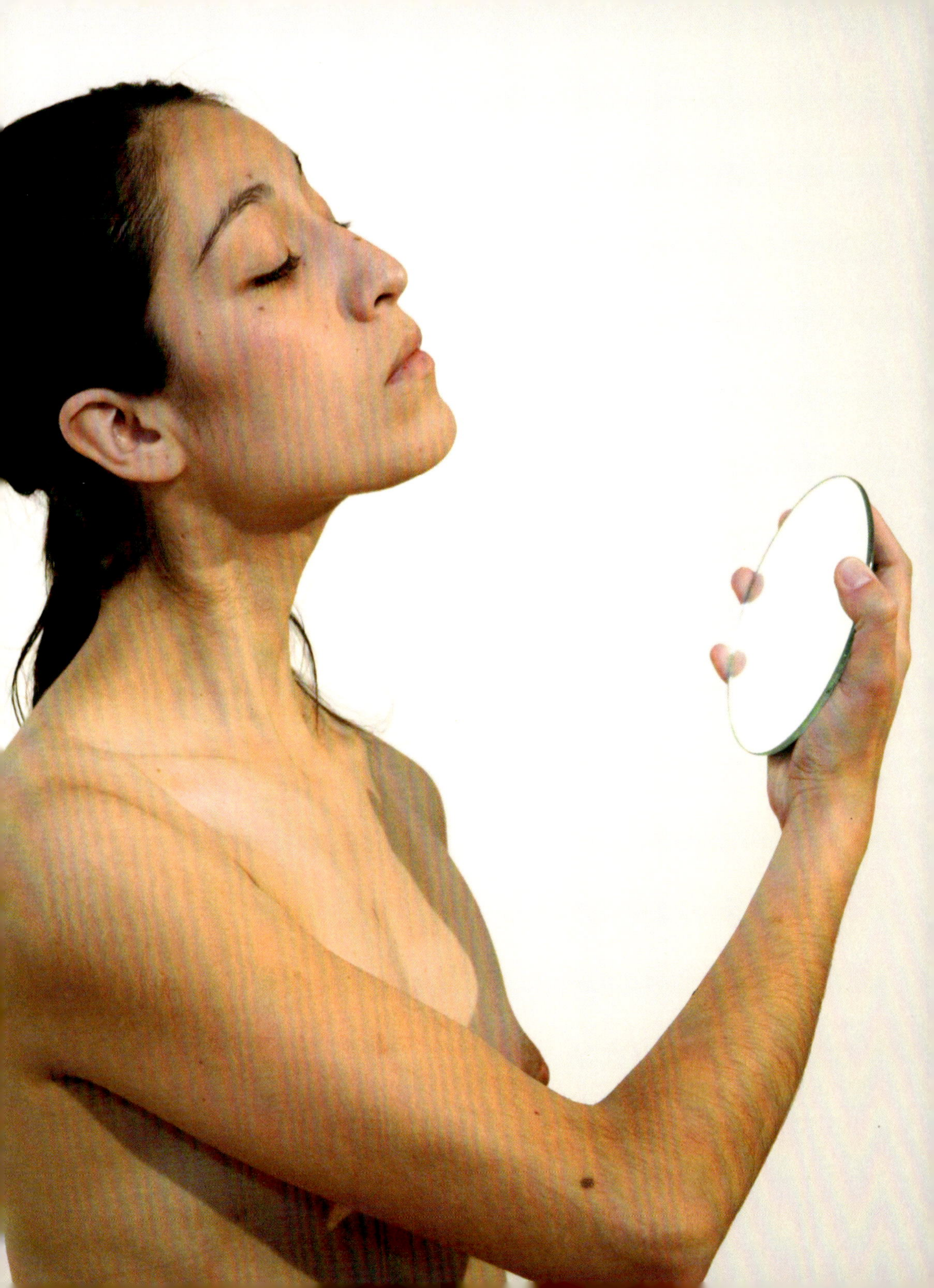

ancy between what the performer can see in the mirror and what the audience can see. A mirror generally represents likenesses, but what does this mirror show and what does it conceal? A tension between illusion and reality, seduction and distance, disguise and nakedness is played out through the ten-minute performance. (SF)

[1] Performed previously in these contexts: 11 Rooms at the Manchester Art Gallery during the Manchester International Festival in 2011; 12 Rooms at the Museum Folkwang during the RUHRTRIENNALE International Arts Festival 2012–14 in 2012; 13 Rooms at Kaldor Public Art Projects during the 27th Kaldor Public Art Project in 2013.
—
p. 47 (detail) Joan Jonas, Mirror Check, 1970.
Performed for 11 Rooms at the Manchester Art Gallery during the Manchester International Festival in 2011.
p. 49 Joan Jonas, Mirror Check, 1970.
Performed for 13 Rooms at Kaldor Public Art Projects during the 27th Kaldor Public Art Project in 2013.

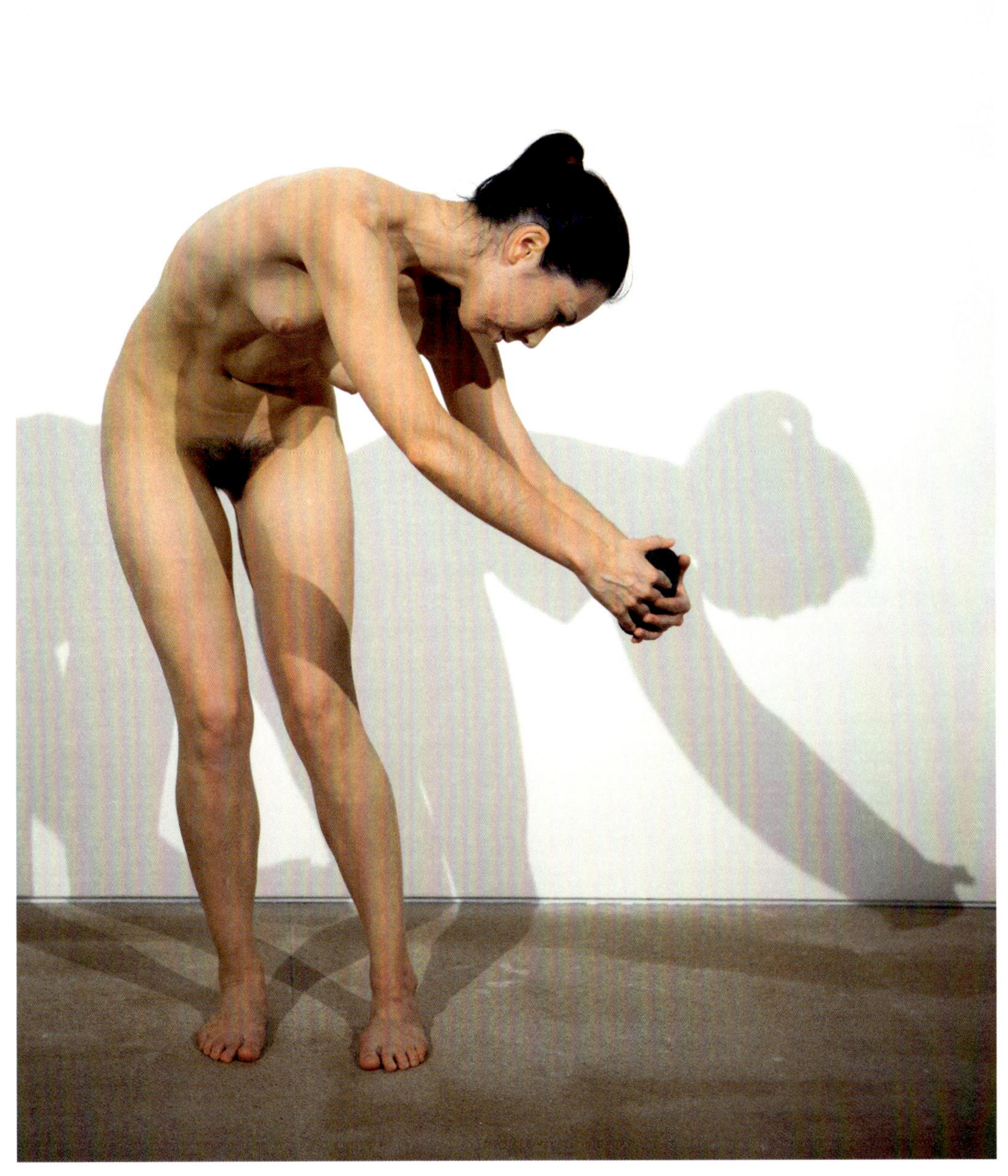

LAURA LIMA
MAN=FLESH/WOMAN=FLESH – FLAT, 1997

IN THIS ROOM THE HEIGHT OF THE CEILING IS ONLY FORTY-FIVE CENTIMETERS. AT THE BACK OF THE ROOM A PHYSICALLY DISABLED PERSON LIES ON THE GROUND, NEXT TO A SINGLE LAMP. THE VIEWER MUST CROUCH OR LIE DOWN TO SEE THE PIECE.

Since the early 1990s Lima has involved live beings in durational work that runs continuously throughout gallery opening hours, under the equation Man=flesh/Woman=flesh. The artist has constructed a personal glossary to discuss the nature of her works, thus avoiding terms such as "performance" or "performer." She never appears herself, instructing others to present pieces she has developed. She has worked with children, old people, men, women, and animals to extract an image out of their existential meaning, investigating the boundaries of autonomy and dependence in human action. Lima explains: "I am interested in the intricate social relationships, the exchange of behaviors that in time serves to alter our perception of language and life."[1]

For her work Doped (1997) a woman clothed in a shroud-like white dress takes a soporific drug and lies sleeping for hours on the floor of the gallery, connected to the wall via a long red woven net that links to her head like a thick cord. In To Age (2004) gallery staff members were made-up with prosthetics to synthesize their future faces, creviced and wrinkled with time. Other works have used animals, such as Gala Chickens (2004), presented for the Lyon Biennial in 2011, in which hens were adorned with the festive-colored feathers used in Brazilian carnival costumes. Costume was also a focus of Lima's work Costumes Store (2003/2006) in which blue and transparent vinyl clothing was made available for sale to visitors who were encouraged to wear these clothes routinely in their daily lives.

In Lima's pieces Man=flesh/Woman=flesh (1994 onwards) the artist assigns the participants (whom Lima calls "fleshperson") a variety of tasks utilizing specially constructed apparatus or settings. Each participant

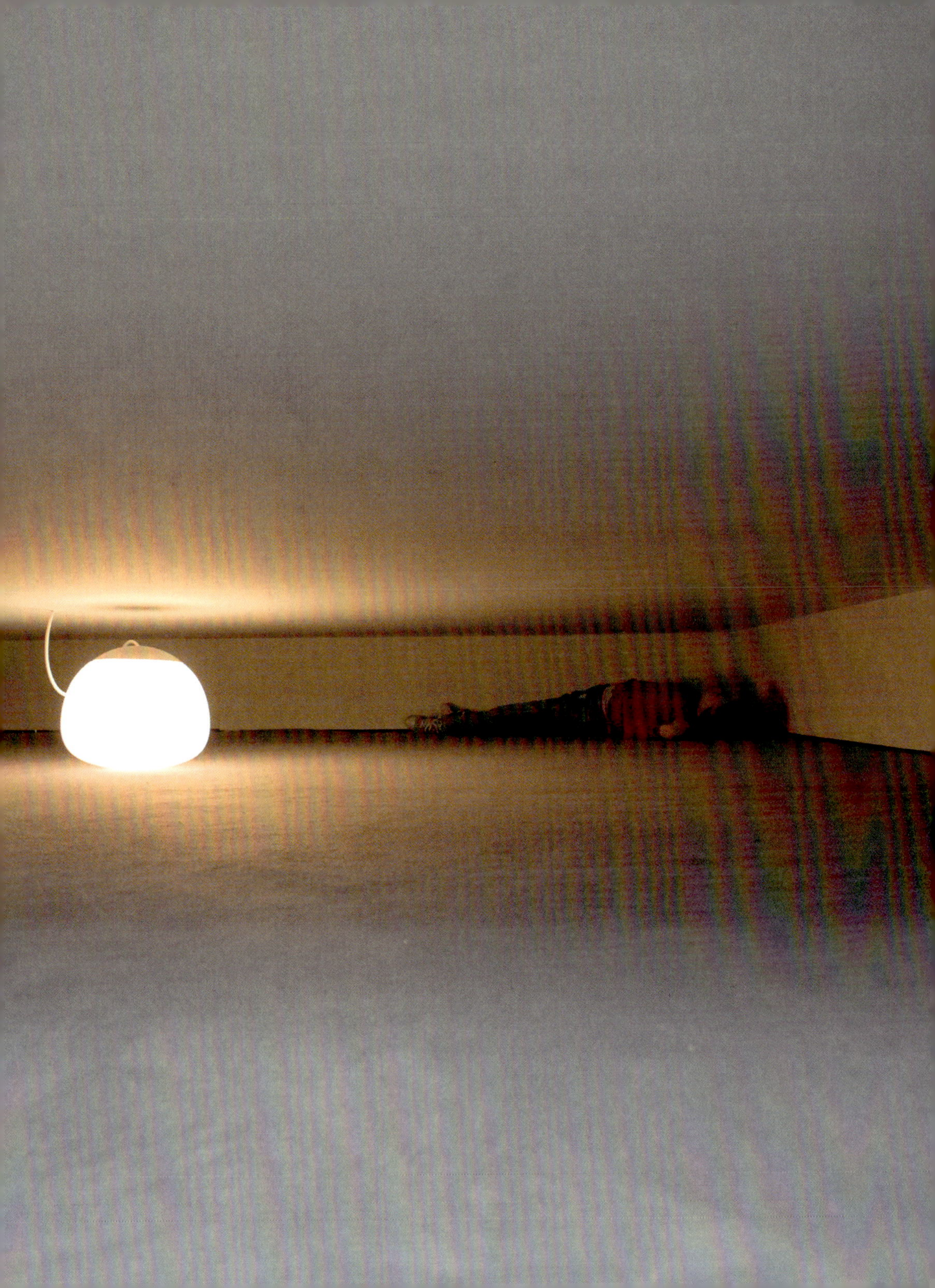

follows Lima's plan of activities—walking, sucking, sleeping, fighting, and pulling—continuously throughout the duration of the exhibition. In Lima's work for <u>14 Rooms</u>,[2] <u>Man=flesh/Woman=flesh – FLAT</u> (1997) flesh is the basic working material, positioned within a confined architectural environment. Beneath a ceiling that is a mere forty-five centimeters off the ground, a person silently lies with just a single lamp to light the small space. The viewer must crouch or lie down to see the participant who, in this case, has some form of physical disability. (SF)

[1] Lima in correspondence with Kaldor Public Art Projects, February 2013.
[2] Performed previously in these contexts: <u>11 Rooms</u> at the Manchester Art Gallery during the Manchester International Festival in 2011; <u>12 Rooms</u> at the Museum Folkwang during the RUHRTRIENNALE International Arts Festival 2012–14 in 2012; <u>13 Rooms</u> at Kaldor Public Art Projects during the 27th Kaldor Public Art Project in 2013.

—

pp. 51, 53 Laura Lima, <u>Man=flesh/Woman=flesh – FLAT</u>, 1997
Performed for <u>12 Rooms</u> at the Museum Folkwang during the RUHRTRIENNALE International Arts Festival 2012–14 in 2012.

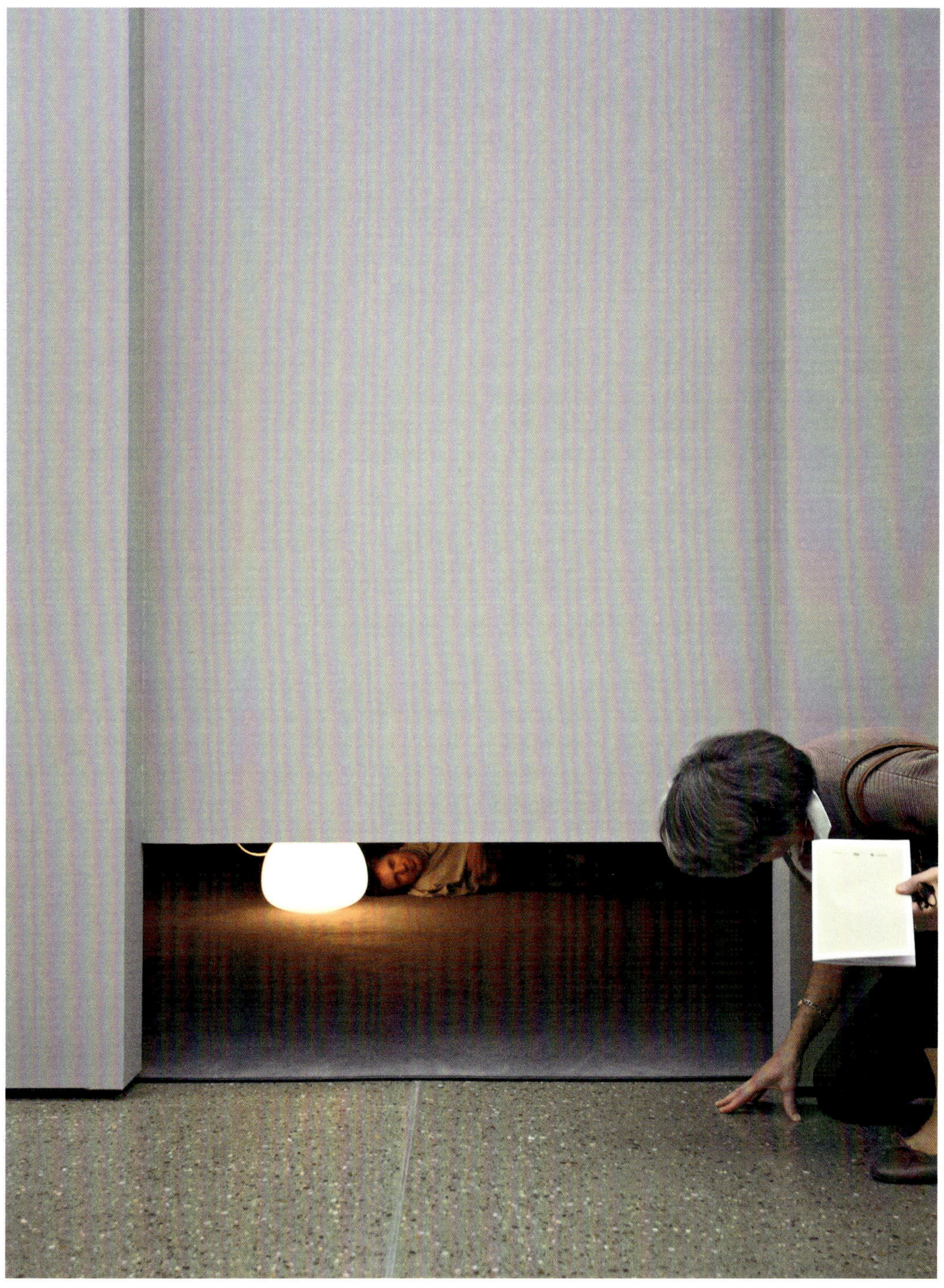

BRUCE NAUMAN
WALL-FLOOR POSITIONS, 1968

A PERFORMER RE-ENACTS A SET OF TWENTY-EIGHT POSITIONS WHICH ARE RELATED TO THE WALL AND THE FLOOR. THE SEQUENCE IS DRAWN FROM ORIGINAL VIDEO FOOTAGE OF THE ARTIST. THE PERFORMER HAS TO STUDY THE ORIGINAL CHOREOGRAPHY FROM THE VIDEOTAPE AND METICULOUSLY COPY THE MOVEMENTS IN THE CORRECT SEQUENCE.

Bruce Nauman is one of the most versatile and influential artists to emerge from his generation. He works in a variety of materials including film, video, performance, interactive environments, neon, photography, printmaking, and sculpture. After first studying mathematics and physics at the University of Wisconsin–Madison from 1960 to 1962, Nauman changed his major to art, graduating in 1964. In pursuit of his MFA at UC Davis, Nauman started to develop an oeuvre that was characterized by its research into the physicality of the body, the psychological aspects of expression, and the ambivalent power that language holds. In his work Nauman further investigated different forms and materials that could heighten the notions of what art and the role of the artist could be. In his first one-man show in Los Angeles in 1966 he created a group of fiberglass sculptures based on the backside of objects

or made from molds of his own body. Later the same year, he took the color photograph Self Portrait as a Fountain, an iconic image which challenged the public's conception of a fountain. By simply spouting water out of his mouth, the artist not only quoted the famous readymade by Marcel Duchamp from 1917—the urinal presented as a fountain—but turned the act into a performative gesture. A conceptual shift occurred where the physical and psychological quality of the artwork moved from object to subject and back.

In the late 1960s, the artist turned his attention to making films and videos. He recorded himself in his studio with rudimentary technology, performing different tasks. A 16mm camera was set up in just one position, from where the artist could be observed executing a number of movements, actions, or happenings. An example of such a film is Bouncing Two Balls between the Floor and

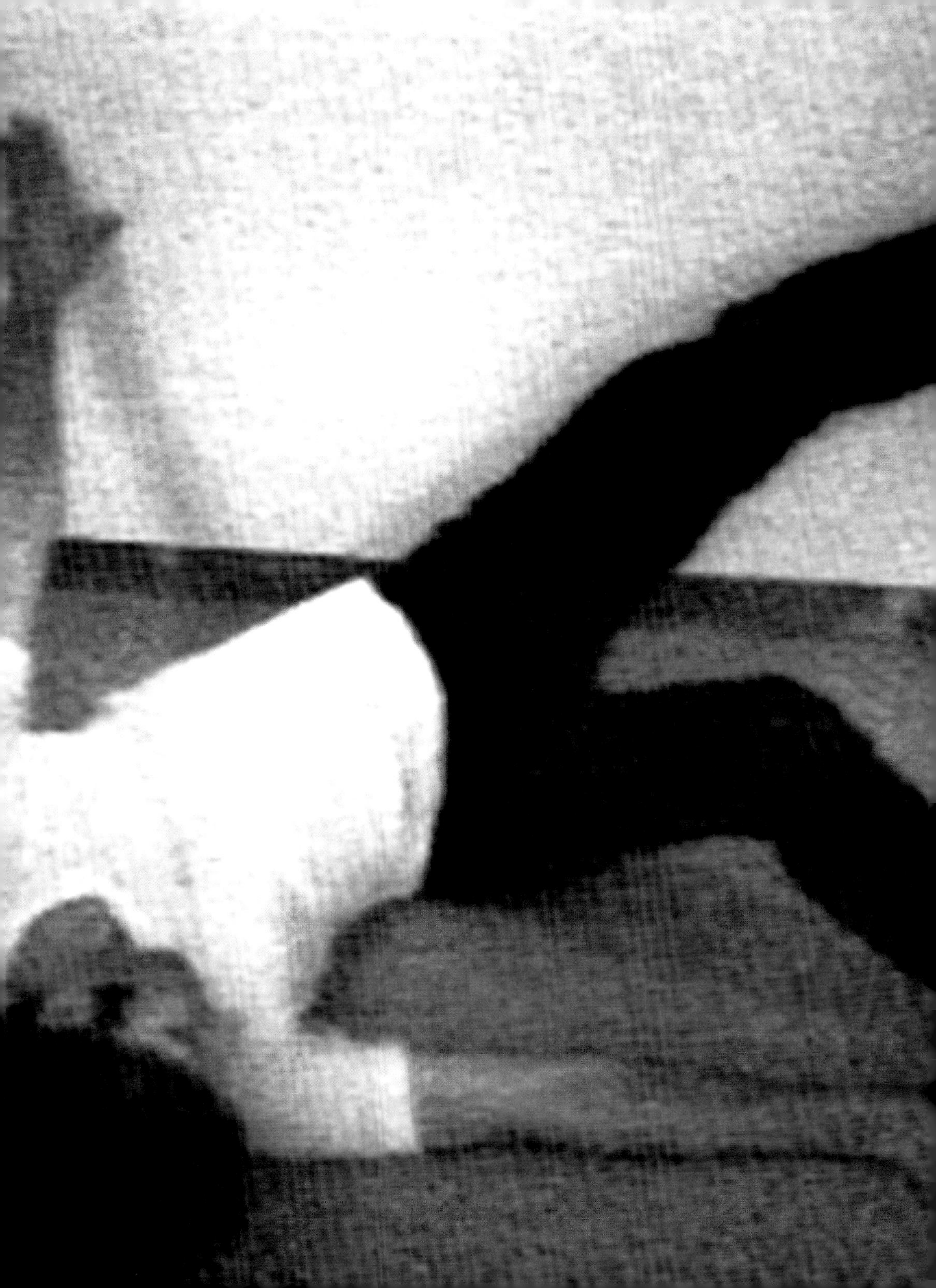

the Ceiling with Changing Rhythms, in which he marked a square on the floor of his studio with white masking tape, bouncing two balls as hard as possible on the floor while trying to maintain a certain rhythm—which kept failing, over and over.

For 14 Rooms, Nauman has approved a re-enactment of Wall-Floor Positions from 1968, a video work based on his 1965 performance of the sequence of movements at UC Davis. He describes it as follows: "standing with my back to the wall for about forty-five seconds or a minute, leaning out from the wall, then bending at the waist, squatting, sitting, and finally lying down. There were seven different positions in relation to the wall and floor. Then I did the whole sequence again standing away from the wall, facing the wall, then facing left and right. There were twenty-eight positions and the whole presentation lasted about half an hour."[1] In 14 Rooms one performer rigidly reenacts this set of twenty-eight positions in relation to wall and floor as seen in the original footage. The performer has to study the original choreography from the videotape and meticulously copy the movements in the correct sequence. Once completed, the performer leaves the room and the next performer enters. Nauman's contribution to this year's edition of 14 Rooms is of paramount importance, not only because he may be contextualized with today's live-art environment but also because of the influence his work had on contemporary artists such as Marina Abramović and Tino Sehgal, both of whom re-interpreted Nauman's work at earlier stages of their careers. (SL)

[1] Artist statement, http://www.eai.org/title.htm?id=4287 (accessed May 2014).

—

pp. 55 (detail), 57 Bruce Nauman, Wall-Floor Positions, 1968. 60 min, black & white video, sound

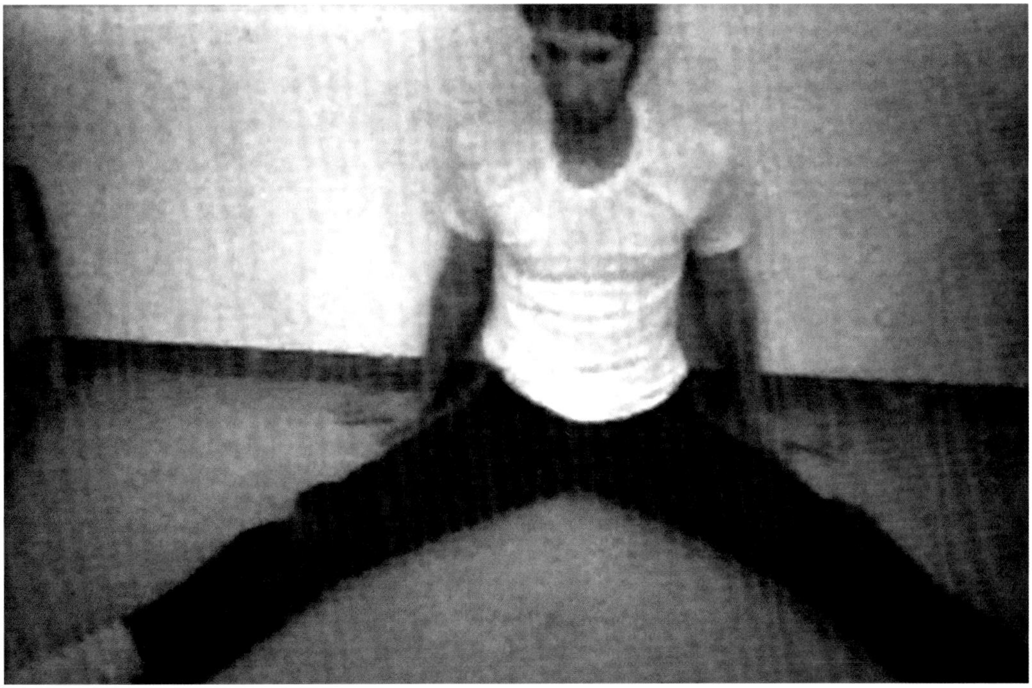

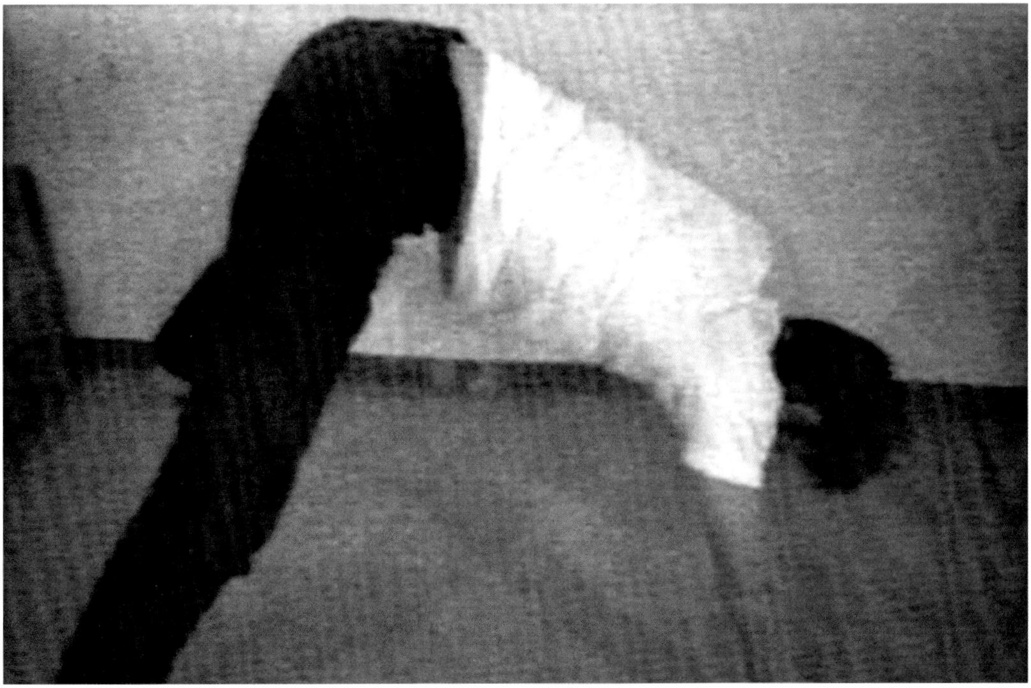

OTOBONG NKANGA
DIASPORE, 2014

THE PERFORMANCE CONSISTS OF ONE TO THREE WOMEN ALWAYS CARRYING THE PLANT CESTRUM NOCTURNUM, ALSO KNOWN AS QUEEN OF THE NIGHT. IN CONSTANT DIALOGUE WITH THE PLANT, THESE WOMEN NAVIGATE THROUGH A TOPOGRAPHICAL MAP ON THE FLOOR, GUIDING THEIR MOVEMENTS THROUGH DIFFERENT TERRITORIES.

Since early 2000, Otobong Nkanga has been working in a variety of media including drawing, photography, installation, and performance art. She observes social and topographical changes in her environment, the complexities that are embedded in these experiences, and how such things as resources, soil, earth, and its potential worth are subjected to regional and cultural scrutiny. "Her work often invites the viewer to engage in a dialogue about the intangibility of identity, memory, perception, observing how these change when presented through a specific arrangement and narration,"[1] through language and her own body. Nkanga was born in Nigeria where she also began her art studies at the Obafemi Awolowo University in Ile-Ife, she continued at the Ecole Nationale Supérieure des Beaux-Arts, Paris and in 2008 obtained a Master's Degree in Performing Arts from Dasarts, Amsterdam.

At the Sharjah Biennale in 2013, Nkanga performed Taste of a Stone: Itiat esa Ufok. For five to nine hours daily she wore a plant on her head and interacted with her audience by means of dance movements, singing, and talking, sometimes passing the plant to a spectator. The plant, Cestrum nocturnum (Queen of the Night), which was native to the West Indies but naturalized in South Asia, illustrates the artist's interest in migration and the dense web of social, political, and economic tensions that can arise when various resources are migrated, displaced, and uprooted from their original source. Interestingly, the plant becomes another performer, someone Nkanga can communicate with, move with, be with. Nkanga likes to draw from her emotions, from her land; and in relation to that land, she explores the role of mapping, notions of ownership, the history of colonialism, and the economical meanings that are associated with it.

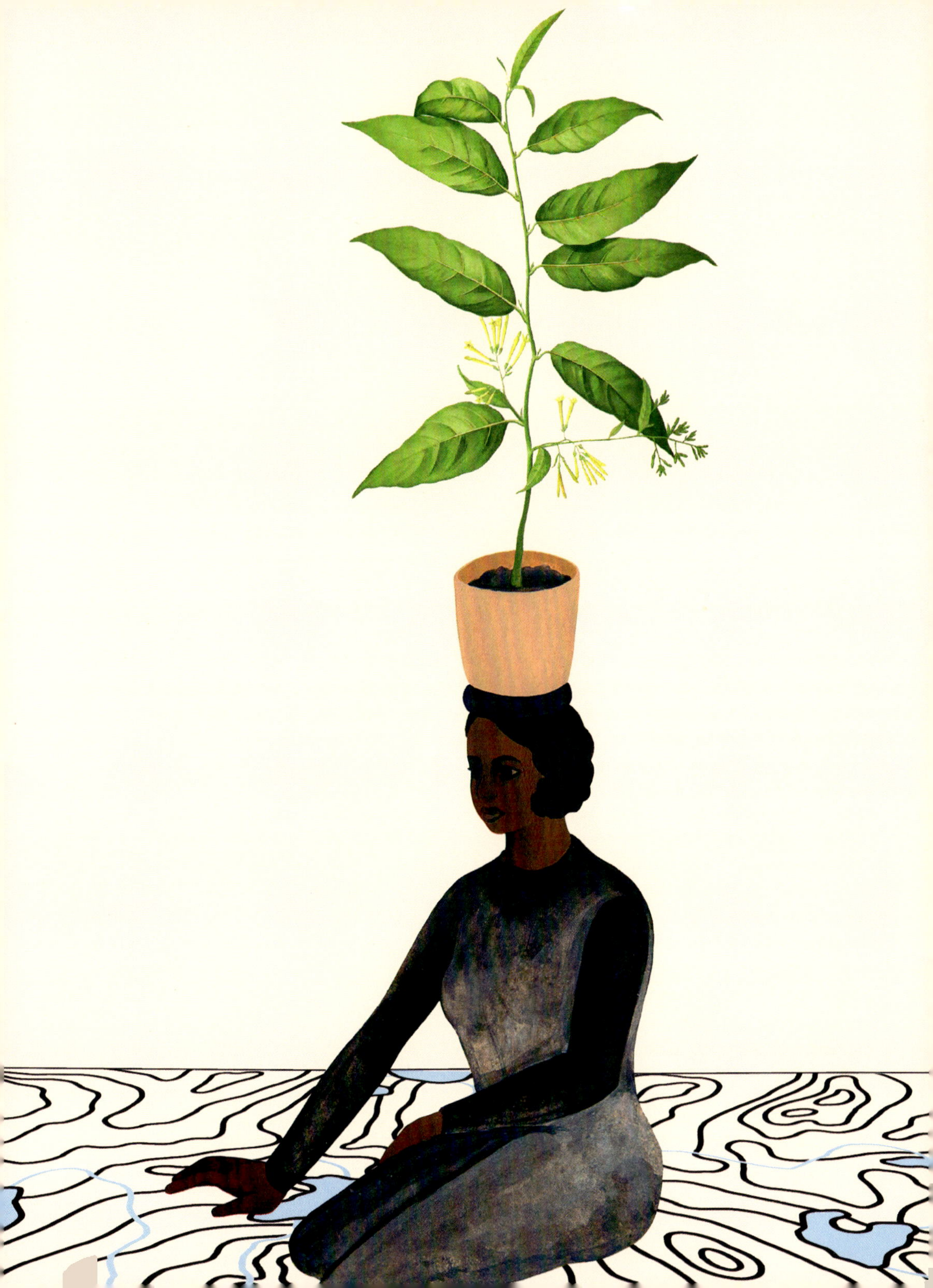

For <u>14 Rooms</u>, Nkanga adapted her choreography, instructing between one and three women from the diaspora to enter the room at various moments, each carrying the plant <u>Cestrum nocturnum</u>. A topographical map on the floor serves as a point for navigation, helping the women to move through the space, through different territories. The artist continues to explore the language of diaspora, of leaving what is called home and facing forwards toward a new future. The same goes for the plants, first uprooted from their natural soil, they leave their spores in new places, creating new identities. The women map the floor, hold conversations, meditate or sit with their plants, move in a rhythm, face away, turn around, stand still. The gaze is upon their journey, on the body as well as on the plant, on the possibility of a symbiosis. Nkanga is interested in shifting the perspectives of things, in trying to capture time through experience, in grabbing the intangible—and in keeping these experiences in constant motion. (SL)

[1] http://www.berliner-kuenstlerprogramm.de/en/gast.php?id=1223 (accessed May 2014).
—
p. 59 Otobong Nkanga, <u>Sketch for Diaspore</u>, 2014
Collage and acrylic on paper, 36 × 27 cm
p. 61 Otobong Nkanga, <u>Sketches for Diaspore</u>, 2014.
Digital print and mixed media on paper, 27 × 36 cm

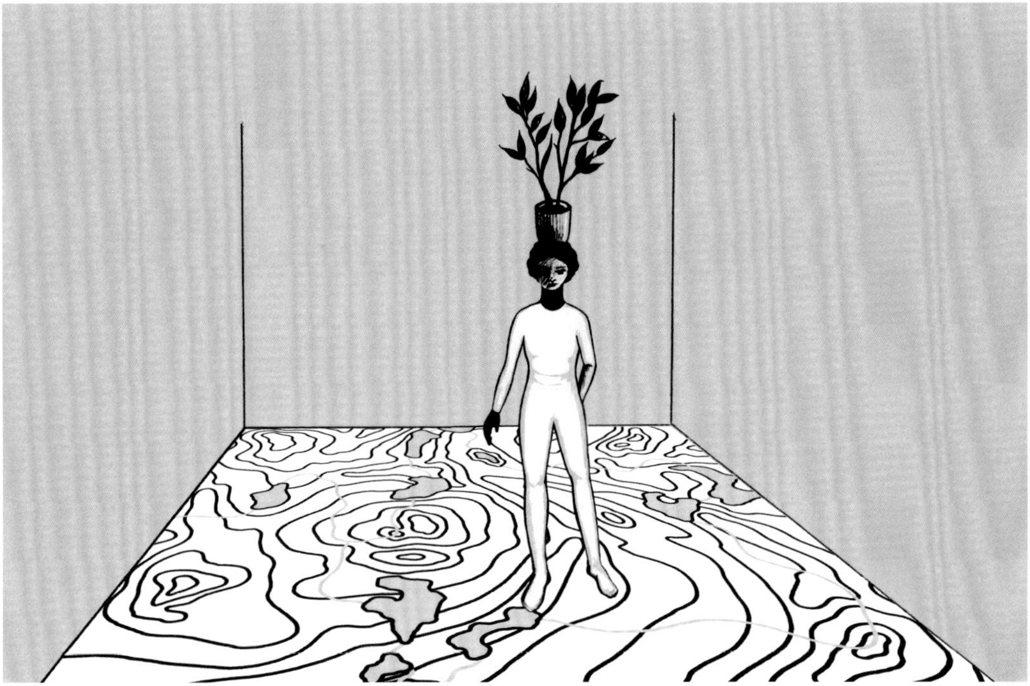

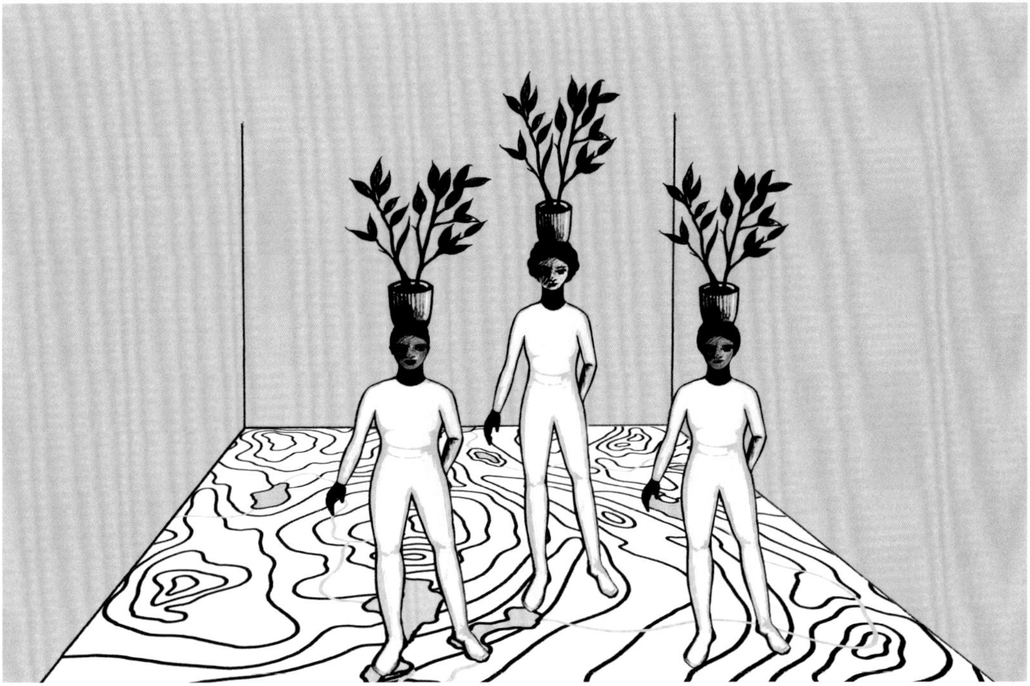

ROMAN ONDÁK
SWAP, 2011

A PERFORMER SITS BEHIND A TABLE LIKE A VENDOR, WITH AN OBJECT HE BRINGS ALONG. ONCE THE FIRST VISITOR ENTERS THE ROOM, THE PERFORMER TRIES TO SWAP HIS OBJECT WITH ANY OBJECT THE VISITOR MIGHT BE CARRYING WITH HIM AND WHICH HE IS WILLING TO GIVE UP IN EXCHANGE FOR THE PERFORMER'S OBJECT. THIS SETS IN MOTION AN ENDLESS CHAIN OF BARTER AND COMMUNICATION WHICH WILL GO ON FOR THE ENTIRE DURATION OF THE EXHIBITION.

Roman Ondák takes the familiar elements of everyday life and reframes them to surprise our expectations and perspectives. He investigates social codes, conventions, rituals, and forms of exchange by discreetly dislocating objects, ideas, and actions from their usual settings. His installations, performances, and interventions are sometimes scarcely distinguishable from the context in which they are presented. Often humorous, they provoke a double take by viewers, making them question their preconceptions and modes of interaction. In a number of performances Ondák has asked participants to follow his instructions while also inviting them to use their creativity. The resulting works are controlled studies of collective imagination.

For his work <u>Passage</u> (2004), he gave chocolate bars to 500 steel factory workers in Japan and asked them to construct sculptures from the foil wrapping after eating the chocolates. Hundreds of tiny silver constructions were displayed together, presenting a vision—far from the production line—of multiplicity and creativity. <u>For Good Feelings in Good Times</u> (2003) people were asked to queue outside an art gallery, creating an artificial line with no destination, while for <u>Teaching to Walk</u> (2002) each day a mother was invited to use the gallery as a location for her child to practice its first steps.

For his celebrated work <u>Measuring the Universe</u> (2007) Ondák started with an empty gallery space and instructed attendants to record the height of each visitor, their first name, and the date by marking the white wall with black felt-tip markers. When it was presented over four months in 2009 at the Museum of Modern Art, New York, thousands of visitors became part of the work and the space was transformed with a multitude of lines, names, and dates. Marking the flow of

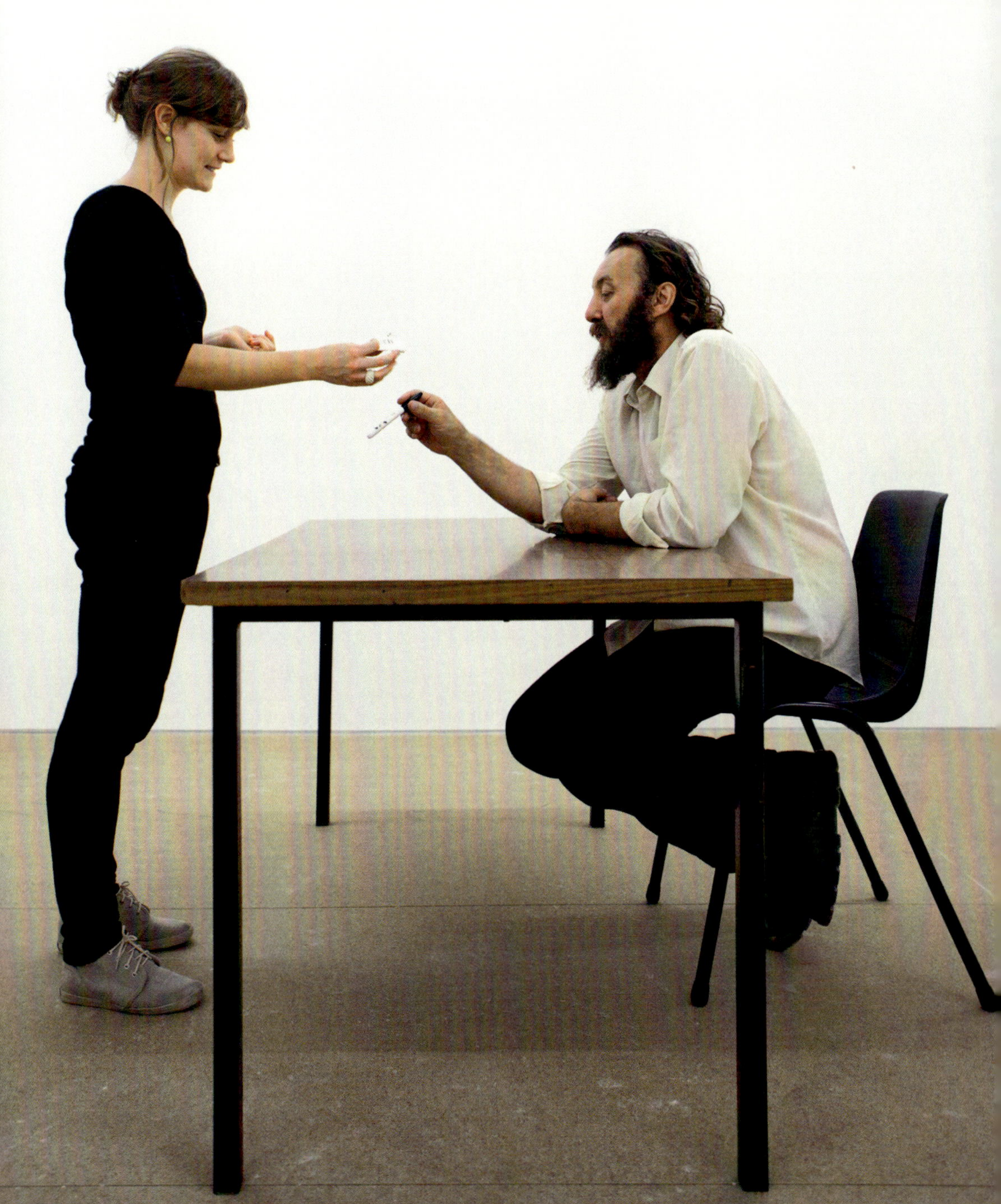

visitors throughout the exhibition, the black strokes merged together to create a dense, dark mass along the wall, congregating at the average height of the visitors and revealing just one of the many generalities that inform our social norms and measures.

Ondák's work for 14 Rooms,[1] titled Swap (2011), merges art with everyday life. Ondák selects a performer to wait behind a table like a vendor in a marketplace. The performer is asked to bring along an object, which sits on the table until the first visitor enters the room. The visitor is then given the opportunity to swap the object with anything else he or she would be willing to exchange—a coin or a watch, a feather or a piece of paper. Setting in motion an endless chain of barter and exchange, the performer continues to ask each visitor to swap an object with the one on the table. Each day the last object remains on the table until the following morning. Finally, at the close of the exhibition, the last performer takes with them the final object of the day. (SF)

[1] Performed previously in these contexts: 11 Rooms at the Manchester Art Gallery during the Manchester International Festival in 2011; 12 Rooms at the Museum Folkwang during the RUHRTRIENNALE International Arts Festival 2012–14 in 2012; 13 Rooms at Kaldor Public Art Projects during the 27th Kaldor Public Art Project in 2013.
—
pp. 63, 65 (top right, bottom) Roman Ondák, Swap, 2011. Performed for 13 Rooms at Kaldor Public Art Projects during the 27th Kaldor Public Art Project in 2013.
p. 65 (top left) Roman Ondák, Swap, 2011. Performed for 12 Rooms at the Museum Folkwang during the RUHRTRIENNALE International Arts Festival 2012–14 in 2012.

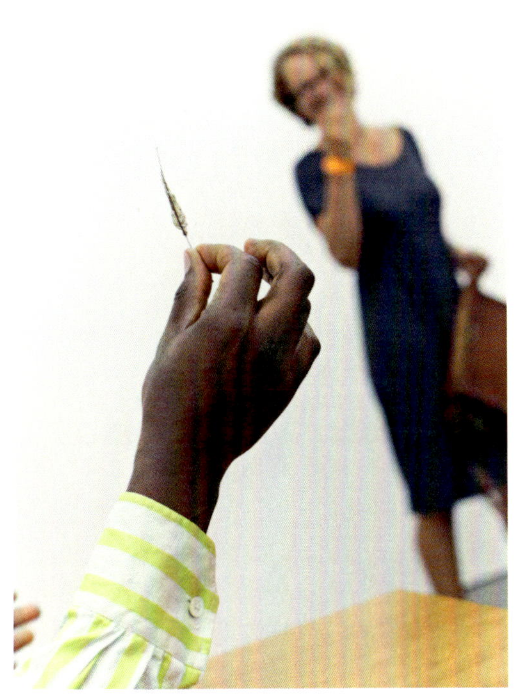

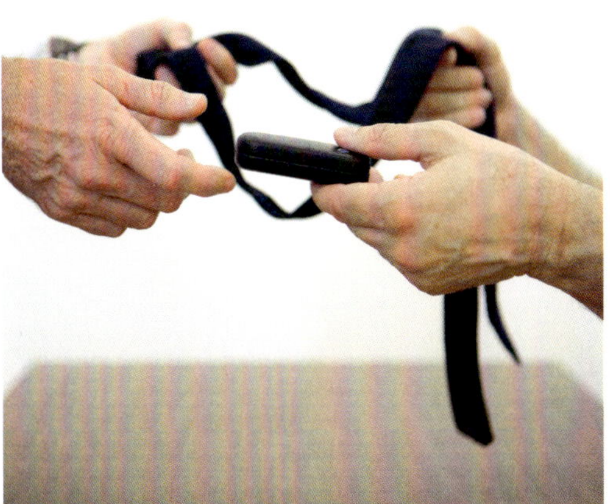

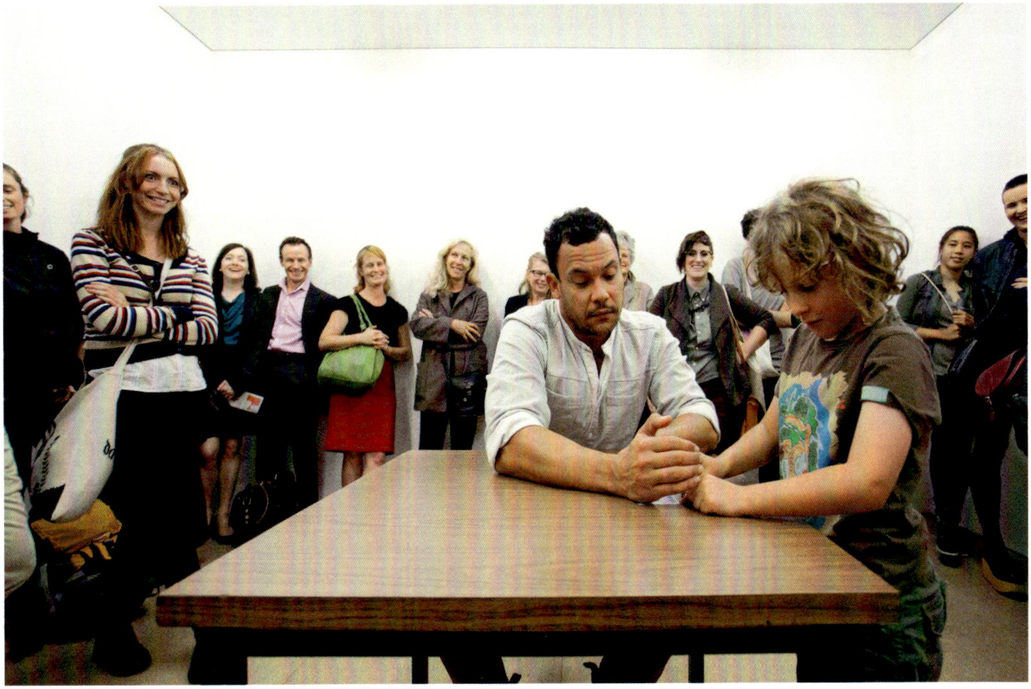

YOKO ONO
TOUCH PIECE, 1963/2014

VISITORS ARE ENCOURAGED TO TOUCH ONE ANOTHER IN THE DARK. SOME MAY BE BLINDFOLDED, OTHERS MAY DISCOVER PENCILS TO WRITE MESSAGES ON THE WALLS, CHALLENGING EACH VISITOR'S SENSE OF INTIMACY AND PRIVACY.

For over five decades, Yoko Ono has been a challenging artist, poet, and musician, as well as a video and performance artist. By examining the complexity of human emotions from loss and conflict to harmony and love, she experiments with her audience's conception of art and the world in general. In her prolific career she has embraced a wide range of media, constantly creating new forms of artistic expression, challenging the relationship between artist and spectator. She moved to New York in the early 1950s and, being a pioneer in conceptual art, became part of the vibrant avant-garde. It was there she began her instruction series. In 1961 she created instruction paintings where, initially, canvases with various materials and verbal or written instructions were exhibited. The following year she exhibited only the written instructions for the paintings for others to execute in their minds. Around the same time, she staged a series of ground-breaking performances around movement and sounds, and in 1964 she performed Cut Piece in Kyoto and Tokyo, a seminal piece which showed the artist kneeling motionless on the floor. The audience was then invited to come up on stage and to cut off Ono's clothing with scissors. This act not only raised questions around gender and identity but also symbolized the internal suffering people experience on a daily basis.

Ono's engagement as a peace activist repeatedly appeared and keeps appearing in her work as a prominent leitmotif. In 1969, together with John Lennon, she realized Bed-In as well as War Is Over! (if you want it), a worldwide billboard campaign for peace. In more recent years she created interactive works such as Wish Tree (1996) which invites visitors to attach personal wishes for peace to the branches. Over one million wishes have been gathered. The Imagine Peace Tower in

TOUCH PIECE

Touch.

Iceland is one of the results of the artist's long-term efforts to promote peace as well as positive thinking and love across the globe. A similarly expansive project is <u>Smilefilms</u>, where her ultimate goal is "to make a film which includes a smiling face snap of every single human being in the world."[1] The interactive piece encourages the public to upload their smiles onto an online database that is in constant growth.

For <u>14 Rooms</u> Ono is presenting her 1963 work <u>Touch Piece</u>, which was first published in her book <u>Grapefruit</u>, a collection of instruction pieces from 1964. The instruction at the entrance of the completely dark room simply reads: "Touch": visitors are invited to touch one another in the dark. Entering the room, the smell of incense welcomes them and they immediately become active participants in the piece. Some visitors may be blindfolded, others may discover pencils to write messages on the walls. Most visitors will feel their way about the room. The piece challenges each visitor's sense of intimacy and privacy and simultaneously breaks with one of the last taboos in our society. (SL)

[1] Artist statement, http://www.smilesfilm.com (accessed May 2014).
—
p. 67 Yoko Ono, <u>Touch Piece</u>, 1963.
Instruction published in <u>Grapefruit</u>, 1964,
Wunternaum Press, Tokyo, Japan
p. 69 Yoko Ono, <u>Grapefruit</u>, 1964.
Artist book, Edition of 500. Published by
Wunternaum Press, Tokyo, Japan

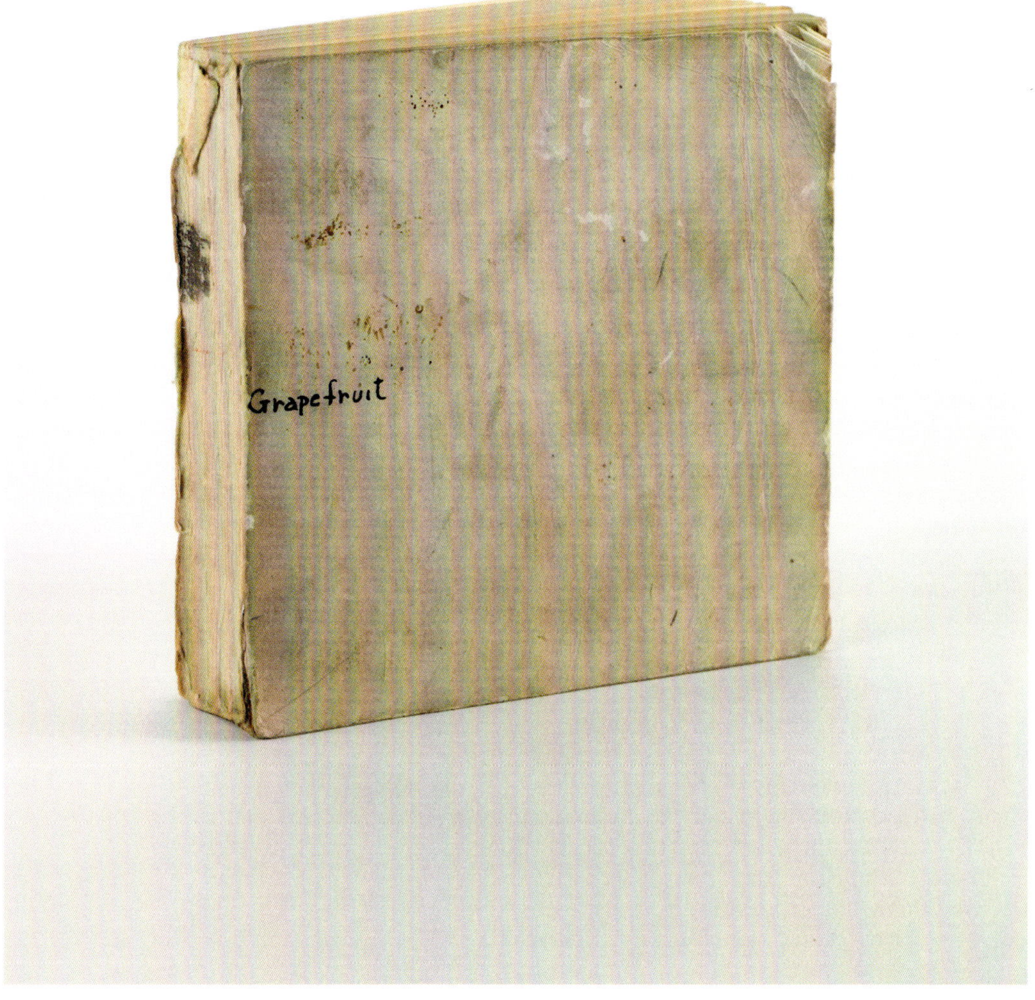

Grapefruit

TINO SEHGAL
THIS IS COMPETITION, 2004

Tino Sehgal's practice is an inspiration for all the <u>Rooms</u> exhibitions (<u>11 Rooms</u> at the Manchester Art Gallery during the Manchester International Festival, <u>12 Rooms</u> at the RUHRTRIENNALE 2012–2014, and <u>13 Rooms</u> at Kaldor Public Art Projects). Since 2000, he has been constructing situations that instigate unique encounters between people through movement, the spoken word, and song; creating vibrant, living artworks that run continuously throughout the opening hours of an exhibition. Taking shape in the moment when the spectator encounters them, Sehgal's artworks are intimate and unique, informed by the responses and perspectives of each visitor.

<u>This is competition</u> was originally shown at Art Basel in 2004 where it received the Baloise Art Prize. It is an algorithmic work that addresses the inner functioning processes of markets. In it, two interpreters attempt to describe works under a particular linguistic constraint: neither can speak more than one consecutive word. This rule structure produces a cybernetic control system that limits the agency of both participants, while rendering the varying outcomes recognizably part of the piece. Technology therefore influences the piece to a considerable degree, even though specific technological apparatuses are absent: the act of subjecting people to an algorithmic rule structure demonstrates the extent to which machine thinking influences human culture. At the same time, this rule structure is revealed as capable of accommodating innovation and imagination, putting rest to notions of mechanical simplicity. (TS)

SANTIAGO SIERRA
VETERANS OF THE WARS OF ERITREA, KOSOVO AND TOGO FACING THE CORNER, 2014

A WAR VETERAN FACES THE CORNER AND NEITHER RESPONDS NOR REACTS TO THE AUDIENCE. THIS CREATES A PROFOUND AND DISQUIETING EXPERIENCE FOR THE VISITOR AS THE PERTINENT QUESTION OF HOW VETERANS SHOULD OR SHOULD NOT BE TREATED WITHIN SOCIETY IS RAISED.

Spanish-born artist Santiago Sierra employs workers as sculptures in his poetic and often confrontational artworks. Drawing on the art-historical tradition of using paid models who were often taken from the streets, Sierra commissioned his models from the unwanted and ostracized—street workers, illegal immigrants, the unemployed, and the dispossessed. Conducted within set parameters, like minimalist investigations of form, Sierra's events test individual and social boundaries to expose social and cultural inequalities.

In 1999 Sierra permanently tattooed a black line across the backs of six unemployed young men in Havana, Cuba. He paid each man 30 USD. For the Venice Biennale in 2001 he paid 133 illegal street vendors—immigrants from China, Senegal, and Bangladesh—to dye their hair blonde and, in 2009, he investigated sexual variations us-ing different couplings of race and gender in his work <u>Los Penetrados</u>. Many of Sierra's works hide his participants' faces through blurring or positioning them away from the camera. In doing this he both protects the participants' identities and imbues them with an elevated symbolic status. Rather than remaining isolated individuals, they become emblematic of a certain class, gender, or culture, and their actions, and those of the artist, become political and social statements.

Sierra has also created a number of works in which individuals and groups are photographed from behind, facing a blank wall. Participants in these works have included a hooded female figure, groups of homeless women, migrant workers, and self-described anarchists. These works ask us to reflect on the struggles of those who fall outside our economic and political sys-

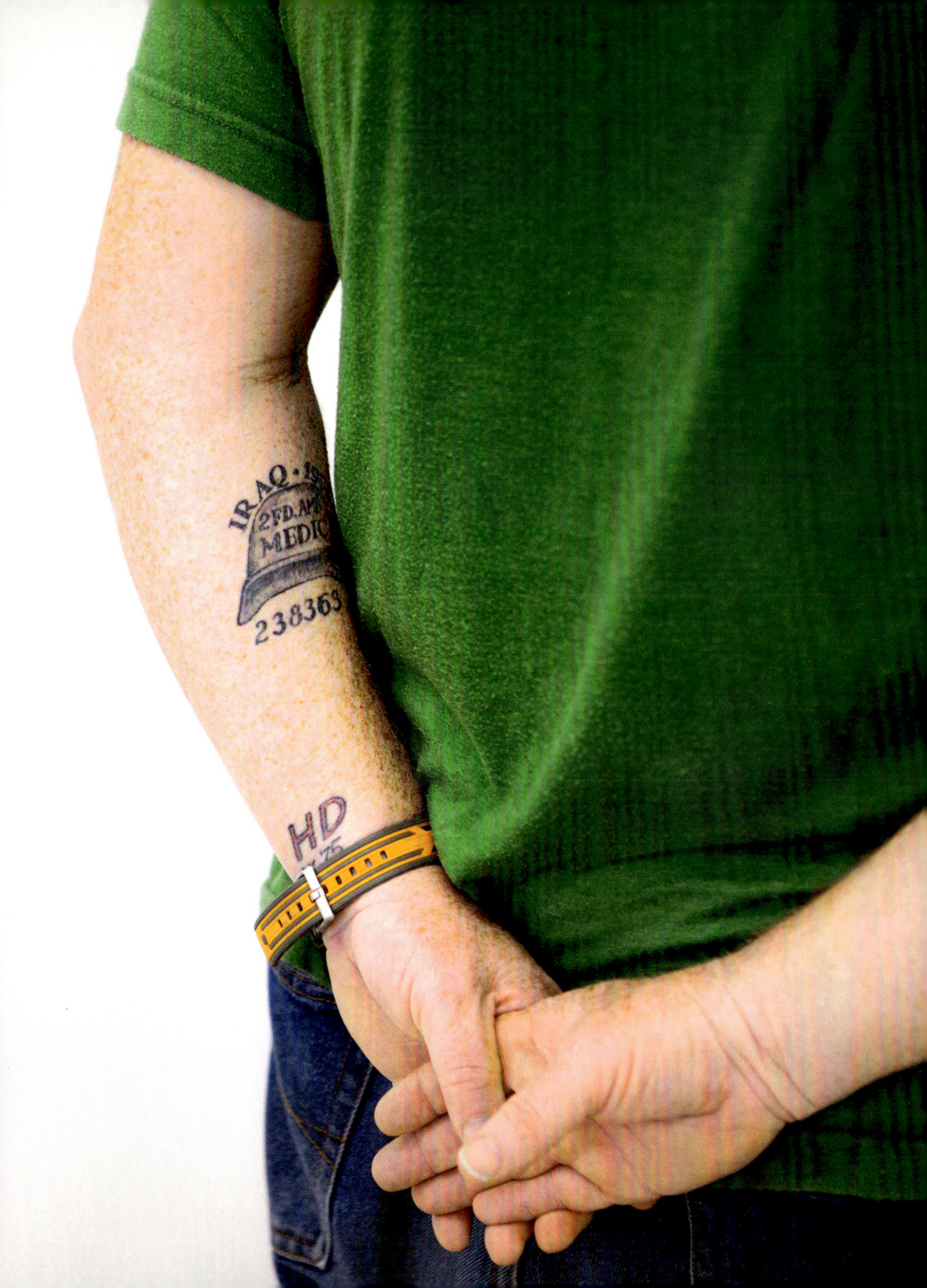
IRAQ · 19
2 FD. AM
MEDIC
238363
HD

tems; those who are not represented within existing power structures.

In <u>14 Rooms</u>, Sierra presents <u>Veterans of the Wars of Eritrea, Kosovo and Togo Facing the Corner</u> (2014)[1] a durational work in which a series of war veterans from varied past conflicts stand facing the corner within the 5-by-5-meter room. Silent and still, not reacting to their audience in any way, they stand as if positioned in a military line. They only move away from their post when they are replaced by another veteran, who solemnly steps in as if changing the guard.

The experience of viewing the work is profound and intentionally disquieting. We might assume that war veterans are remembered for their selfless, perhaps even heroic service, but Sierra gives us figures of far greater complexity. He evokes the trauma, guilt, and fear that often go unacknowledged within both mainstream and military culture. Are the ex-soldiers facing the wall as a form of punishment? Why can't we see their faces? What is running through their minds? (SF)

[1] Performed previously in these contexts: <u>11 Rooms</u> at the Manchester Art Gallery during the Manchester International Festival in 2011; <u>12 Rooms</u> at the Museum Folkwang during the RUHRTRIENNALE International Arts Festival 2012–14 in 2012; <u>13 Rooms</u> at Kaldor Public Art Projects during the 27th Kaldor Public Art Project in 2013.
—
p. 73 Santiago Sierra, <u>Veterans of the Wars of Afghanistan, Timor-Leste, Iraq and Vietnam Facing the Corner</u>, 2013. Performed for <u>13 Rooms</u> at Kaldor Public Art Projects during the 27th Kaldor Public Art Project in 2013.
p. 75 Santiago Sierra, <u>Veterans of the Wars of Northern Ireland, Afghanistan and Iraq Facing the Corner</u>, 2011. Performed for <u>11 Rooms</u> at the Manchester Art Gallery during the Manchester International Festival in 2011.

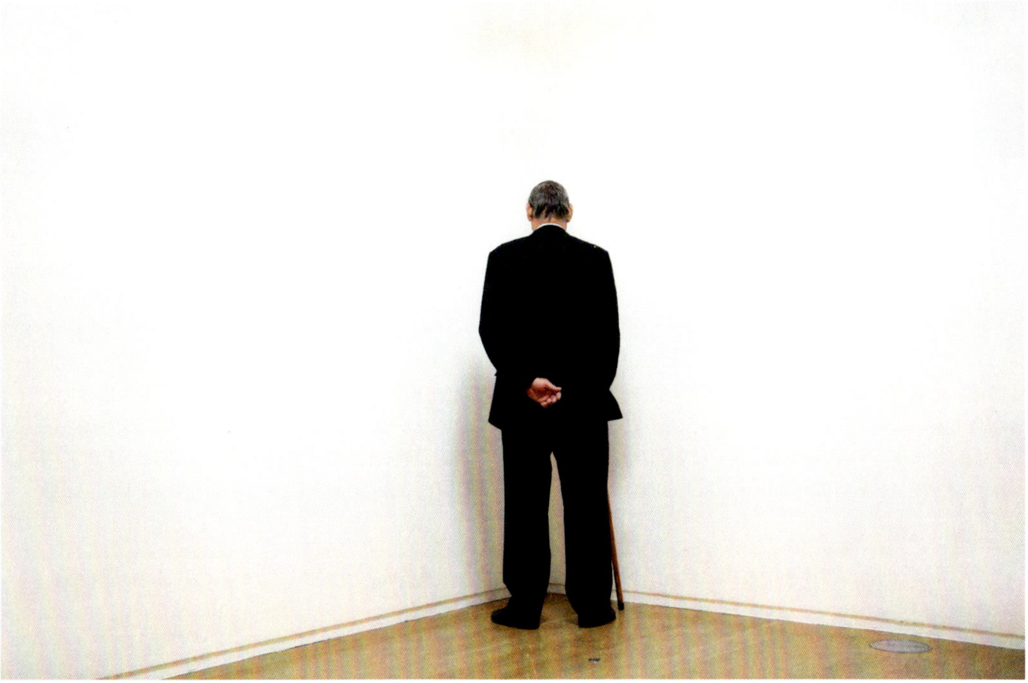

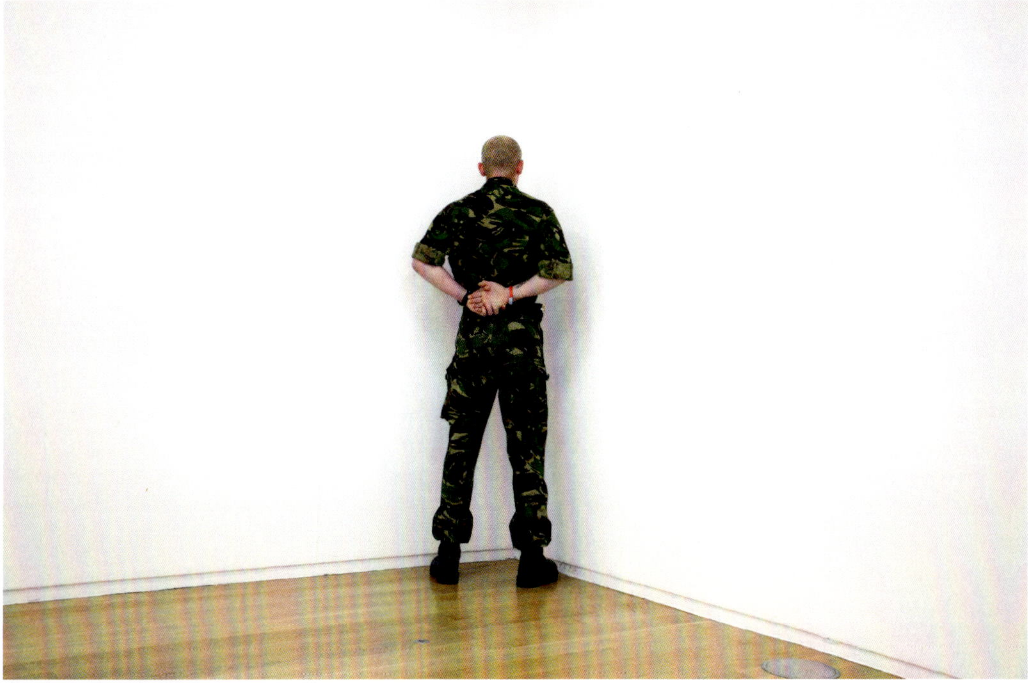

XU ZHEN
IN JUST A BLINK OF AN EYE, 2005

A PERSON FLOATS MYSTERIOUSLY IN MID-AIR, FROZEN IN TIME AND SPACE AS IF DEFYING THE CONSTRAINTS OF PHYSICS. THE WORK ENGAGES WITH THE NOTIONS OF THE BODY AS MATERIAL AND THE MATERIALITY OF THE BODY, TESTING THE LIMITS OF PHYSICAL AND COGNITIVE POSSIBILITIES AS WE TRY TO COMPREHEND WHAT WE SEE.

A prolific and controversial artist, Xu Zhen has established a conceptually-driven practice that encompasses a vast range of media and often employs humor, irony, and sophisticated trickery. For In Just a Blink of an Eye (2005),[1] presented in 14 Rooms, a breathing body floats mysteriously in mid-air, frozen in time and space as if defying the constraints of physics. The work engages with the notions of the body as material and the materiality of the body, testing the limits of physical and cognitive possibilities as we try to comprehend what we see. We wait for movement, for the performer to stand up or to continue falling, but instead time seems to stretch on impossibly and there is no resolution. In previous iterations of the work, Zhen employed members of marginalized communities, such as migrant workers, to undertake the performance. In these instances the literal suspension became a metaphor for liminal civil status.

Part of Zhen's practice is the illumination of the mechanics of observation and perception, particularly foreign perceptions of his homeland China. One of his best known works, 8848 – 1.86 (2005), is a mockumentary of the artist purportedly scaling Mount Everest—the title referring to the height of the mountain minus the height of the artist. In the work, the artist and his team chop off the peak of the world's highest mountain to bring it back to China like a trophy. This tongue-in-cheek piece was actually filmed on a set on the roof of Zhen's Shanghai studio and the installation includes climbing equipment from the expedition, as well as the snowy peak triumphantly presented in a huge refrigerated vitrine. The work tests the limits of gullibility so effectively that the reduced height of Mount Everest actually received news coverage. Through and beyond its humor the work speaks to China's current Tibet policy, which refuses to recognize

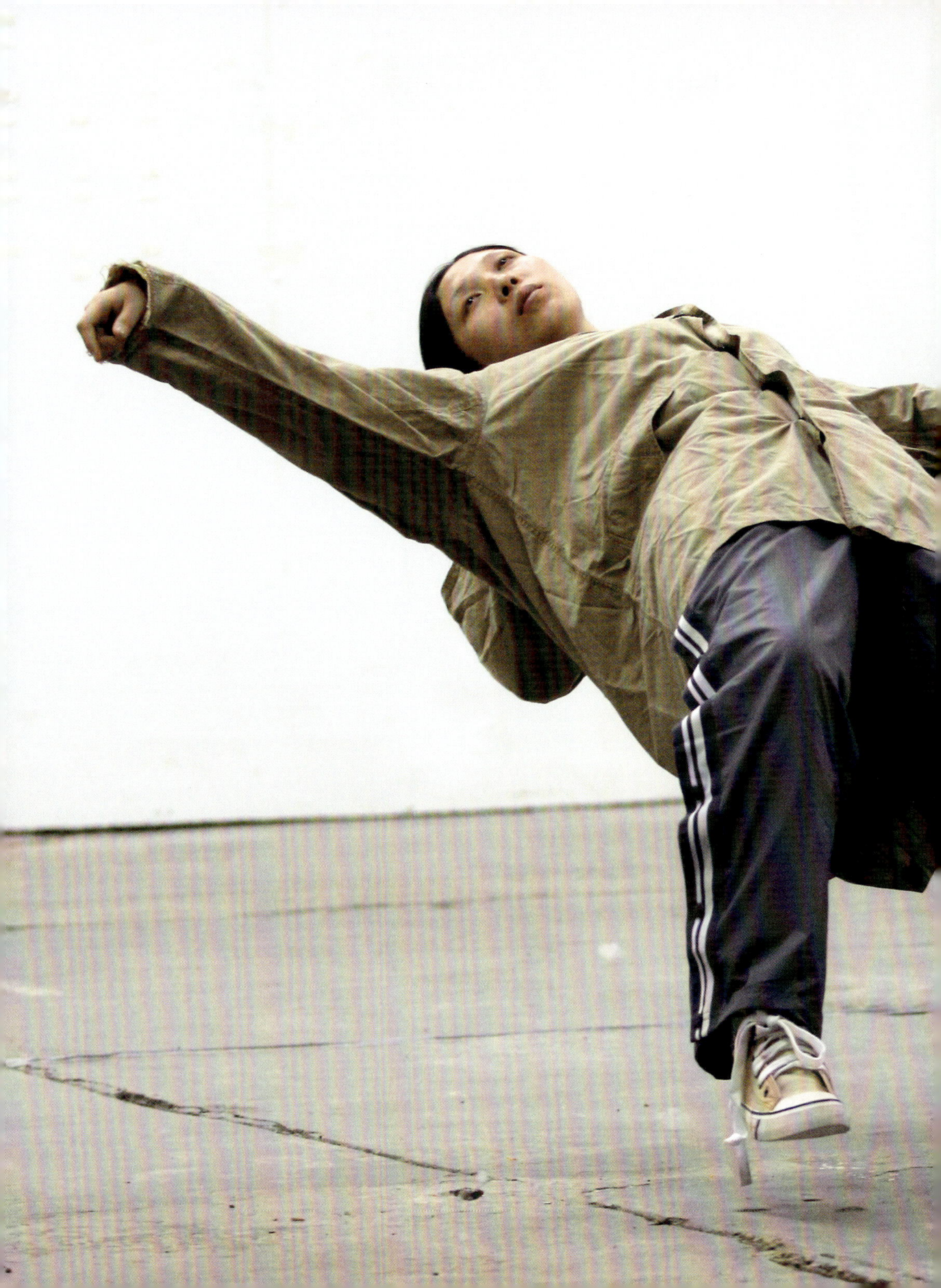

Tibet's struggle for self-determination. In an imperial-like campaign, her proud peak is callously cut off.

Zhen's work is often described as provocative and controversial, exemplified by the piece <u>The Starving of Sudan</u> (2008), an installation at Long March Space in Beijing that recreated photojournalist Kevin Carter's 1993 prize-winning photograph of a vulture stalking a starving Sudanese child. In Zhen's version, the vulture was animatronic and the child (a paid actor supervised by her mother) from an immigrant Guinean family living in Guangzhou. The installation was completed by the reactions of visitors, many of whom retrieved their phones to take photographs. By implicating the audience and casting them in Carter's role, Zhen's work raised complex ethical questions about bearing witness. (TL)

[1] Performed previously in these contexts: <u>11 Rooms</u> at the Manchester Art Gallery during the Manchester International Festival in 2011; <u>12 Rooms</u> at the Museum Folkwang during the RUHRTRIENNALE International Arts Festival 2012–14 in 2012; <u>13 Rooms</u> at Kaldor Public Art Projects during the 27th Kaldor Public Art Project in 2013.

—

p. 77 (detail) Xu Zhen, <u>In Just a Blink of an Eye</u>, 2005
p. 79 (top) Xu Zhen, <u>In Just a Blink of an Eye</u>, 2005
Performed for <u>13 Rooms</u> at Kaldor Public Art Projects during the 27th Kaldor Public Art Project in 2013.
p. 79 (bottom) Xu Zhen, <u>In Just a Blink of an Eye</u>, 2005
Performed for <u>11 Rooms</u> at the Manchester Art Gallery during the Manchester International Festival in 2011.

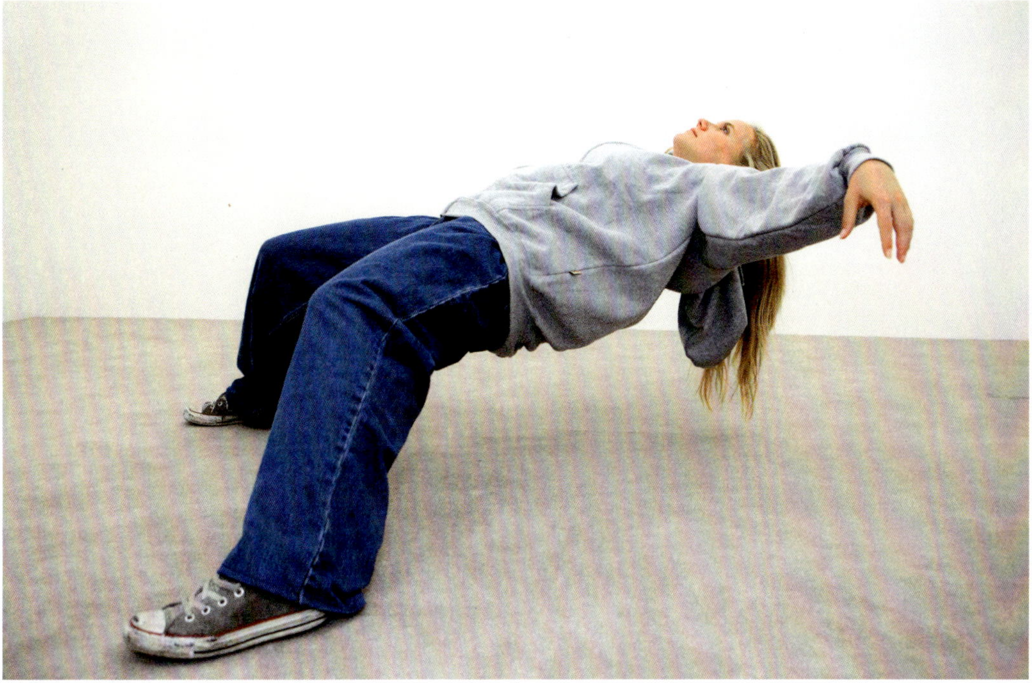

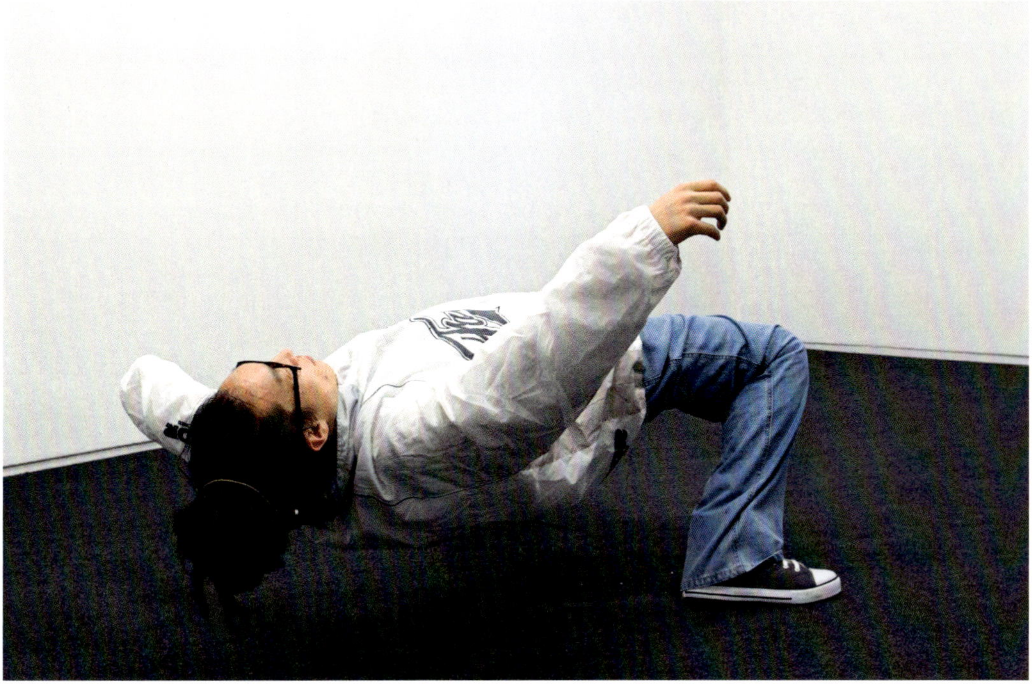

EPILOGUE
JORDAN WOLFSON

ARCHIVE
JOHN BALDESSARI

JORDAN WOLFSON
(FEMALE FIGURE) 2014, 2014

AN ANIMATRONIC DANCER MOVES LASCIVIOUSLY IN FRONT OF A LARGE MIRROR. SHE TRIES TO CATCH THE EYE OF THE SPECTATOR WHILE AT THE SAME TIME WATCHING HERSELF, MUCH IN THE WAY THAT VIEWERS ARE CONFRONTED WITH THEIR OWN MIRROR IMAGES.

Jordan Wolfson belongs to a younger generation of artists whose work cannot be ascribed to any one specific medium. The artist works with installation, video, sculpture, and performance. His interests are situated within a larger discussion about the contemporary human condition and how we define ourselves within an environment that resists such definitions. An important point of departure for Wolfson's work is technology, which the artist implements less as a means of generating cold machines with purely utilitarian applications and more as a way of creating new "contemporary" characters. Born from a world dominated by communication, advertising, and marketing, these figures are developed in narratives that forcefully convey the artist's view and that address how we portray ourselves.

Wolfson began developing in 2009 three video works including Con Leche (2009), Animation, masks (2011), and Raspberry Poser (2012), which use animation to convey various narrative sequences. He not only draws from the aesthetics of animation, recalling Disney renderings, but he also generates stories that resemble typical documentaries. In Con Leche animated bottles of Diet Coke filled with milk march in rows through the streets of Detroit. The images of the city were filmed on site, the Coke bottles are cartoons. The commercial product and the scenery are infused with the codes of marketing and media—as the refreshment drink and as a bankrupt city that has become emblematic of poverty in the United States. A global product poses a contradiction to the decline of a city that once forged American history. The video is one of Wolfson's psychologically complex works in which images and language undergo dreamlike repetitions and experimental configurations.

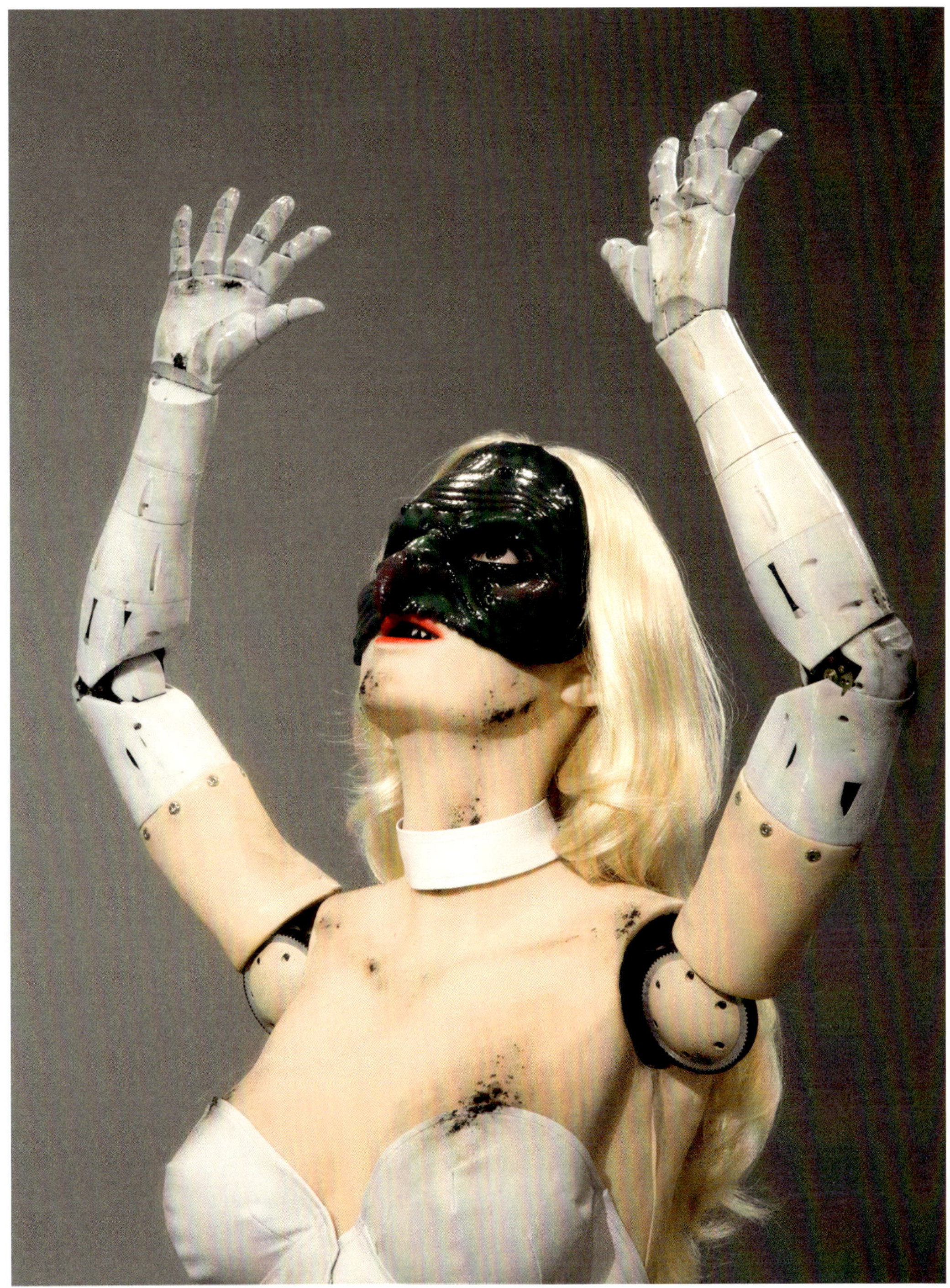

For <u>14 Rooms</u> Wolfson presents his installation <u>(Female figure) 2014</u> (2014), an animatronic robot. Placed in the final room of the exhibition, it can be seen as an epilogue to the project. The female robot moves lasciviously back and forth, up and down while standing in front of a large mirror. She is watching herself, much in the way that viewers are confronted with their own mirror images. This produces, if indirectly, a communication between individuals, other visitors, and the robot. Based on the guiding concept of <u>14 Rooms</u> to offer a real and visually immediate encounter with works of performance, Wolfson's work can be read as a step into the future. When entering the room we are alone and we are confronted by ourselves and the machine, which tries to make eye contact with us through motion detectors in her eyes. In a highly evocative manner this work deals with our own self-presentation. Whereas we put more and more images of ourselves on the Internet, if we count all the selfies on social networks, the robot represents the future of technology as a machine which is infused with human qualities and watches and observes herself—confronting us with this situation. The machine becomes a constantly functional, always available subject within a society of constant accessibility. With <u>(Female figure) 2014</u> Wolfson creates a machine that portrays narcissism in a natural and physical constellation, enabling this device to become a mirror of who we are. Perhaps this is the very reason that Wolfson's installation captivates us, pulling us into the world of the mechanical unconscious, into the depths of our most intimate fears. (FS)

—

pp. 83, 85 Jordan Wolfson, <u>(Female figure) 2014</u>, 2014
Mixed media. 229.9 × 182.9 × 73.7 cm

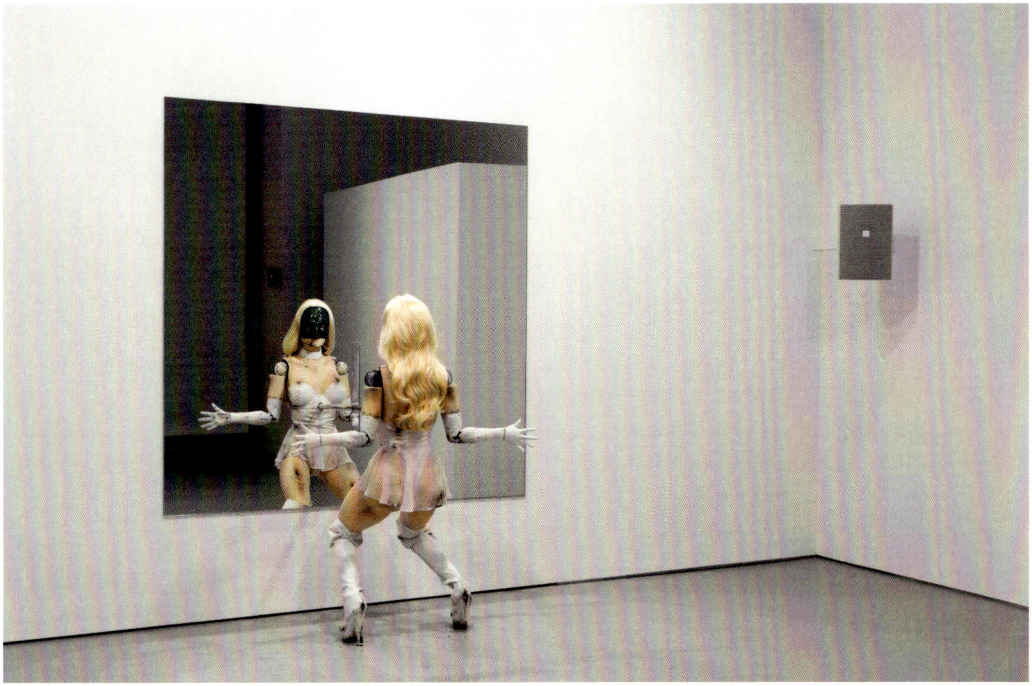

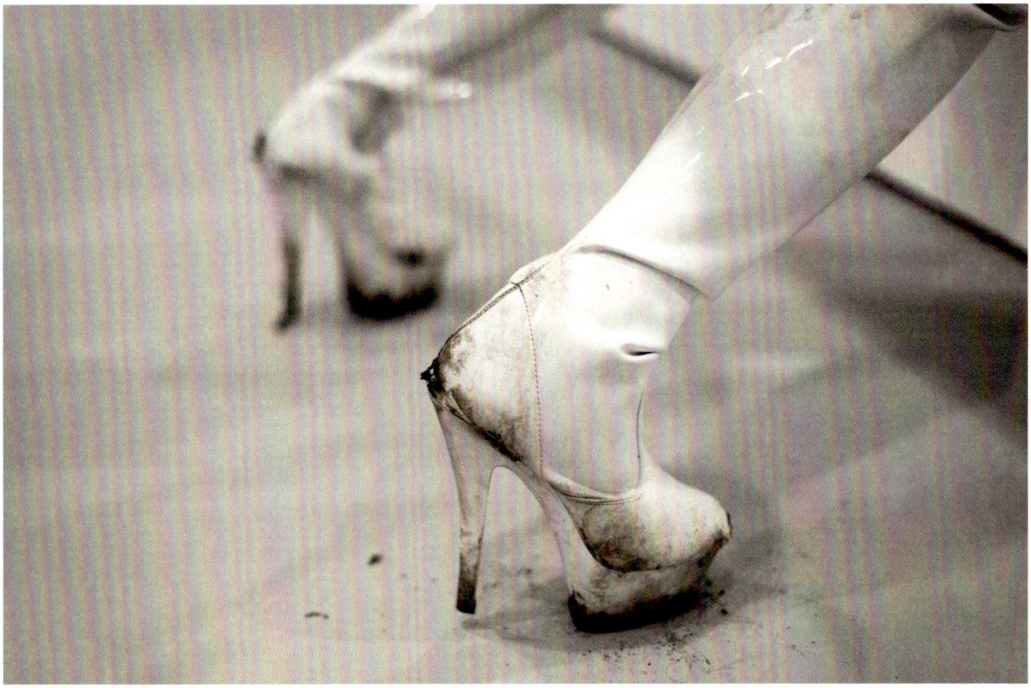

JOHN BALDESSARI
UNREALIZED PROPOSAL FOR CADAVER PIECE, 1970

IN 1970 THE ARTIST PROPOSED SHOWING A CORPSE IN THE CONTEXT OF THE <u>INFORMATION</u> EXHIBITION AT MOMA IN NEW YORK, A PROVOCATIVE AND CHALLENGING WORK THAT WOULD ADDRESS HOW THE ART WORLD—AND SOCIETY AS A WHOLE— DEAL WITH DEATH. THIS REMAINS AN UNREALIZED PROJECT, AS ETHICAL AND LEGAL CONCERNS HAVE BEEN A RECURRENT HINDRANCE.

John Baldessari is one of the most influential artists of his generation. In 1970 he proposed a provocative and challenging work that addresses how the art world—and society as a whole—deal with death. This intensely poignant work references Andrea Mantegna's painting <u>Lamentation of Christ</u> (c. 1490) and Marcel Duchamp's three-dimensional tableau <u>Étant donnés</u>, completed just before the artist's death in 1968.

Baldessari's proposal to present a cadaver recalls Mantegna's realistic representation of Christ. Viewers would see a recumbent figure through a viewing hole from the same perspective as the Mantegna and Duchamp works—from the feet upwards. This unusual use of perspective brings the body so close to the viewer that it elicits a powerful emotional reaction and profound sense of pathos, as the reality of our own mortality comes to the fore. However, the cadaver is not the subject of the work. The piece addresses how death is represented in art and how artistic conventions such as lighting and staging can be used to create aesthetic distance.

It was only in 2010 that an effort by Manchester International Festival and Manchester Art Gallery to finally realize this concept brought the project to fruition within the context of <u>11 Rooms</u>. Until then no institution had seriously attempted to present it. A range of international professionals and academics in the fields of pathology, medical ethics, and law were consulted about the legal and ethical issues that this work raises. However, it has still not been possible to secure consent to display a body within the frame of an exhibition. There is an on-going dialogue with the artist and a serious commitment by Manchester International Festival, Manchester Art Gallery, The International Arts Festival RUHRTRIENNALE, and the curators to realize this important and profound work in the future.

PROPOSAL: Possibly an impossible project.
The idea is to exhibit a cadaver, rather than
a facsimile person. What is intended is a
double play of sorts. One would possbly be
appalled at seeing the corpse, i.e., the
factor of aesthetic distance would be broken
down; but by controlling the lighting, staging, etc., so that it approximates Andrea
Mantegna's _Dead Christ_ (making it look like
art, refer to what is established as art) the
shock would be cancelled and one might be
able to look at the tableaux with little or
no discomfort. The subject is not the cadaver. The subject is rather the issue of a
breaking and mending aesthetic distance.

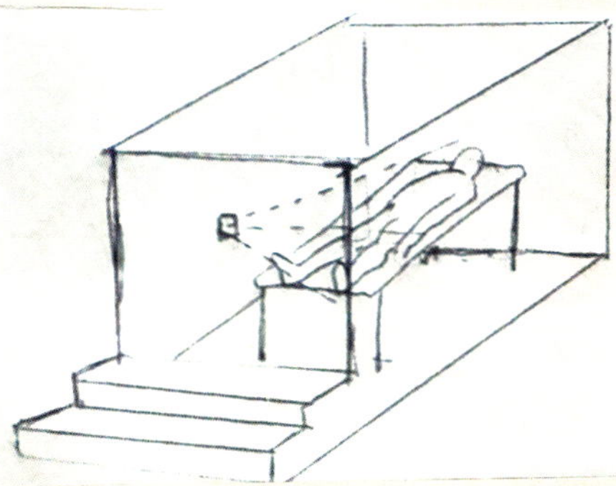

Special room would be built with a glass
peephole. Rheostat lighting, refrigeration
unit would be concealed.

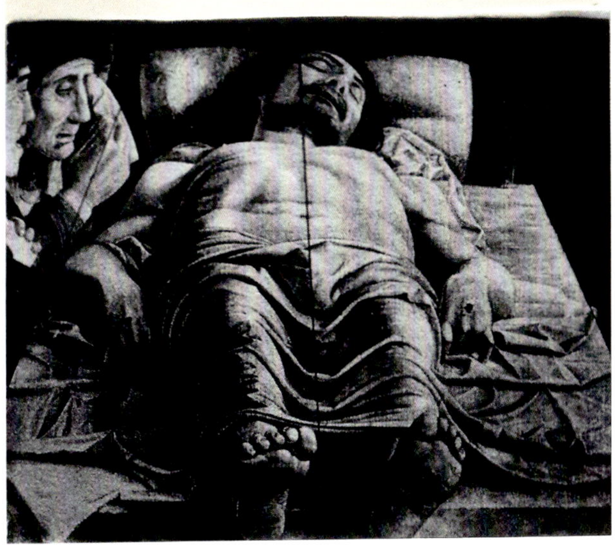

Hundreds of emails and calls between the festival, gallery, exhibition staff, curators, artist's studio, and consulted professionals document the process thus far. This documentation, shown on the occasion of <u>14 Rooms</u>,[1] acts as testament to the serious effort that has been made to realize the concept in a sensitive and respectful way. (FC/MBW/MP/DN/RC)

[1] Presented previously in these contexts: <u>11 Rooms</u> at the Manchester Art Gallery during the Manchester International Festival in 2011; <u>12 Rooms</u> at the Museum Folkwang during the RUHRTRIENNALE International Arts Festival 2012–14 in 2012.

—

p.87 John Baldessari, <u>Cadaver Piece (Proposal for Information Show)</u>, 1970. B+W Photographs, 11 × 8.5 inches
p.89 (top) John Baldessari, <u>Unrealized Proposal for Cadaver Piece</u>, 1970/2011. Dimensions variable.
Presented at <u>11 Rooms</u> at the Manchester Art Gallery during the Manchester International Festival in 2011.
p.89 (bottom) John Baldessari, <u>Unrealized Proposal for Cadaver Piece</u>, 1970/2011. Dimensions variable.
Presented at <u>12 Rooms</u> at the Museum Folkwang during the RUHRTRIENNALE International Arts Festival 2012–14 in 2012.

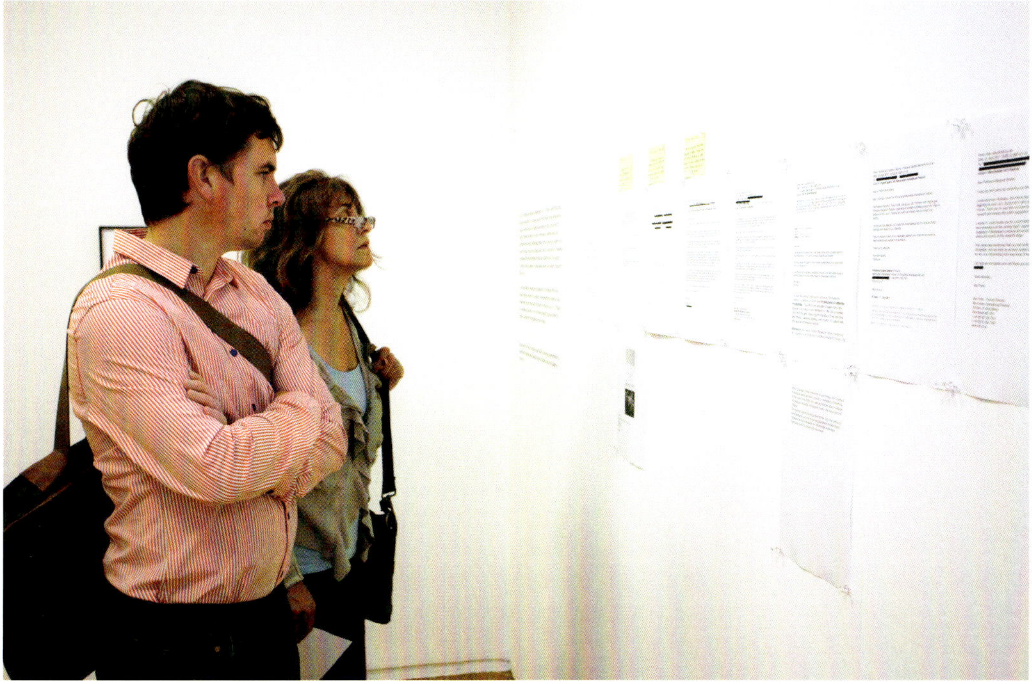

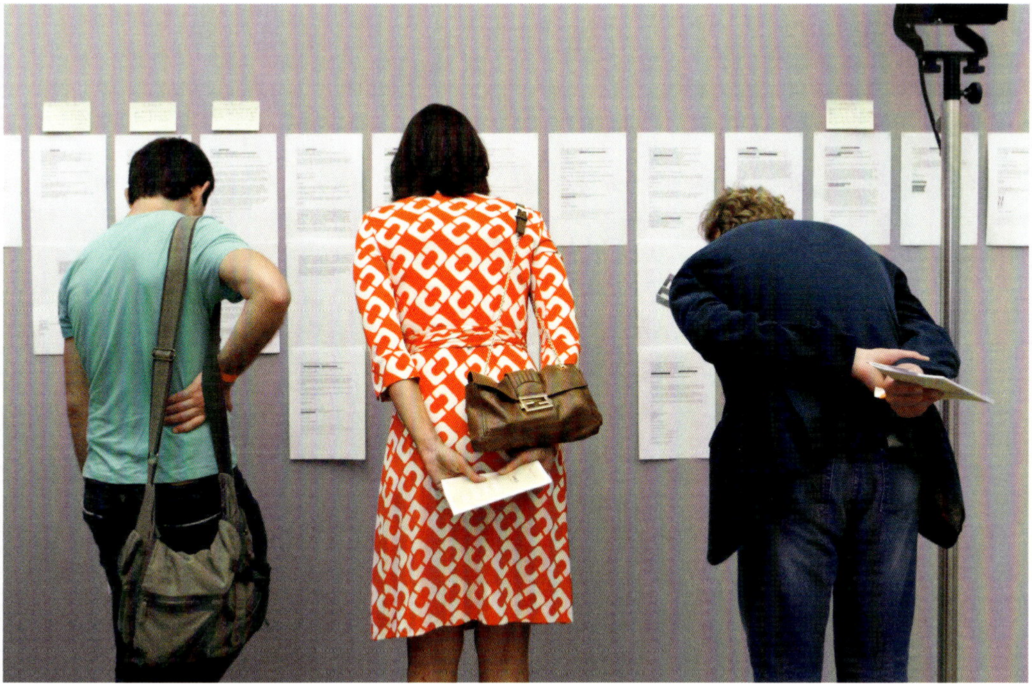

ARCHITECTURE

HERZOG & DE MEURON

HERZOG & DE MEURON

14 Rooms is taking place in the same hall where we designed a temporary architectural installation in 2001—a concert hall for the European Month of Music. Now, in 2014, there will be fourteen rooms for fourteen artists to present live performances for small groups of people. This spectacular artistic project, already organized in various cities, will continue to take place in the coming years. Last year there were thirteen rooms, this year there will be fourteen and next year fifteen. The overall temporary installation of the rooms is variable but the basic properties of each one are always the same: a floor area of 5-by-5 meters, a height of 3.5 meters, a door, and no windows. Earlier on, the rooms were laid out like scattered or compact settlements with lanes and plazas in between. We have opted for a stringent, linear arrangement of two parallel facades, painted white, each with seven doors. A mirrored wall placed at the two narrow ends optically extends the white facades and the doors to infinity. Instead of fourteen doors, there seem to be two, three, or four times as many. Fourteen is a chance number; it will be fifteen in 2015 and possibly 100 in the year 2100.

The location and the city where this exhibition takes place are not relevant in this temporary installation; the white walls and doors could be anywhere—unlike the HERE and NOW of the encounter between artworks and visitors.

The temporary installation is therefore an extreme abstraction, almost like a typological sculpture—a lane as broad as a plaza, typical of a small town in South America or China or Europe. Only the wooden handles used by visitors to enter the room vary slightly from door to door—fourteen different handles, digitally cut out of wood, minimally distinguishable at first sight but each somewhat different in feeling.

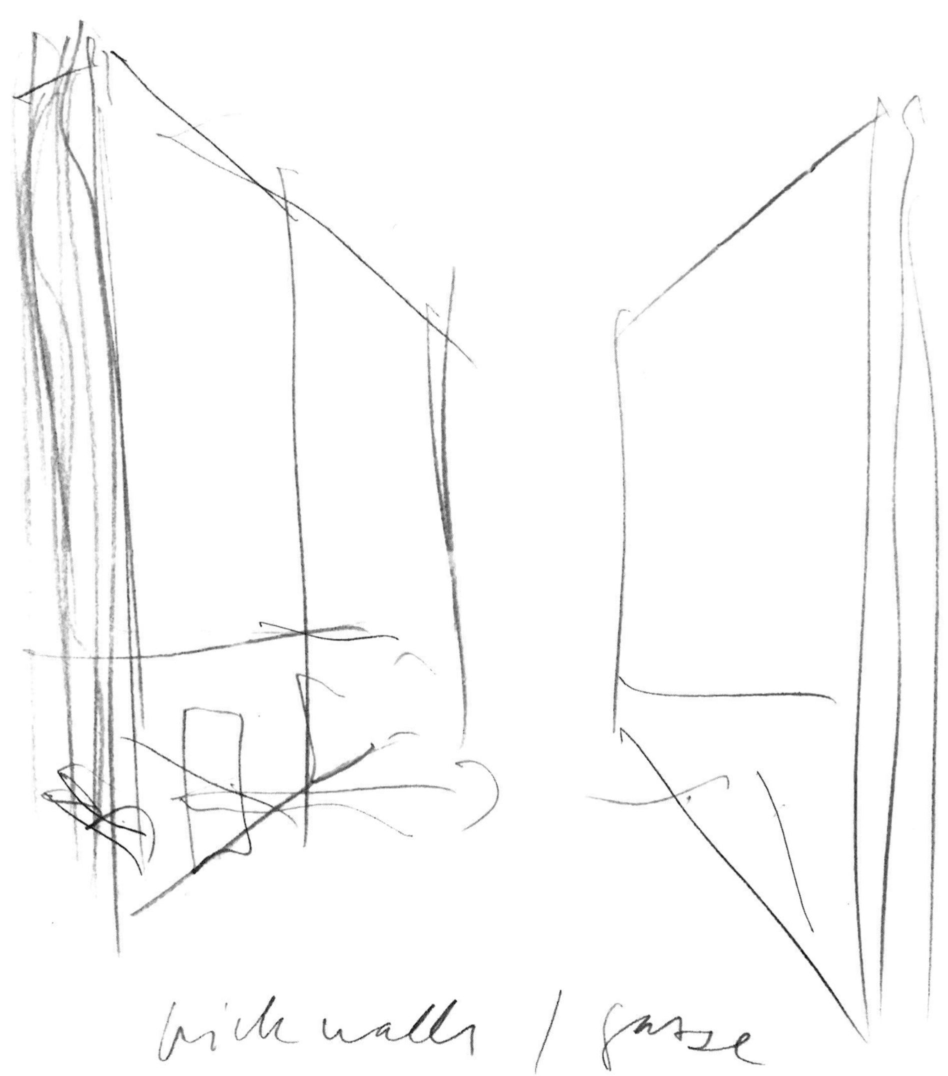
brick walls / gasse

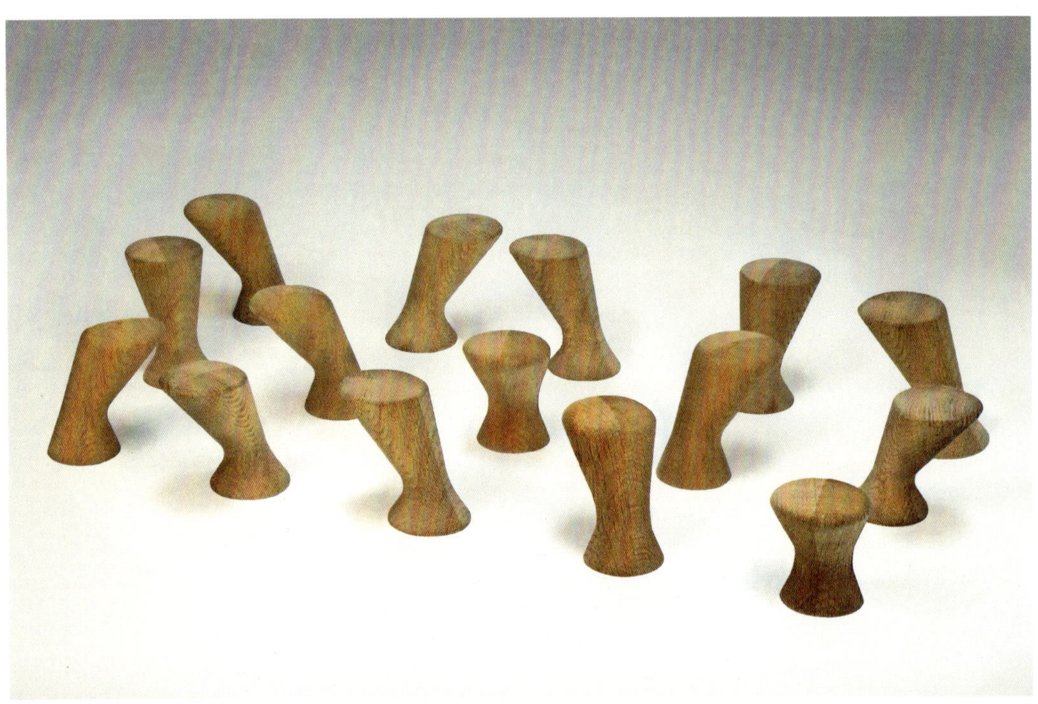

The specificity of the location is not perceived unless visitors look up at the ceiling where they see a load-bearing structure whose archaic appearance testifies to the oldest surviving trade fair hall in Basel. (H&dM)

—

p. 93 Herzog & de Meuron, Sketch for <u>14 Rooms</u>, Basel, Switzerland, 2014
p. 94 Herzog & de Meuron, Photograph of digitally cut wooden door handles of varying textures and shapes for <u>14 Rooms</u>, Basel, Switzerland, 2014
p. 95 Herzog & de Meuron, Model and rendering for <u>14 Rooms</u>, Basel, Switzerland, 2014

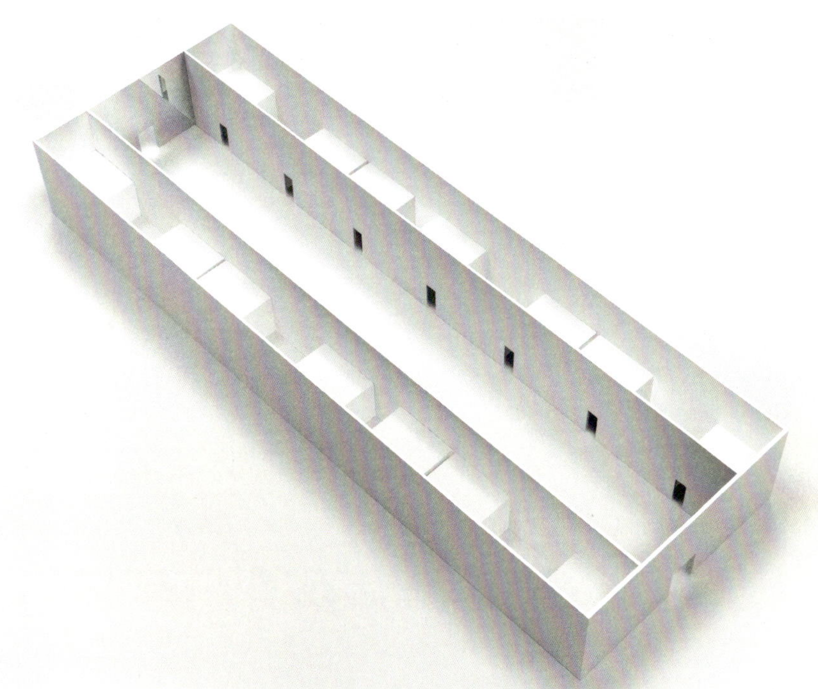

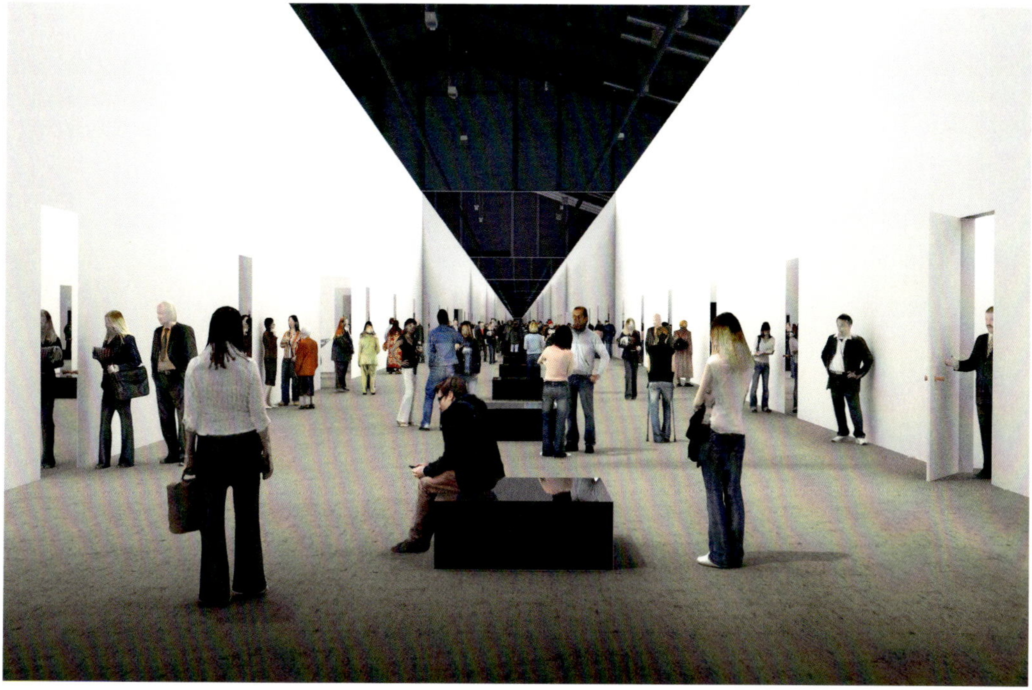

ESSAY
PASSING SHOW

DAVID MALOUF

DAVID MALOUF

John Keats, in one of his last and greatest poems, addresses the Grecian urn that is his model of transcendent art:

Thou, silent form, dost tease us out of thought,
As dost eternity. Cold Pastoral!
When old age shall this generation waste,
Thou shalt remain . . .

The special quality he isolates in the work of art is its permanence against the passing seasons and the actions and generations of men, and this insistence on "endurance" goes back to the beginnings of aesthetic thinking. Shakespeare, in claiming for what is merely written (printed) the permanency of metal or stone,

Not marble, nor the gilden monuments
Of princes shall outlast my powerful rhyme

is echoing a poet of 1500 years before, the Horace of Ode 30, Book III:

Exigi monumentum aere perennius
regalique situ pyramidum altius

(I have made a monument more enduring
than bronze and taller than a pyramid)

The claim, itself an enduring one, is that the work of art, the object carved in marble, struck in bronze, raised in stone, or painted or in mosaic on a wall, belongs not to time and "occasion" but to what Yeats, in "Sailing to Byzantium" called "the artifice of eternity."

Of course there has from the beginning been another form of artistic action that makes no such claim. Opposed to objects that exist solidly in space, in an eternal presence that resists time, are works of performance that belong only in time, and to a single, if endlessly repeatable, occasion; dependent, as they are, on the immediate energy and interaction of the actors, singers, dancers, musicians who produce them, but also on the chemistry of each particular audience and on the spatial or other qualities, indoors or out, of the venue. No performance is fixed or perfect—that is a good part of its attraction—or free of contingency or risk; and since it cannot, like the object in space, be returned to, it endures—that is its special poignancy—only as a trace in the memory (or memoirs) of those who were there to experience it.

Later, in the sixteenth century, such traces of performance were also searched out in some works of the other, non-performative kind; as brushstrokes for example, signs of action and presence, in Venetian painters, and in Velásquez and Rubens, and later again in the plein air works of the Impressionists. But essentially the distinction between works made or performed was, till the early twentieth century, an orthodoxy. Made works were always the real thing, and clearly superior.

In fact painters, sculptors, and architects often worked in genres that were "occasional" and ephemeral: mediaeval floats and processions that celebrated civic or religious festivals; the triumphal arches and tableaux that welcomed Renaissance princes; later, stage designs, such as the ones Inigo Jones created for court masques and ballets, and the transformation scenes of baroque opera. Bernini, in 1638, was the producer of an extraordinary spectacle, <u>The Flooding of the Tiber</u>, that ended with the revelation of two audiences, two "theaters," facing one another as in a mirror, and Jacques-Louis David, at the height of the Terror, organized vast outdoor celebrations of the days of the Revolutionary Calendar. But artists continued to make a distinction between occasional art and art that was intended to endure.

Bernini's Cornaro Chapel, theatrical as it may be, and dependent for its effect on the moment and on illusion, takes place in a theater of eternity—that is its whole point. The several generations of the Cornaro family, who as spectators of the <u>Ecstasy of Saint Teresa</u> occupy boxes on either side of the altar, are frozen in a single moment of presence, and are of marble. They are always available to view, as is the spectacle of the saint itself, which is "fixed" as Saint Teresa and the angel float in an eternal moment before them.

Even Pozzo's vast ceiling in Il Gesù, which is occasional in that it springs fully into existence only when a single spectator moves to a particular spot on the church floor, is made to endure.

The challenge to this orthodoxy, and the hierarchy on which it was based, comes only with the Dadaist performances at Cabaret Voltaire, and later at the Odeon, in 1916, first in Zurich, later in Paris, Berlin, and elsewhere; then in the 1930s, in the vast spectacles arranged for the Nazis by Albert Speer, culminating at Nuremberg in 1934, and to some extent "preserved" on film by Leni Riefenstahl; then in the many installations and happenings of the 1960s, and increasingly in works such as Christo's wrapping of sites and public buildings, the gallery performances of Gilbert & George, and locally of Mike Parr and Ken Unsworth, and in Deborah Warner's <u>The Angel Project</u> at the 2000 Perth Festival.

A large part of what now constitutes contemporary art runs counter to previous orthodoxies. In line with an outlook and sensibility that sees in immediacy and presence something more essential to art than what is fixed and permanent—"the imperfect," to quote Wallace Stevens, "is so hot within us"—contemporary artists have embraced contingency, performance, play, but also wit, humor, anguish, provocation, affront, and the pathos of transience and error, as being more properly truthful to the world as it is than older verities. They invite us in—as they do to the fourteen rooms that make up the latest collaboration between Fondation Beyeler, Art Basel, and Theater Basel—to occupy the spaces they create and become the players and spectators, and sometimes both, who will amplify with our presence the occasions they offer and make a living theater of them.

BIOGRAPHIES

MARINA ABRAMOVIĆ
ALLORA & CALZADILLA
ED ATKINS
DOMINIQUE GONZALEZ-FOERSTER
DAMIEN HIRST
JOAN JONAS
LAURA LIMA
BRUCE NAUMAN
OTOBONG NKANGA
ROMAN ONDÁK
YOKO ONO
TINO SEHGAL
SANTIAGO SIERRA
XU ZHEN

JORDAN WOLFSON
JOHN BALDESSARI

KLAUS BIESENBACH
HANS ULRICH OBRIST

HERZOG & DE MEURON

MARINA ABRAMOVIĆ

BORN 1946, BELGRADE.
LIVES IN NEW YORK.

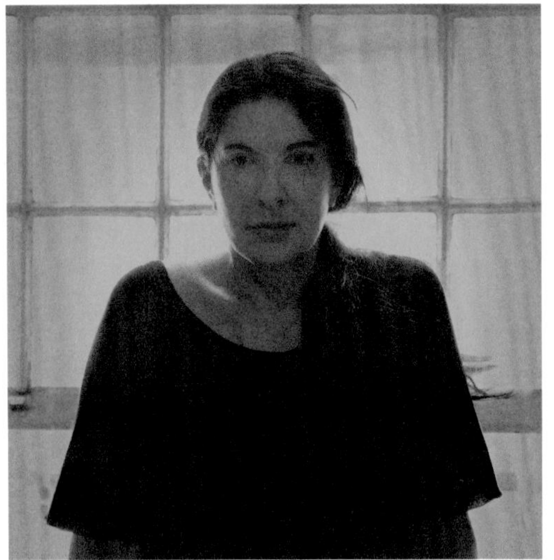

ALLORA & CALZADILLA

JENNIFER ALLORA: BORN 1974, PENNSYLVANIA.
LIVES IN SAN JUAN.
GUILLERMO CALZADILLA: BORN 1971, HAVANA.
LIVES IN SAN JUAN.

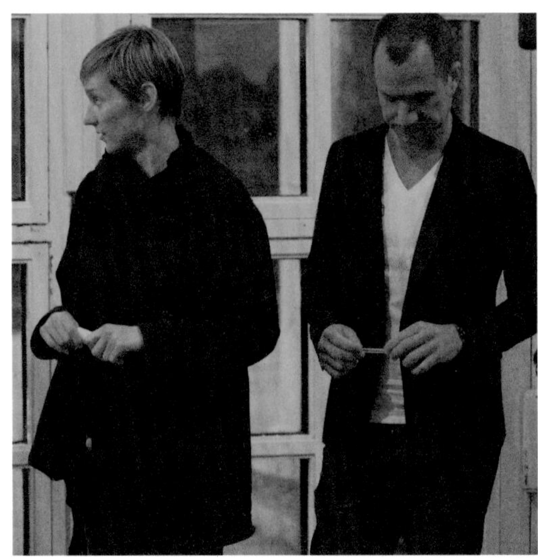

In 2014, Abramović is showing at the CAC Malaga; Kistefos Museet, Oslo; and The Serpentine Galleries in London. She is planning to open the Marina Abramović Institute for the Preservation of Performance Art (MAI) in New York in 2015. In 2012, the documentary Marina Abramović: The Artist is Present premiered at the Sundance Film Festival. In 2011 she was the subject of a major retrospective at the Garage Center in Moscow and she participated in Robert Wilson's The Life and Death of Marina Abramović, a critically acclaimed re-imagination of Abramović's biography. She was the subject of The Artist is Present, a major retrospective at the Museum of Modern Art, New York (2010). Abramović was awarded the Golden Lion at the 1997 Venice Biennale for her piece Balkan Baroque. Her work has been included in many international exhibitions such as the Venice Biennale (1997, 1976) and documenta, Kassel (1992, 1982, 1977).

Allora & Calzadilla have participated in numerous group exhibitions, biennials, and events around the world, such as documenta 13 in 2012. One year earlier they represented the United States at the 2011 Venice Biennale. Their selected solo exhibitions include: Fondazione Nicola Trussardi, Milan (2013); Indianapolis Museum of Art (2012); Museum of Modern Art, New York (2011); National Museum of Art, Oslo (2009); Temporäre Kunsthalle, Berlin (2009); Haus der Kunst, Munich (2008); Stedelijk Museum, Amsterdam (2008); San Francisco Art Institute (2007); Kunsthalle Zürich, Zurich (2007); The Renaissance Society at The University of Chicago (2007); Serpentine Gallery, London (2007); Whitechapel Gallery, London (2007); Center for Contemporary Art Kitakyushu, (2007); Palais de Tokyo, Paris (2006); Dallas Museum of Art (2006); and the Institute of Contemporary Art, Boston (2004).

ED ATKINS
BORN 1982, OXFORD.
LIVES IN LONDON.

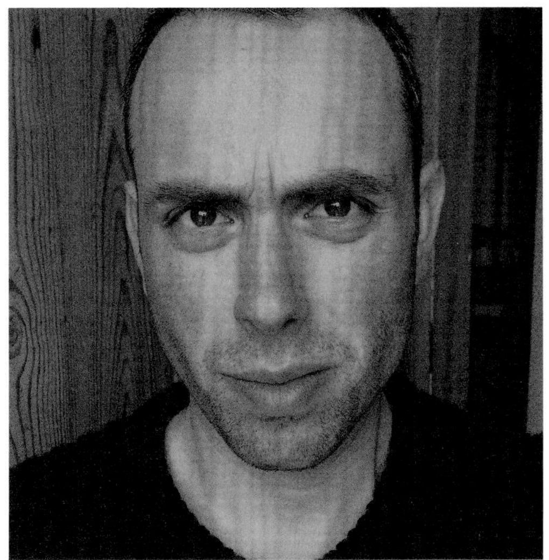

In 2014 Atkins will present solo exhibitions at the Palais de Tokyo, Paris; Kunsthalle Mainz (with Bruce Nauman); and the Serpentine Gallery, London. His recent solo presentations include Chisenhale Gallery, London; MoMA PS1, New York; Julia Stoschek Collection, Düsseldorf; and Kunsthalle Zürich, Zurich. He was included in both the Venice and Lyon Biennials, and the recent group exhibitions <u>Teen Paranormal Romance</u>, The Renaissance Society, Chicago (2014); <u>Speculations on Anonymous Materials</u>, Fridericianum, Kassel (2013–14); and <u>Frozen Lakes</u>, Artist Space, New York (2013).

DOMINIQUE GONZALEZ-FOERSTER
BORN 1965, STRASBOURG.
LIVES IN PARIS AND RIO DE JANEIRO.

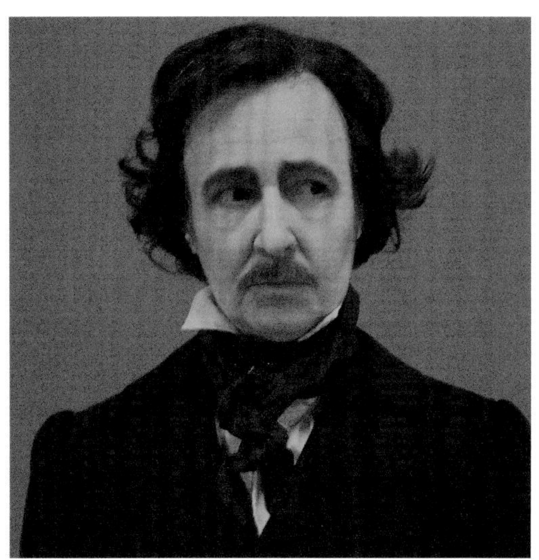

Dominique Gonzalez-Foerster is currently preparing for an upcoming show at the Centre Pompidou in Paris. Previously she has exhibited widely in, among others, <u>SPLENDIDE – HOTEL</u>, Palacio de Christal, Parque del Retiro, organized by the Museo Nacional Centro de Arte Reina Sofia, Madrid (2014); <u>Cloud Illusions I Recall</u> (a collaboration with Cerith Wyn Evans), Irish Museum of Modern Art, Dublin (2013); <u>M.2062 (Scarlett)</u>, The Museum of Kyoto (2013); <u>T.451</u>, Tensta Konsthall and the Asplund Library, Stockholm (2012); <u>chronotopes & dioramas</u>, Dia Art Foundation, New York (2009); <u>TH.2058</u>, Tate Modern Turbine Hall, London (2008); <u>Expodrome</u>, Musee d'Art Moderne de la Ville de Paris/ARC, Paris (2007); and <u>Multiverse</u>, Kunsthalle Zürich, Zurich (2004).

DAMIEN HIRST

BORN 1965, BRISTOL.
LIVES IN LONDON, DEVON, AND GLOUCESTERSHIRE.

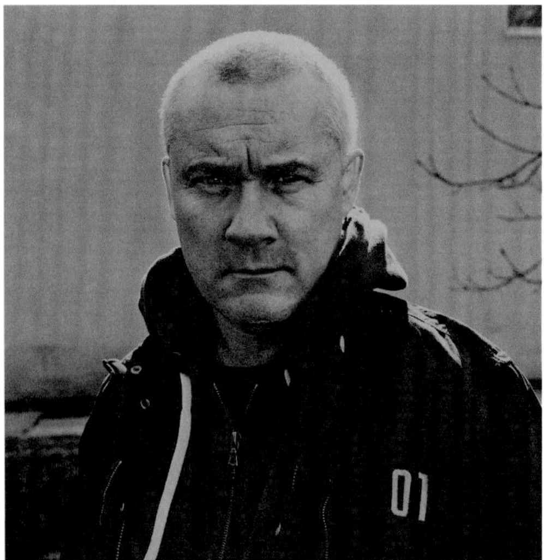

JOAN JONAS

BORN 1936, NEW YORK CITY.
LIVES IN NEW YORK.

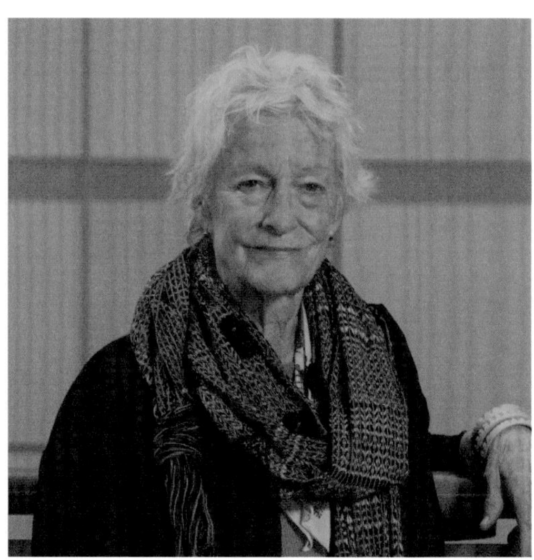

Since 1987 Hirst has been in over 80 solo and 250 group exhibitions worldwide and has been the subject of more than twenty-five monographs. He was awarded the coveted Turner Prize in 1995 and in 2012 the Tate Modern held <u>Damien Hirst</u>, a major retrospective spanning twenty-five years of the artist's practice.

Jonas will make a new work for the American Pavilion in the Venice Biennale in 2015 and will have a retrospective in 2014 at Hangar Bicocca, Milan. In 2009 she was awarded the Guggenheim Museum's Lifetime Achievement Award in New York. She has presented numerous works and performances at museums and galleries around the world, in recent years these have included the Museum of Modern Art, New York; Museu d'Art Contemporani de Barcelona; Centre d'Art Contemporain, Geneva; Castello di Rivoli, Turin; Museo Nacional Centro de Arte Reina Sofia, Madrid; Witte de With, Rotterdam; Whitney Museum of American Art, New York; and Tate Modern, London. Major retrospectives of Jonas's work were held at the Queens Museum, New York, (2003); Galerie der Stadt Stuttgart (2000); and the Stedelijk Museum, Amsterdam (1994). She took part in the Venice Biennale in 2009 and has participated in six of the prestigious documenta exhibitions in Kassel.

LAURA LIMA
BORN 1971, MINAS GERAIS.
LIVES IN RIO DE JANEIRO.

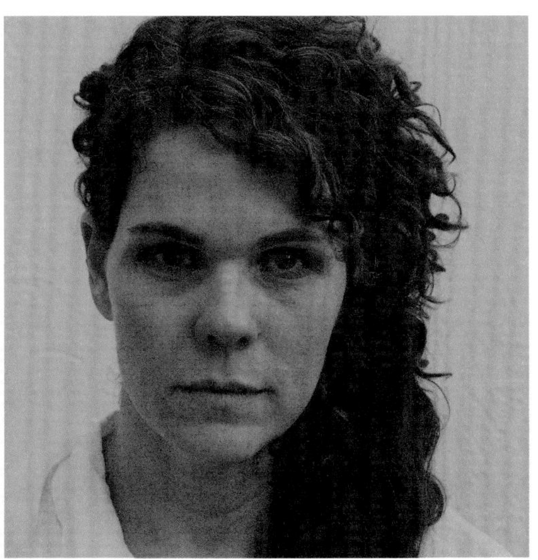

BRUCE NAUMAN
BORN 1941, FORT WAYNE, INDIANA.
LIVES IN NEW MEXICO.

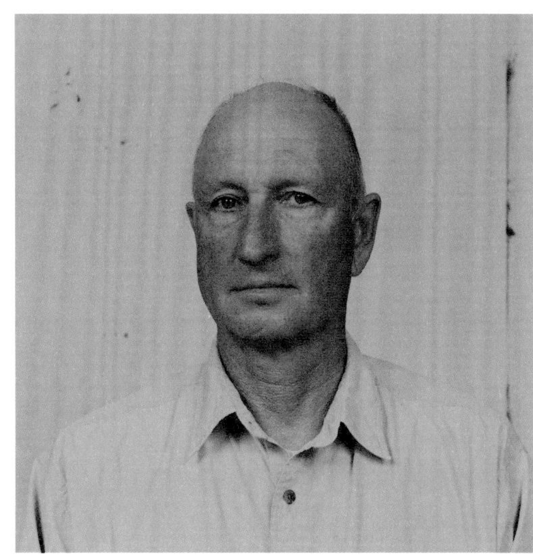

Lima has had solo exhibitions at Museu de Arte da Pampulha, Belo Horizonte, Brazil; Galeria Luisa Strina, São Paulo; Hardcore Art Contemporary Space, Miami; Casa França Brasil, Rio de Janeiro; Museo Universitario Arte Contemporáneo (MuAC), Mexico City; Chapter Arts Centre, Cardiff; and Migros Museum für Gegenwartskunst, Zurich. She is preparing solo shows at the Bonnefanten Museum, Maastricht; the Bonniers Konsthall, Stockholm; and the Lilith Performance Studio, Malmo. Her work has been included in group shows and festivals around the globe, including the 11th Biennale de Lyon (2011); the 7th Mercosul Biennial, Porto Alegre, Brazil (2009); and the São Paulo Biennial (2006 and 1998). Winner of the BACA Laureate, Netherlands, 2014.

Nauman represented the United States at the Venice Biennale (2009). The exhibition was awarded the Golden Lion for Best National Participation. His solo and group exhibitions include: <u>A Rose Has No Teeth</u>, Berkeley Art Museum, Castello di Rivoli, and Menil Collection (2007–08); <u>Raw Materials</u>, Tate Modern Turbine Hall (2004); <u>Bruce Nauman</u>, a major retrospective co-organized by The Walker Art Center and the Hirshhorn Museum, which traveled to the Museo Nacional Centro de Arte Reina Sofia, Madrid; Museum of Contemporary Art, Los Angeles; Museum of Modern Art, New York; and Kunsthaus Zürich, Zurich (1993–95); <u>Bruce Nauman 1972–1981</u>, Rijksmuseum Króller-Müller, Otterlo, Netherlands and Staatliche Kunsthalle Baden-Baden (1981); <u>Bruce Nauman: Work from 1965 to 1972</u>, organized by the Los Angeles County Museum of Art and the Whitney Museum of American Art, New York (1972–73); documenta, Kassel (1968).

OTOBONG NKANGA
BORN 1974, KANO, NIGERIA.
LIVES AND WORKS IN ANTWERP.

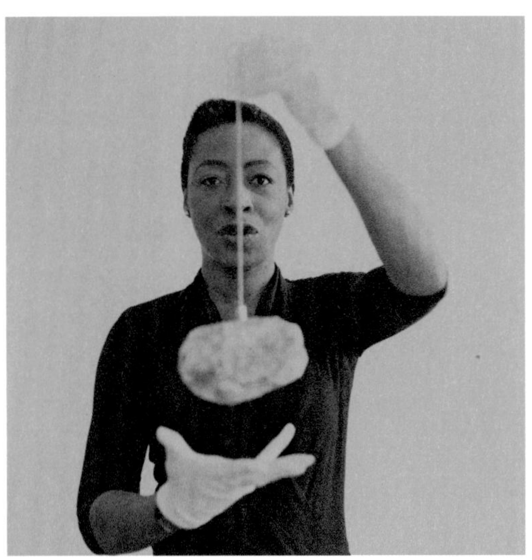

ROMAN ONDÁK
BORN 1966, ŽILINA.
LIVES IN BRATISLAVA.

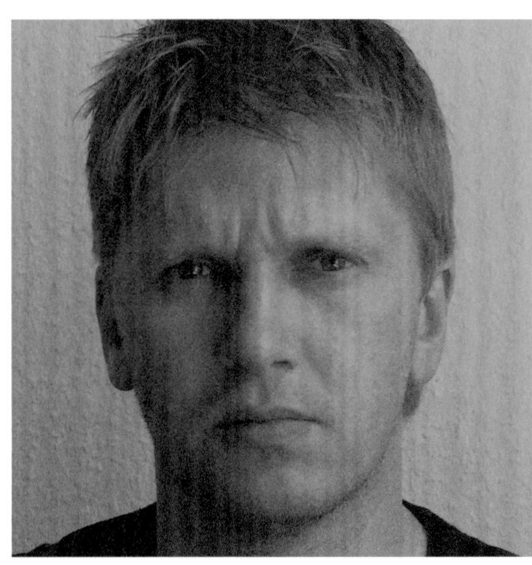

Nkanga has exhibited widely internationally and her recent shows and performances include: In Pursuit of Bling, 8th Berlin Biennale (2014); Glimmer Fragments in Symposium: Landing and Confessions, Stedelijk Museum, Amsterdam (2014); Foreign Exchange (or the stories you wouldn't tell a stranger), Weltkulturen Museum, Frankfurt am Main (2014); Taste of a Stone: Itiat Esa Ufok, Sharjah Biennial 11, United Arab Emirates (2013); Contained Measures of Shifting States in Across the Board: Politics of Representation, The Tanks at Tate Modern, London (2012); Contained Measures of a Kolanut in Tropicomania: The Social Life of Plants, Bétonsalon, Paris (2012); Contained Measures of Tangible Memories: Indigo Regina, L'Appartement 22, Rabat, Morocco (2012); Inventing the World: The Artist as Citizen, Biennale Benin, Cotonou, Benin (2012); ARS 11, Kiasma Museum of Contemporary Art, Helsinki (2011).

Ondák has had solo exhibitions at The Common Guild, Glasgow (2013); the Museo Nacional Centro de Arte Reina Sofía, Madrid (2013); the Deutsche Guggenheim, Berlin (2012); K21, Düsseldorf (2012); the Musée d'Art Moderne de la Ville de Paris (2012); Kunsthaus Zürich, Zurich (2011); and the Museum of Modern Art, New York (2009). He has participated in group exhibitions at the Centre Pompidou, Paris (2014 and 2010); Palais de Tokyo, Paris (2013); Fundación Jumex, Mexico City (2013); documenta 13, Kassel (2012); the Venice Biennale (2011, 2009, and 2003); the Berlin Biennale (2010); Hamburger Bahnhof, Berlin (2009); and Tate Modern, London (2007).

YOKO ONO
BORN 1933, TOKYO.
LIVES IN NEW YORK.

TINO SEHGAL
BORN 1976, LONDON.
LIVES IN BERLIN.

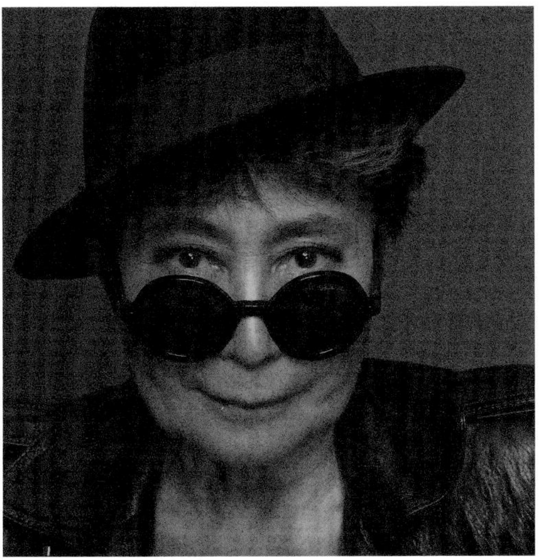

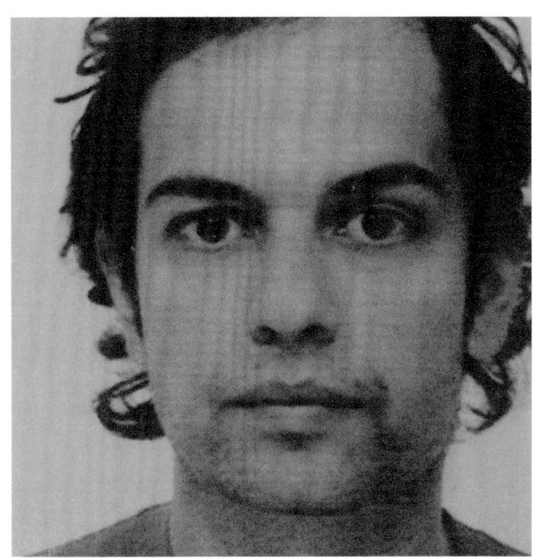

Yoko Ono has had numerous exhibitions in museums, including traveling exhibitions organized by the Museum of Modern Art, Oxford and the Japan Society, New York. Most recently <u>Yoko Ono: Half-A-Wind Show: A Retrospective</u> was exhibited at the Schirn Kunsthalle, Frankfurt; the Louisiana Museum, Humlebaek, Denmark; the Kunsthalle Krems, Austria; and the Guggenheim Museum, Bilbao (2013–14). In 2009, she received a Golden Lion Award for lifetime achievement from the Venice Biennale, which recognized her lifelong goal of pursuing the freedom to act, create, and love.

Solo exhibitions of Sehgal's work have been held around the world. In 2014 he had his first major show in Brazil at the Centro Cultural Banco do Brasil in Rio de Janeiro. Sehgal won the Golden Lion for Best Artist in the International Exhibition at The 55th Venice Biennale (2013). His largest work to date, <u>These associations</u>, was constructed for Tate Modern's Turbine Hall as the final installment of the Unilever Series (2012). For documenta 13 he presented <u>This variation</u> (2012). New York's Guggenheim Museum dedicated an extensive solo show to Sehgal that was celebrated by audiences and critics alike (2010). In 2005, he represented Germany at the Venice Biennale.

SANTIAGO SIERRA
BORN 1966, MADRID.
LIVES IN MADRID.

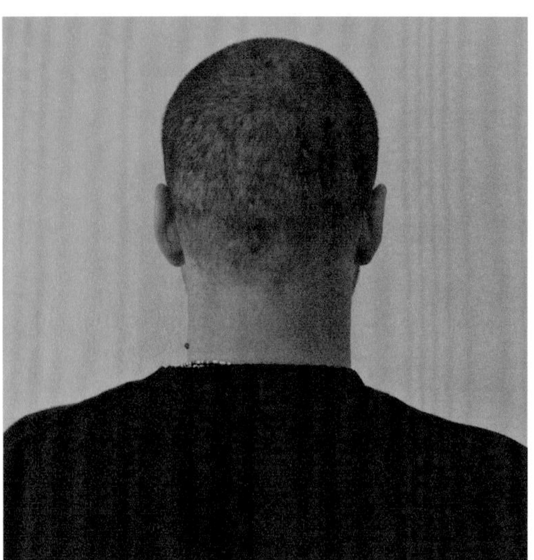

In 2013 Sierra held his first major retrospectives at the Kunsthalle Tubingen and Deichtorhallen Hamburg Sammlung Falckenberg. In 2010 he created Kaldor Public Art Project 22 at the Queensland Art Gallery | Gallery of Modern Art, Brisbane. He has created many unique projects in public space and was commissioned to make an installation in the Tate's Turbine Hall in 2008. Sierra's work has been exhibited in numerous solo and group exhibitions around the world, including MoMA PS1, New York; KW Institute for Contemporary Art, Berlin; Ikon Gallery, Birmingham; the 2007 Moscow Biennale; Kunsthalle Wien, Vienna; and the 2005 Sharjah Biennial. Sierra was chosen to represent Spain at the 2003 Venice Biennale and to create a new work for the Arsenale for the 2005 event.

XU ZHEN
BORN 1977, SHANGHAI.
LIVES IN SHANGHAI.

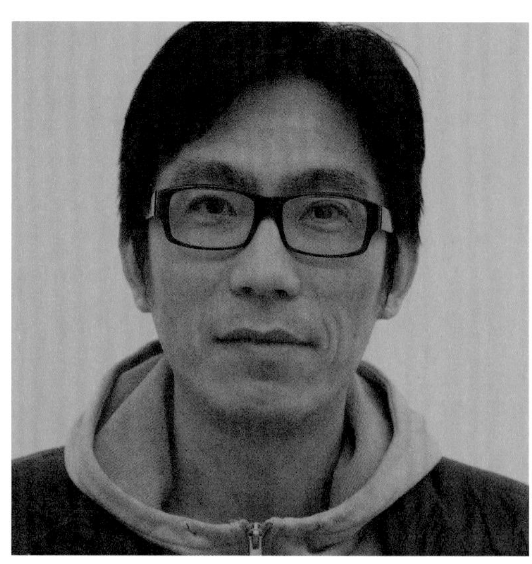

Zhen's work has been included in numerous exhibitions internationally, including Tate Liverpool (2007); MoMA PS1, New York (2006); the Mori Art Museum, Tokyo (2005); and the Venice Biennale (2005 and 2001). In 2004, he won the prize for Best Artist at the China Contemporary Art Awards. He has also shown at the Guangzhou Triennial, <u>The Real Thing: Contemporary Art from China</u> (2005). In 2012, Zhen held solo exhibitions at Contemporary Art Gallery, Vancouver and Museum Montanelli, Prague. In 1998 Zhen co-founded the influential artist-run space BizArt Art Center, Shanghai and in 2009 formed the MadeIn Company (a riff on the ubiquitous "Made in China" moniker) with a group of collaborative practitioners who explore notions of authorship, ethics, and commerce, particularly within the art system.

JORDAN WOLFSON

BORN 1980, NEW YORK.
LIVES IN NEW YORK AND LOS ANGELES.

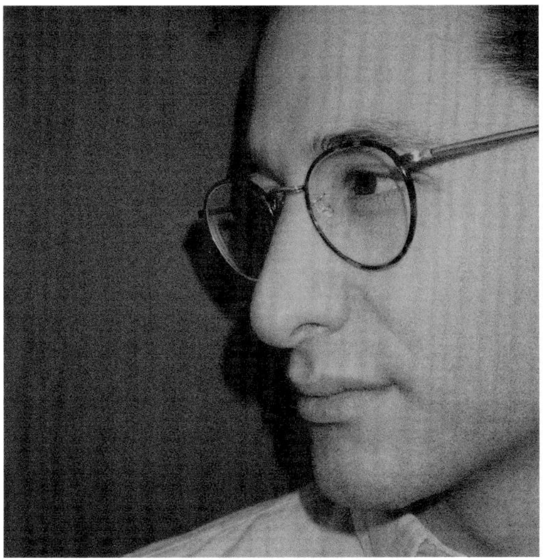

Wolfson's work has been shown internationally in solo exhibitions at venues including the Glasgow International, McLellan Galleries, Glasgow (2014); Stedelijk Museum voor Actuele Kunst (S.M.A.K.), Ghent (2013); Center for Contemporary Art Ujazdowski Castle, Warsaw (2013); Chisenhale Gallery, London (2013); Kunsthalle Wien, Vienna (2012); Schmela Haus, Kunstsammlung Nordrhein-Westfalen, Düsseldorf (2011); CCA Wattis Institute, San Francisco (2009); Swiss Institute of Contemporary Art, New York (2008); Galleria d'Arte Moderna e Contemporanea di Bergamo, Bergamo (2007); and Kunsthalle Zürich, Zurich (2004).

JOHN BALDESSARI

BORN 1931, NATIONAL CITY.
LIVES IN SANTA MONICA.

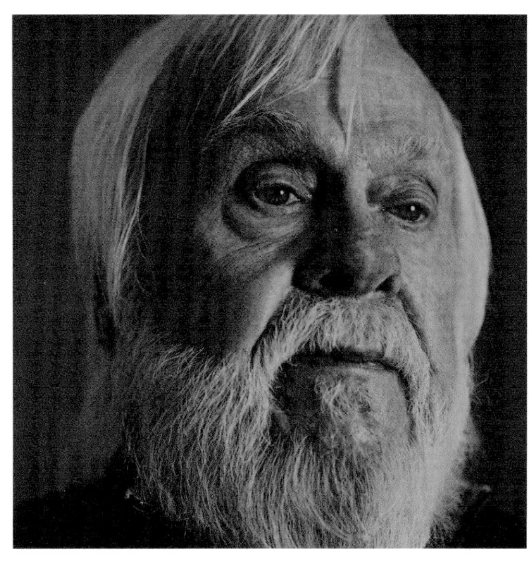

In 2013 Baldessari had his first solo show in Russia at the Garage Center, Moscow. Between 2012 & 2011, he shown at the Van Abbemuseum, Eindhoven, Stedelijk Museum Amsterdam among others. In 2011, he created Kaldor Public Art Project 23, <u>Your Name in Lights</u>. A major retrospective: <u>Pure Beauty</u>, opened at the Tate Modern, London (2009) and toured to the Museu d'Art Contemporani de Barcelona (2010); the Los Angeles County Museum of Art (2010) & the Metropolitan Museum of Art, New York (2010). Exhibitions were held at Kunstmuseen Krefeld: Museum Haus Lange, Krefeld (2009). In 2005 he had a retrospective at the Museum Moderner Kunst Stiftung Ludwig Wien, Vienna (<u>Works 1962–1984</u>) and the Kunsthaus Graz (<u>Works 1984–2005</u>). His work has been exhibited in the Venice Biennale (1997, 2009); the Carnegie International, Pittsburgh (1985–86); the Whitney Biennial, NY (1983) & at documenta (1972, 1982).

KLAUS BIESENBACH & HANS ULRICH OBRIST

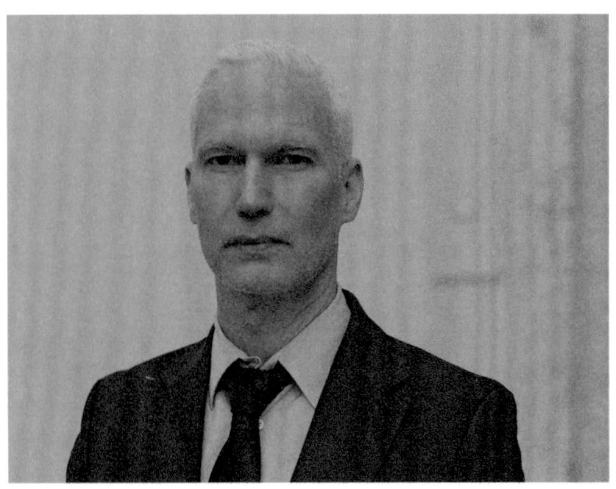

KLAUS BIESENBACH
BORN 1966, KÜRTEN.
LIVES IN NEW YORK.

Klaus Biesenbach is Director of MoMA PS1 and Chief Curator at Large at the Museum of Modern Art, New York, where he has curated groundbreaking retrospectives of Kraftwerk (2012) and Marina Abramović (2010). Prior to this he founded the Kunst-Werke (KW) Institute for Contemporary Art in Berlin (1991) and the Berlin Biennale (1996). In 2006, Biesenbach was named founding Chief Curator of MoMA's newly formed Department of Media and in 2009 founding Chief of the Department of Media and Performance Art. Among the many exhibitions Biesenbach has organized or co-organized internationally are Korakrit Arunanondchai, MoMA PS1 and MoMA (2014); Christoph Schlingensief, Berlin and New York (2013 and 2014); EXPO1, New York and Rio de Janeiro (2013 and 2014); Cyprien Gaillard (2013); Antony and the Johnsons (2012); Ryan Trecartin (2011); Francis Alys (2011); Laurel Nakadate (2011); 100 Years of Performance, Garage Center for Contemporary Culture, Moscow (2010); Andy Warhol (2010); Performance 9: Allora & Calzadilla (2010); Greater New York (2000, 2005, and 2010); Performance 4: Roman Ondák (2009); Performance 1: Tehching Hsieh (2009); Jonathan Horowitz (2009); 100 Years (version 2) (2009); Pipliotti Rist (2008); Doug Aitken (co-commissioned with Creative Time) (2007); Fassbinder: Berlin Alexanderplatz (2007); Douglas Gordon (2006); Into Me/Out of Me (2006); Regarding Terror: The Red Army Faction Exhibition (2005); the Shanghai Biennale (2002); Mexico City: An Exhibition about the Exchange Rate of Bodies and Values (2002); Disasters of War (2000); Hybrid Workspace at documenta (1997); Projected Images at the Venice Biennale (1995); and 37 Rooms (1992) in Berlin.

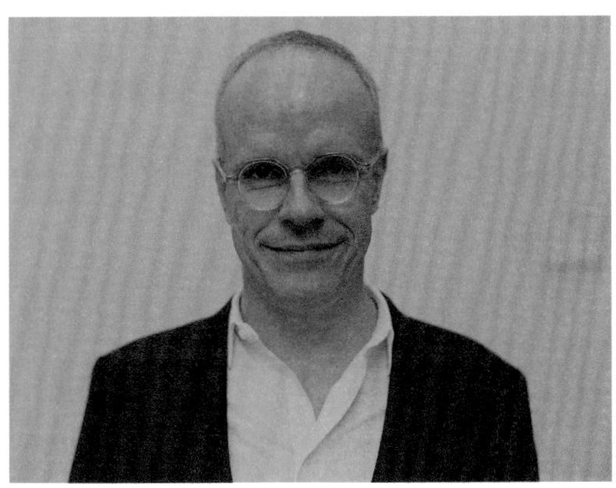

HANS ULRICH OBRIST
BORN 1968, ZURICH.
LIVES IN LONDON.

Hans Ulrich Obrist is co-director of the Serpentine Galleries, London. Prior to this, he was the Curator of the Musée d'Art Moderne de la Ville de Paris. Since his first show <u>World Soup (The Kitchen Show)</u> in 1991 he has curated more than 250 shows. In 2014 Obrist will be the guest curator of Gerhard Richter's exhibition at Fondation Beyeler, Riehen. In 2013, he co-curated the following exhibitions at the Serpentine Galleries: <u>Sturtevant: Leaps Jumps and Bumps</u>, <u>Adrian Villar Rojas: Today We Reboot the Planet</u>, <u>Marisa Merz</u>, <u>Wael Shawky</u>, and <u>Jake and Dinos Chapman: Come and See</u>. In addition, he co-curated <u>13 Rooms</u> with Klaus Biesenbach and Kaldor Public Art Projects, <u>Do It 20th Anniversary Show</u> at ICI New York, along with the ongoing <u>Art of Handwriting</u> project taking place on Instagram and Twitter.

In addition, Obrist is co-founder of 89+, a long-term, international, multi-platform research project, conceived as a mapping of the generation born in or after 1989. In 2009 Obrist was made Honorary Fellow of the Royal Institute of British Architects (RIBA), and in 2011 received the CCS Bard Award for Curatorial Excellence. Obrist has lectured internationally at academic and art institutions, and is contributing editor to several magazines and journals. Obrist's recent publications include <u>A Brief History of Curating</u>, <u>Project Japan: Metabolism Talks with Rem Koolhaas</u>, <u>Everything You Always Wanted to Know About Curating But Were Afraid to Ask</u>, <u>Do It: The Compendium</u>, <u>Think Like Clouds</u>, <u>Ai Weiwei Speaks</u>, <u>Sharp Tongues – Loose Lips – Open Eyes – Ears to the Ground</u>, along with new volumes of his Conversation Series.

HERZOG & DE MEURON

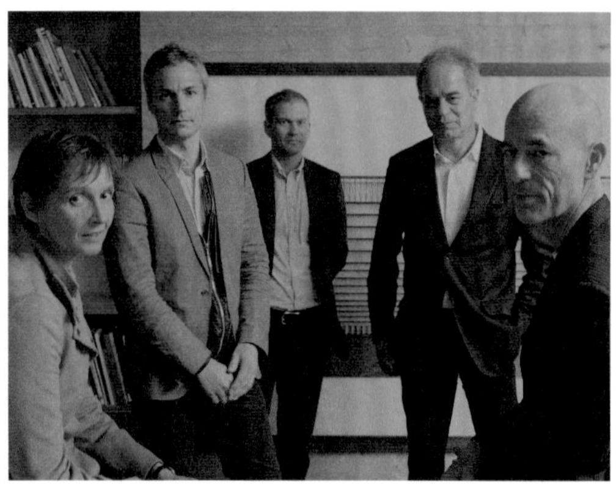

Herzog & de Meuron is a partnership led by five Senior Partners—Jacques Herzog, Pierre de Meuron, Christine Binswanger, Ascan Mergenthaler, and Stefan Marbach.

Jacques Herzog and Pierre de Meuron established their office in Basel in 1978. The partnership has grown over the years—Christine Binswanger joined the practice as Partner in 1994, successively followed by Robert Hösl and Ascan Mergenthaler in 2004, Stefan Marbach in 2006, David Koch in 2008, Esther Zumsteg in 2009, Andreas Fries in 2011, Vladimir Pajkic in 2012, and Jason Frantzen and Wim Walschap in 2014. An international team of 38 Associates and about 360 collaborators is working on projects across Europe, North and South America. The firm's main office is in Basel with additional offices in Hamburg, London, Madrid, New York, and Hong Kong. Herzog & de Meuron have designed a wide range of projects from the small scale of a private home to the large scale of urban design. While many of their projects are highly recognized public facilities, such as the Tate Modern in London (2000) and the development of its extension (2016), as well as the National Stadium in Beijing for the 2008 Olympic Games, they have also completed several distinguished private projects including apartment buildings, offices, and factories. In many projects Herzog & de Meuron have worked together with artists, eminent examples of that practice include the collaborations with Rémy Zaugg, Thomas Ruff, and more recently with Chinese artist Ai Weiwei, with whom Herzog & de Meuron worked on a contribution to the Venice Architecture Biennale in 2008 and the 2012 Serpentine Gallery Pavilion in London's Kensington Gardens. The practice has been awarded numerous prizes including The Pritzker Architecture Prize (USA) in 2001, the

RIBA Royal Gold Medal (UK), and the Praemium Imperiale (Japan), both in 2007. Jacques Herzog and Pierre de Meuron are both visiting professors at Harvard University, Graduate School of Design (GSD), USA, since 1994 (and in 1989). They are professors at the Swiss Federal Institute of Technology Zurich (ETH) —Department of Architecture, Network City and Landscape, since 1999, and co-founders of the ETH Studio Basel—Contemporary City Institute.

DEUTSCHE ÜBERSETZUNGEN

VORWORT

SAM KELLER
MARC SPIEGLER
GEORGES DELNON

Für alle drei Veranstalter von <u>14 Rooms</u> – die Fondation Beyeler, die Art Basel und das Theater Basel – stellt diese zehn Tage dauernde Ausstellung den letzten Schritt in einer Neudefinition ihres kulturellen Terrains dar. Indem wir dieses einzigartige Projekt – kuratiert von Klaus Biesenbach, Direktor des MoMA PS1 und Chief Curator at Large des Museum of Modern Art in New York, und Hans Ulrich Obrist, Co-Director and Director of International Projects der Serpentine Galleries in London – nach Basel gebracht haben, betrachten wir das Verschwimmen der Verbindung zwischen Publikum und Kunstwerk, während wir damit gleichzeitig die Überzeugung vertreten, dass ein bildender Künstler seine Kunstwerke ebenso gut durch die Arbeit mit Menschen wie durch den Einsatz von Bronze, Leinwand, Tintenstrahldrucker, Ölfarben, Video oder jede andere Methode physischer Produktion erzeugen kann.

Dies markiert unsere zweite Zusammenarbeit mit dem Manchester International Festival. Im Jahr 2009 veranstalteten die gleichen drei Organisationen die Basler Version von <u>Il Tempo del Postino</u>, co-kuratiert von Hans Ulrich Obrist und Philippe Parreno. Ursprünglich von Alex Poots vom Manchester International Festival initiiert, erwies sie sich als ein Highlight des Jahres im Kalender der internationalen Kunstszene. Für <u>14 Rooms</u> erwarten wir die gleiche Wahrnehmung, da das Projekt einem ähnlichen Weg folgt. Co-kuratiert von Alex Poots und Heiner Goebbels von der Essener RUHRTRIENNALE debütierte es in Manchester im Jahr 2011 als <u>11 Rooms</u> und wurde dann als <u>12 Rooms</u> im Rahmen der RUHRTRIENNALE 2012 inszeniert. Im Jahr 2013 zeigte der australische Mäzen John Kaldor <u>13 Rooms</u> als Teil der Langzeitserie Kaldor Public Art Projects in Sydney. Indem wir nun eine neue und leicht vergrößerte Version in der Woche der bedeutendsten Kunstmesse der Welt nach Basel bringen, stellen wir <u>14 Rooms</u> direkt ins Rampenlicht der globalen Kunstwelt.

Für jede Ausgabe überarbeiteten die Kuratoren ihre Liste von Künstlern im Hinblick auf den Kontext des jeweiligen Austragungsortes. Von den vierzehn in Basel präsentierten Stücken sind vier völlig neue Auftragswerke, fünf sind das erste Mal mit dabei und bei fünf weiteren handelt es sich um wahrhaft historische Arbeiten, die bis ins Jahr 1963 zurückreichen. Angesichts der internationalen Ausrichtung der Art Basel bietet das Programm natürlich ein erstaunlich vielfältiges Aufgebot an Talenten und umspannt damit drei Generationen und fünf Kontinente: Marina Abramović, Allora & Calzadilla, Ed Atkins, Dominique Gonzalez-Foerster, Damien Hirst, Joan Jonas, Laura Lima, Bruce Nauman, Otobong Nkanga, Roman Ondák, Yoko Ono, Tino Sehgal, Santiago Sierra und

Xu Zhen. Zudem wird es rund um <u>14 Rooms</u> zwei Sonderprojekte geben, darunter eine Installation von Jordan Wolfson in Form eines Epiloges und eine historische Dokumentation eines nicht realisierten Projektes von John Baldessari von 1970. Wir möchten uns bei allen teilnehmenden Künstlern für ihren Enthusiasmus in der Zusammenarbeit an diesem einzigartigen und anspruchsvollen Projekt bedanken und wollen besonders den Kuratoren unseren tiefempfundenen Dank für die Möglichkeit ausdrücken, diese Schau in Basel zu präsentieren. Mehr als siebzig Performer arbeiteten an dieser Produktion mit, und wir danken auch ihnen für ihren maßgeblichen Beitrag.

Die Liste an Unterstützern, die dieses einzigartige Ereignis ermöglicht haben, ist ebenso lang, mit Repräsentanten aus zahlreichen unterschiedlichen Sektoren. Die Regierung von Basel trug kräftig zum Projekt bei und erlaubte es uns, die öffentliche Komponente zu erweitern. Unser besonderer Dank gilt Regierungspräsident Guy Morin und Philippe Bischof, Leiter der Abteilung Kultur der Stadt. Wichtige Unterstützung aus dem Unternehmenssektor kam sowohl von UBS als auch der MCH Group, dem Mutterunternehmen der Art Basel. Die privaten Förderer, die das Projekt unterstützen, stellen die oberste Riege bedeutender internationaler Sammler und Philanthropen dar: Cristina Bechtler, Denise und Rolando Benedick, Joop van Caldenborgh, Ulla Dreyfus-Best, Nicoletta Fiorucci, Wendy Fisher, Francesca von Habsburg, Maja Hoffmann, Guillaume Houzé, Pierre de Labouchere Michael Ringier, Tony Salamé, Gerd Schepers Franz Wassmer und Dasha Zhukova.

Mit einem hohen Grad an direktem persönlichen Einsatz vonseiten der beiden Gründungspartner, spielt Herzog & de Meurons eigens errichtete Architektur eine bedeutende Rolle bei der Ausformung der Ausstellung und dient als Zwischenräume bildende Struk-

tur, die eine Reihe intimer Erfahrungen im öffentlichen Raum miteinander verbindet und auch die Erfahrung des Betrachters formt. Wir danken auch dem hart arbeitenden Team von <u>14 Rooms</u> unter dem Projektmanagement von Ann-Christin Rommen, Marc Bättig und Associate Curator Samuel Leuenberger, das sich aus Mitarbeitern der drei organisierenden Institutionen sowie aus Experten aus aller Welt zusammensetzt.

Schließlich gilt unser Dank Ihnen, den Besuchern, die dieses einzigartige Projekt erst zum Leben erwecken, indem sie die Anweisungen von vierzehn Künstlern in einen Meilenstein in der Geschichte der Performancekunst verwandeln.

Sam Keller, Direktor Fondation Beyeler
Marc Spiegler, Direktor Art Basel
Georges Delnon, Direktor Theater Basel

DIE KURATOREN IM GESPRÄCH SYDNEY, 2013

KLAUS BIESENBACH HANS ULRICH OBRIST

KLAUS BIESENBACH (KB) Stellen Sie sich vor, Sie sind mit Ihren Kollegen zusammen und plötzlich sagt jemand: „Bitte kommen Sie in mein Büro und schließen Sie die Türe hinter sich". Die Stimmung der Situation ändert sich völlig. Oder stellen Sie sich vor, Sie befinden sich in einem Hochhaus und benutzen den Fahrstuhl. Die Türen schließen sich. Der Fahrstuhl fährt in den nächsten Stock, die Türen öffnen sich und jemand steigt ein. Diese Person ist nackt. Die Fahrstuhltüren schließen sich wieder. Sie sind nun für einige Minuten mit dieser nackten Person alleine. Oder stellen Sie sich vor, Sie kommen zu spät zu einer Theateraufführung und sollen links entlang gehen und dann durch die rechte Türe. Sie folgen den Anweisungen und stehen plötzlich mit den Schauspielern auf der Bühne.

Im Vorfeld zu Marina Abramovićs Einzelausstellung im Museum of Modern Art (2010) fanden zwei Jahre lang Workshop-Sessions unter dem Titel <u>The Performance Workshop</u> statt, in denen es um Performancekunst, Live-Art, Interpretationen von choreografischen Anweisungen und darum ging, wie Museen diese Kunstformen erhalten, sammeln und ausstellen sollten. Wir saßen alle um einen großen Tisch und dieser Tisch wurde zu einer Bühne, auf der jeder gleichberechtigt war. Keiner stand am Podium, keiner wurde auf ein Podest gestellt, wir waren alle Mitwirkende, wie wir es auch in <u>13 Rooms</u> sind.

Was also äußerst wichtig für <u>13 Rooms</u> ist, steckt schon im Titel. Es heißt nicht <u>13 Performances</u>, weil es keine 13 Performances sind. Es heißt auch nicht <u>13 Artists</u>, weil das irritierend wäre. Es heißt nicht <u>13 Sculptures</u>, weil das missverständlich wäre. Stattdessen heißt es <u>13 Rooms</u>: Wenn man Pier 2/3 in Sydneys Walsh Bay betritt, entdeckt man eine sehr große, weitläufige Lagerhalle, die in 13 Räume aufgeteilt ist, mit Türen, die man öffnen und durch die man eintreten kann.

HANS ULRICH OBRIST (HUO) Viel an Inspiration für diese Ausstellung entsprang der Vorstellung, dass es sich bei Live-Art auch um Skulptur handelt und dass sie einen ähnlichen zeitlichen Umfang wie ein physisches Objekt aufweisen kann, das heißt, vom Morgen bis zum Abend, während der gesamten Öffnungszeit einer Galerie. Wenn aber die letzten Besucher gegangen sind und die Galerie ihre Pforten für die Nacht schließt, dann verlassen auch die Skulpturen das Gebäude.

Eine der wichtigsten Inspirationen sind Gilbert & George. Sie haben, mehr als alle anderen Künstler, diese Idee wirklich ausgelotet. Wann immer sie einen Raum betreten, sind sie lebendige Skulptur, und unter Anwendung dieses Konzeptes schufen sie einige erstaunliche frühe Werke. Für Weihnachten 1969 schlugen sie der Tate zum Beispiel ihre Idee einer Skulptur vor – einer lebendigen Skulptur – wo man dann anstelle von Jesus Gilbert & George sah, für die gesamte Weihnachtszeit während der Öffnungszeiten der Galerie. Oder <u>The Singing Sculpture</u>, die John Kaldor 1973 nach Australien brachte, wo sie auf einem Tisch in der Galerie standen und stundenlang <u>Underneath the Arches</u> sangen.

Dies führt uns zu Tino Sehgal, der sich in erster Linie von seinem tänzerischen Hintergrund inspirieren lässt und nicht so sehr von der traditionellen Plastik. Wie Tino im Gespräch meinte: „Während die bildende Kunst davon ausgeht, dass wir Material aus natürlichen Ressourcen gewinnen können, um es dann zu transformieren und ein Produkt erhalten, das überdauert, transformiert Tanz Handlungen, um ein Produkt oder Kunstwerk zu erhalten, und gleichzeitig produziert und de-produziert er dieses Produkt.“

Von daher – und im Gegensatz zu natürlichen Ressourcen – können Tinos Arbeiten niemals verbraucht oder erschöpft sein. Ich werde mich immer an ein Gespräch mit Eugène Ionesco, dem großen Dramatiker und Pionier des absurden Theaters erinnern. Als wir uns in den 1980er-Jahren in der Schweiz kennenlernten, erzählte er mir, dass – während wir miteinander sprachen – sein Stück <u>La Cantatrice Chauve</u> in Paris aufgeführt würde. Mehr als vierzig Jahre lang war es in Paris jeden einzelnen Abend aufgeführt worden. Damals war ich noch ein Kind und ich war wirklich beeindruckt, da dieses Stück ebenso beständig war wie all die Kunstwerke aus Bronze, Marmor oder Stein, es lief seit Tausenden von Tagen.

KB Die ursprüngliche Ausstellung <u>11 Rooms</u> war zunächst im Jahr 2011 vom Manchester International Festival in Auftrag gegeben worden. Die Organisatoren des Festivals sind sehr progressiv, sie beauftragten Björk mit ihrer ersten Performance, wo sie doch normalerweise Konzerte machte, sie gaben Antony den Auftrag, sein Album <u>Swanlights</u> zu performen, und sie baten Hans Ulrich Obrist, Philippe Parreno und eine Gruppe von Künstlern 2010 <u>Il Tempo del Postino</u> zu präsentieren. <u>Il Tempo del Postino</u> war eine Ausstellung, in der die zeitgenössischen Künstler Doug Aitken, Matthew Barney und Jonathan Bepler, Tacita Dean, Trisha Donnelly, Ólafur Eliasson, Liam Gillick, Dominique Gonzalez-Foerster, Douglas Gordon, Carsten Höller, Pierre Huyghe, Koo Jeong-a, Arto Lindsay, Philippe Parreno, Anri Sala, Tino Sehgal und Rirkrit Tiravanija Ausstellungsstücke schufen, die auf der Bühne und nicht im Inneren eines Museumsraumes präsentiert wurden. Jeder Künstler hatte ein Zeitfenster im Theater.

Dominique Gonzalez-Foerster zeigte dieses wunderschöne Stück, in dem ein Orchester Musik spielte und dann, einer nach dem anderen, jedes Mitglied des Orchesters hinausging. Doug Aitken initiierte eine Liveauktion. Ich weiß nicht, was er versteigerte, doch im ganzen Theater waren Auktionatoren, es war unglaublich. Douglas Gordon verdunkelte das gesamte Theater, es war stockfinster und dann wurde der Joy-Division-Song <u>Love Will Tear Us Apart</u> a capella gesungen. Als das Festival Hans Ulrich Obrist und mich dann fragte, ob wir im darauffolgenden Jahr etwas tun würden, waren wir ziemlich ahnungslos, wie wir da nachziehen könnten.

Dann kamen die Spielregeln. Ich besuchte die Villa Borghese und ich gehöre eigentlich nicht zur der Sorte Kurator, die Dinge in Rahmen oder auf einem Podest präsentieren, aber ich ging dort durch und sah eine Skulptur hier und eine Skulptur da und ich machte kehrt und ging von vorne vorbei, betrachtete sie von hinten und von vorne. Wenn man sich in dieser Phase erhöhter Aufmerksamkeit befindet, dann ist man sich seiner eigenen Zeit, seines eigenen Volumens, seiner eigenen Schritte in diesem Raum, seiner Proportionen bewusst. Man fragt sich, ist diese Skulptur tatsächlich lebensgroß oder doch überlebensgroß? Ist die als Skulptur dargestellte Person älter als ich oder handelt es sich um eine jüngere Person? Ich erinnere mich also, dass ich Hans Ulrich Obrist anrief und sagte: „Ich bin in der Villa Borghese. Vielleicht sollten wir eine Ausstellung machen, wo wir einen Raum haben, in dem wir nur eine Skulptur betrachten, und dann einen anderen Raum mit einer weiteren Skulptur, und dann noch einen Raum mit noch einer Skulptur". Vor der Villa Borghese war einer dieser Akrobaten, der stillstand wie eine Skulptur und ganz silbern angemalt war.

Als Hans Ulrich und ich telefonierten, wurde diese Idee von einem Wort zu einem Satz und wir beschlossen, ja, wir würden eine Skulpturengalerie machen, ein Raum nach dem anderen, aber in jedem Raum würde es eine „lebendige Skulptur" geben, jeweils einen Menschen oder mehrere Personen, jedoch nicht die Künstlerin oder den Künstler selbst.

HUO Uns gefiel auch die Möglichkeit, eine Ausstellung zu organisieren, die später wieder aufgenommen werden konnte. Diese Idee interessierte uns, da sie, wie Musik, Teil eines Kataloges von Arbeiten werden konnte, die man in unterschiedlichem Kontext wieder inszenieren könnte. Die Vorstellung der Wiederholbarkeit, die Vorstellung, dass eine Ausstellung – wie Duchamps <u>Boîte-en-valise</u> – offen gehalten und neu inszeniert werden kann, ist etwas, das Philippe Parreno und ich sicherlich mit <u>Il Tempo del Postino</u> beim Manchester International Festival 2007 erreichen wollten. Dort versuchten wir, die Ausstellung neu zu konzipieren, als Weg, um Zeit anstatt bloß Raum in Besitz zu nehmen. Von unserer Seite gab es ein bewusstes Bemühen, gegen den einengenden Raum- und Zeitrahmen traditioneller Ausstellungen anzugehen. Wir wollten die Ausstellung und all ihre Elemente neu durchdenken, als so etwas wie eine fruchtbare, sich entwickelnde, offene choreografische Anweisung. Als Kurator macht man oft Ausstellungen, wo man für einen begrenzten Zeitraum einige Objekte, Quasiobjekte oder Nichtobjekte zusammenträgt – und dann ist die Schau vorbei. Ausstellungen werden normalerweise nicht von Museen gesammelt. Ausgewählte Stücke aus Ausstellungen schon, aber nicht ganze Ausstellungen. Also gefiel uns diese Idee wirklich, besonders, da es so viele Künstler gibt, die mit dieser Vorstellung von Instruktionen arbeiten und mit zeitbasierter Kunst, die es dir ermöglicht, Ausstellungen gemäß einer choreografischen Anweisung zu kuratieren.

Viele Künstler schaffen Werke, in denen sie im Grunde genommen etwas an andere Menschen delegieren oder ihnen Anweisungen geben. Wir haben diese Idee nicht erfunden, wir haben sie da draußen beobachtet. Es ist etwas, das wir endlos reproduzieren können und wir glauben, dass diese Qualität für Ausstellungen extrem interessant ist. Kunst kann die Zeit überdauern, nicht nur durch Objekte und nicht nur durch Dokumentation. Die Malerei war stets eine dauerhafte, geschätzte Kunstform. Dann gibt es das Quasiobjekt, das ebenfalls bis zu einem gewissen Grad die Zeit überdauert. Oder es gibt ephemere Performances von Künstlern, die zwar nicht repliziert, aber auf Film, Fotografie und so weiter dokumentiert werden können. Dann ist da auch noch die Option, die wir hier erforschen, die Idee der Instructional Art, die der Kunst eine berechtigte Möglich-

keit bietet, sich fortzubewegen und zu überdauern. 13 Rooms ist genauso: Ausgehend vom grundlegenden Text können wir es an unterschiedlichen Orten auf der ganzen Welt neu inszenieren, und das kann auch in fünfzig Jahren wieder geschehen oder in hundert, wenn wir alle tot sind. Es kann ganz woanders auf der Welt sein und es kann für verschiedene Orte überarbeitet werden.

Von dem Augenblick an, in dem wir uns für dieses Konzept entschieden hatten, war es einfach, aber es passte noch nicht sofort alles zusammen. Ich glaube, kuratieren ist ein langsamer Prozess, man braucht Zeit, um eine Menge unterschiedlicher Geografien zu erforschen. Wie man in dieser Ausstellung sieht, kommen die Künstler von vielen verschiedenen Kontinenten. Wir wollten wirklich herausfinden, ob es in Lateinamerika Arbeiten gibt, die mit dieser Vorstellung in Zusammenhang zu bringen sind. Gibt es Arbeiten in Asien? In Australien? In Afrika? Wir sind noch nicht fertig und deshalb ist es großartig, dass diese Ausstellung für viele Jahre touren kann, da wir dann weiterhin lernen und ein Archiv aufbauen können. In Australien haben sich zum Beispiel die jungen Künstlerinnen Clark Beaumont dem Projekt angeschlossen, auch John Baldessari wird eine Arbeit ausführen und ein vergessenes Projekt mit einer lebenden Skulptur zutage fördern, das er erstmals in den späten 1970er-Jahren umgesetzt hat.

Langsamkeit ist nicht nur wichtig für den kuratorischen Prozess sondern auch für die Erfahrung der 13 Rooms-Ausstellung. Es ist überraschend, aber normalerweise verbringen die Menschen nicht viel Zeit vor den Kunstwerken in Museen. Der Louvre hat das einmal analysiert. Sogar vor der Mona Lisa verbringen die Besucher im Durchschnitt nur einige Sekunden – das ist ziemlich schockierend. Sehr oft rennen die Menschen nur durch. Die Erfahrung von 13 Rooms erzeugt jedoch das Gegenteil dieser Beschleunigung: ihre Entschleunigung. Die Bewegung wird durch die Tatsache verlangsamt, dass man die Türe öffnen muss – es ist so, als ob man in jemandes Haus eintreten würde. Es ist ein intimes Zusammentreffen.

Es kann ein Zusammentreffen im dunklen oder im hellen Raum sein. Bei Marina Abramović ist es schmerzhaft hell. Bei Xavier Le Roy fast völlig finster. Bei einem Künstler wie Tino Sehgal ist es ein Gespräch. Bei Santiago Sierra das Gegenteil: völlige Stille. Bei Roman Ondák geht es um die grundlegende Erfahrung des Austausches. Bei Lucy Raven, deren Arbeit in 11 Rooms und in 12 Rooms präsentiert wurde, ging es um eine von Technik vermittelte Interaktion. Es gibt also alle Arten von unterschiedlichen Interaktionen, die geschehen können. Sie brauchen Zeit und verlangsamen die Dinge. Ausstellungen sind im Grunde genommen ein Medium der sozialen Begegnung. Deshalb ist Romans Arbeit, wie er mir erzählt hat „ziemlich medienspezifisch für die Ausstellung". Er meint: „Bei der Ausstellung geht es immer auch um Individuen, die einander auch sehen … Es geht viel eher um Menschen als um Dinge".

KB Als wir mit der Konzeption der Ausstellung begannen, sahen wir uns die vielen verschiedenen Konzepte an. Allora & Calzadilla hatten mit ihrem kreisförmigen Raum für Revolving Door ein etwas anderes Konzept. Es gab Santiago Sierra, der sich auf die Ecken des Raumes konzentriert. Bei Marina war es klar, dass es ein wenig zu intim werden würde, wenn der Raum ein perfekter Kubus wäre. Die meisten der Räume messen tatsächlich 5 mal 5 mal 3 Meter, und diese Dimensionen bewahren den „domestic" Eindruck der Räume. Es ist uns sehr wichtig, dass es sich anfühlt, als würde man ein Zimmer mit einer Türe betreten und nicht eine Galerie. Es

schuf einen gewissermaßen menschlichen Maßstab, den Maßstab des Körpers, und das war genau das, was wir für die Performances brauchten. Ich glaube, dass diese Dimensionen sowohl einen intimen, menschlichen Maßstab, als auch den Fluss der Stücke gewährleisten. Beim Öffnen der Türe tritt man über eine Schwelle und betritt auch jemandes Privatsphäre – wie ich schon zu Beginn mit der Fahrstuhlszene erwähnt habe.

HUO Es ist uns wichtig zu erwähnen, dass sich 13 Rooms, was den Schauplatz von Pier 2/3 in der Walsh Bay in Sydney betrifft, sehr von 11 Rooms in Manchester und 12 Rooms in Essen unterscheidet. Für 13 Rooms wurde die Architektur innerhalb dieses denkmalgeschützten Piers von Harry Seidler und Associates Architects entworfen und wir sind sehr erfreut über den Quantensprung, den die Ausstellung damit gemacht hat.

Die Räume haben weiterhin die gleichen Dimensionen und, wie Klaus Biesenbach sagt, ist ihre Intimität mit Sicherheit sehr wichtig. Also haben wir im Inneren von Pier 2/3 die Räume eines Hauses errichtet, fast so, als würde man einen Raum von der Größe eines Salons in einen Ausstellungskontext transferieren. Natürlich wird das Haus, wenn die Ausstellung an verschiedenen Orten neu inszeniert wird, wachsen und wir werden immer mehr Räume haben. Schlussendlich ist es vielleicht ein großes Winchester Mystery House mit Hunderten von Räumen. Es könnte zur größten Gruppenausstellung der Geschichte werden, wenn es die nächsten fünfzig Jahre weiter reist! Wer weiß? Wir sind sehr optimistisch.

KB Ich glaube, dass Ausstellungen manchmal wie Handlungsabläufe, wie periodisch auftretende Geschichten sind. Du hast eine Vorstellung von der Geschichte, du hast den Entwurf der Geschichte, du hast die Zusammenfassung der Geschichte, du hast die Langversion der Geschichte, du hast die Version mit zusätzlichen Kapiteln. Ich glaube, dass eine Ausstellung immer eine Kombination bestimmter Geschichten und Handlungen ist. Hans Ulrich Obrist ist zum Beispiel sehr bekannt für die Ausstellung Do It, eine Schau, die nur aus Instruktionen besteht. Sie ist sehr konzeptuell: Es sind keine Objekte, es sind nur Anweisungen, was ich in der heutigen, marktorientierten Wirtschaft für sehr wichtig halte. Dann gibt es auch noch andere Ausstellungen, die als „Live-Art"-Ausstellungen oder „Live-Ausstellungen" oder „Performance-Ausstellungen" gelten oder wie immer man sie nennen möchte.

Wir haben beobachtet, dass es viele Künstler gibt, die mit „Instruction pieces" arbeiten, die körperliche Arbeit, Performance, Neuinterpretation, Tanz oder Schauspiel umfassen. Dann dachten wir, dass wir die Idee von Kunst als Instruktion auch vorschlagen könnten, also auch Künstlern, die bis jetzt nicht auf diese Art und Weise gearbeitet hatten, weil es eine wichtige künstlerische Praxis ist. Man bringt also das Motiv der Instruction-Ausstellung mit dem Motiv der Performance-Ausstellung zusammen und herausgekommen ist – zusammen mit dem intimen Maßstab, den Türen und der Ausstellungserfahrung – 13 Rooms. Die Ausstellung bietet Raum für Erfahrungen und Beteiligung und die Möglichkeit direkter Auseinandersetzung – wie auch immer man das definiert.

Wiederabdruck des Gesprächs aus: 13 Rooms, Ausst.-Kat. 27. Kaldor Public Art Project in Sydney, Australien, April 2013.

DIE KURATOREN IM GESPRÄCH BASEL, 2014

KLAUS BIESENBACH HANS ULRICH OBRIST

HANS ULRICH OBRIST (HUO) Ein Jahr nach Sydney und drei Jahre nach dem ersten Projekt in Manchester präsentieren wir hier in Basel 14 Rooms! Dabei fühlt es sich immer noch an, als ob alles erst gerade begonnen hat!

KLAUS BIESENBACH (KB) Es mag immer wieder so aussehen, als hätten wir mit unserer Arbeit erst begonnen, aber es ist auch wichtig festzuhalten, dass wir aus jedem der drei vergangenen Projekte viel gelernt und mitgenommen haben. So haben wir am Beispiel von Sydney gelernt, wie sich eine Ausstellung in den städtischen Kontext ausbreiten kann: Wir waren in einer Werft im Hafen, nahe dem Museum und der Oper. Täglich bildete sich eine lange Schlange vor der Ausstellung. Durch diese Schlange breitete sich die Ausstellung in organischer Art und Weise in Richtung Stadt aus und brachte die Ausstellung ins Gespräch. Wo sich größere Ansammlungen von Menschen aufhalten, entsteht ein neuer öffentlicher und urbaner Raum, der neue Gesprächsebenen bietet. Diese Idee des öffentlichen Raumes in Verbindung mit der Ausstellung wollten wir nach Basel mitnehmen.

HUO Wichtig für 14 Rooms ist nicht nur die Ausstellungsarchitektur der 14 Räume, sondern auch das städtische Umfeld, wo die Ausstellung implementiert wird.

Bei der ersten Ausgabe des Projektes in Manchester bauten wir einfache, fast schon spartanisch reduzierte Räume in der Manchester City Art Gallery. In Essen beherbergte David Chipperfields Museum Folkwang die Ausstellung, welches dem Projekt eine besondere Atmosphäre verlieh. In Sydney konzipierte mit Harry Seidler erstmals ein Architekt selber die Ausstellung. In seiner Version ähnelte das Konzept einem kleinen Dorf. Die Idee für Basel, die wir uns im Dialog mit Marc Spiegler und Sam Keller ausgedacht haben, war, dass man wieder Architekten gewinnt, die ein architektonisches Konzept ausarbeiten.

Wir luden Herzog & de Meuron ein, deren Architektur sich freilich nicht nur auf das konzentriert, was in der Ausstellung zu sehen ist. Es geht nicht nur um das, was in der Ausstellung geschieht, sondern es geht auch darum, wie sich das Geschehen rund um eine Ausstellung mit dem städtischen Gewebe verflicht. Obschon Herzog & de Meuron die eindrucksvolle neue Messehalle Basel mit dem Okulus gebaut haben, schlugen sie vor, das Projekt in einer der alten Messehallen stattfinden zu lassen. Diese liegt etwas abseits des großen Kunst- und Messerummels und ist deshalb auch ganz anders in den städtischen Kontext eingeschrieben.

KB Für uns war wichtig, dass Herzog & de Meuron, die ja überall auf der Welt so hervorragende Museen gebaut haben, hier plötzlich in eine alte Struktur gehen, in eine Art öffentlichen, zivilen Stadtraum – im Gegensatz zur neuen Messe, wo der öffentliche Raum nur für potenzielle Käufer und für potenziellen Handel bestimmt ist.

Interessant ist, dass DIE globalen Museumsarchitekten an einem Ort der Welt auch einfach nur lokal sind, weil sie aus Basel stammen. Ich finde das eine schöne Metapher, und auch, dass an diesem Ort der Welt DIE lokale Größe, wofür die Stadt meistbekannt ist, der Kunstmarkt ist. Basel ist die Mutter der Kunstmessen, und es wurde uns bewusst, dass wir diese Tatsache in unsere Überlegungen einbauen müssen. Nun ist es so, dass aufgrund der architektonischen Situation 14 Rooms zwar während der Zeit des größten Kunsthypes stattfindet, aber aufgrund der architektonischen Situation ganz bewusst nicht Teil davon ist, sondern abgesondert als eigenständige Ausstellung organisiert und situiert ist.

HUO Es gibt in unseren Städten immer weniger öffentliche Räume, wo man sein Dasein nicht über Konsum rechtfertigen muss. Genau deswegen ist es die Idee von Herzog & de Meuron, die Messehalle zu einem öffentlichen Raum werden zu lassen. Die Halle wird nach allen Seiten geöffnet und kostenlos begehbar sein.

KB Es wird ein öffentlicher, ziviler Bürger-Raum sein, wo nicht Dinge verkauft werden, sondern – inspiriert von Tony Bennett – es wird ein Ort sein, der einfach sozial ist, wo man hingeht, wo man nichts kaufen muss, aber vielleicht verbal Gegenstände verhandelt. Bei uns kann man einerseits eine seriös kuratierte Kunstausstellung anschauen. Andererseits wird ein sozialer Raum gegeben, wo man sich über die Ausstellung mitteilen und austauschen kann. In Manchester, Essen und Sydney fand dies jeweils dort statt, wo die Leute vor der Ausstellung gewartet haben. Douglas Gordon hat einmal gesagt, dass Kunst oftmals eine Entschuldigung ist, über essenzielle Themen wie Einsamkeit, Cyborgs oder „Selfies", Angst, Scham oder Eitelkeit zu reden. Ich glaube, dass unsere Ausstellung Kunst über Leben und nicht Kunst über Kunst zeigt.

HUO Das Konzept ist nicht nur von Tony Bennett inspiriert, sondern auch von Richard Sennett, der das Verschwinden des öffentlichen Raumes in seinen Büchern diskutiert. Auch uns geht es um diese Idee der Öffnung nach außen, der Entstehung von öffentlichen Räumen und wie man solche Räume schaffen kann. Das neue Konzept der Spiegelwandelhalle trägt seinen Teil dazu bei: Der Besucher/Besucherin wandelt zwischen den Räumen und wird mit seinem/ihrem Spiegelbild selbst Teil von 14 Rooms. Rund um die eigentliche Ausstellung wird es andere Attraktionen geben, die für alle Interessierten frei zugänglich sind. Neben diversen Verpflegungsmöglichkeiten und Sitzgelegenheiten wird das Archiv von Baldessari gezeigt. Die Arbeit besteht aus der Dokumentation über ein Frühwerk von John Baldessari, welches er 1970 fürs MoMA vorgeschlagen hatte. Mit Unrealised Proposal for Cadaver Piece wollte Baldessari einen Leichnam ausstellen, um so den Umgang mit dem Tod in der Kunst und Gesellschaft zu thematisieren. Es war nicht überraschend, dass dieses Projekt bis heute noch nicht realisiert werden konnte, obwohl wir es in Manchester versucht haben. Das Archiv stellt im Grunde die endlose Kommunikation mit den lokalen und globalen Behörden und Instanzen dar.

KB Mit Otobong Nkangas Werk nimmt die Thematik der Öffnung des öffentlichen Raumes eine weitere Dimension an. Ihre Arbeit Diaspore befasst sich mit Migration, Exil und Entwurzelung, dem Blick zurück auf die verlassene Heimat und dem Blick nach vorn auf ein neues Land. Sie lässt entwurzelte Exilantinnen mit einer aus ihrer jeweiligen Heimat stammenden Pflanze „Königin der Nacht" auftreten, einer Pflanze, die ursprünglich aus Südasien kam und den Prozess der Migration bereits erfuhr. Der öffentliche Raum heutzutage muss einer bunt durchmischten Bevölkerung zur Verfügung stehen und sich immer weiter öffnen. Darauf spielt auch das Werk von Santiago Sierra an. Er stellt Kriegsveteranen in die Ecke und konfrontiert den Besucher mit der Frage, wie eine Gesellschaft mit solchen Menschen umgehen soll und wie weit sie sich dazu öffnen muss.

HUO Das digitale Zeitalter, indirekt präsent in 14 Rooms, muss wieder Live-Erfahrung herstellen: Es ist als Reaktion auf die Digitalisierung zu interpretieren, dass sehr viele Künstler heutzutage wieder diese Live-Erfahrung haben wollen, genau so, wie das Livekonzert in der Musik wieder wichtig ist. Vielleicht ist dies sogar als eine Form von Widerstand zu interpretieren. Aber direkt sichtbar war das digitale Zeitalter bis dahin nicht. Deshalb zeigen wir neu Ed Atkins mit seinem Avatarprojekt. Atkins projiziert eine ihm sehr ähnliche digitale Figur und und stellt einen lebenden Doppelgänger vor die Projektion. Mit Ed Atkins kommt die Idee des Avatars zum ersten Mal in die 14 Räume. Weiter haben wir im Dialog mit Tino Sehgal entschlossen, seine Arbeit von 2004, This is competition, zu zeigen. In der Arbeit geht es um eine Form von Reziprozität, einem sich konstant gegenseitigen Ergänzen zweier Personen, die versuchen, über ein und dasselbe Werk zu reden mit der Bedingung, sich stets in der Wortsequenz abzuwechseln. Basierend auf einem Algorithmus analysiert es das Innenwerk des Marktes und seine Prozesse. Die Konkurrenten sind gezwungen, aufeinander einzugehen, und zusammen zu arbeiten. Daraus ergibt sich ein „feedback loop", eine Rückkoppelungsschleife, die nie aufhört. Diese Idee bricht das Thema der Cybernetics an, was bereits für den britischen Architekten Cedric Price mit seiner visionären Idee des Fun Palace eine integrale Rolle spielte, einen Ort zu schaffen der partizipatorisch, offen und stets veränderbar bleibt.

Das führt uns zur Idee mit Jordan Wolfson: Sein Roboter wird einen der Räume bewohnen.

KB Jordan Wolfson zeigt einen animatronischen Roboter, der vor einem Spiegel steht, der über Motion Control auf jeden einzelnen Besucher reagiert. Auch der Besucher steht vor dem Spiegel und sieht sowohl den Roboter als auch sich selbst. Der weibliche Roboter spiegelt sich, und über einen Bewegungsmelder guckt sie dem Besucher direkt in die Augen. Dies ist ganz konkret die Fortsetzung in das 21. Jahrhundert, auch wenn wir sagen, dass 14 Rooms zurückgeht auf die Kontemplation, auf die direkte, unmediatisierte Erfahrung. Man kommt nämlich wirklich an einen Ort und hat dort einen wirklichen Performer, der vor einem eins zu eins tanzt oder eine extrem anstrengende oder konzentriert choreografierte Performance zeigt. Das ist ein ungeheurer Luxus! So eins zu eins gleichberechtigt mit einem Performer, Interpreten oder Schauspieler … Im Gegensatz dazu steht dieser Roboter, der verwischt nun diesen Unterschied zwischen wirklichem Performer und Mediatisierung auf irritierende Weise. Etwas Ähnliches geschieht bei Ed Atkins: Das auf Video aufgenommene Bild des Künstlers erscheint auf dem Flachbildschirm, von dem Simultan eine Liveperformance, Live-Erfahrung stattfindet, sozusagen gleichzeitig reproduziert wird, was ja eigentlich die Umkehrung der Digitalisierung ist. Der Cyborg von Jordan Wolfson, dieser Einzelgänger in seiner Isolation, führt uns zudem vor Augen, was in Realität aus uns wird, wenn wir vor einem digitalen Gerät sitzen: Wir isolieren uns vollkommen.

Ein weiterer interessanter Aspekt bei Jordan Wolfson ist die Obsession, sich selber abzubilden. Zu diesem Thema gibt es eine weitere Arbeit, die schon seit Jahren in der Ausstellung ist, nämlich Joan Jonas' Mirror Check, wo eine junge Frau sich mit einem Handspiegel ihren Körper anschaut. Heutzutage würde man sich mit dem iPhone mustern. Man dreht die Kamera um und schaut sich über das iPhone an. Es ist sehr wichtig, dass wir diese Ebene des „Selfie", des Selbstbildes, thematisieren.

Ein ganz anderer Hinweis auf das digitalisierte 21. Jahrhundert sind Arbeiten wie diejenige von Yoko Ono. Sie hat bereits in den 1960er-Jahren Grapefruit geschrieben, ein Buch voller Handlungsanweisungen. Man könnte dies als eine Urform von Twitter bezeichnen. Yoko Ono hat 4,7 Millionen Twitter-Followers, wahrscheinlich, weil sie als Profi schon vor vierzig Jahren eine Art Twitter gemacht hat. Diese kleinen prägnanten Wahrheiten aus 140 Zeichen, die einem unter die Haut gehen, das macht Yoko Ono seit vierzig Jahren.

Nochmals zurück zu Ed Atkins: Das auf Video aufgenommene Bild des Künstlers erscheint auf dem Flachbildschirm und daneben wird eine Liveperformance aufgeführt, als eine Live-Erfahrung angeboten, das Video sozusagen wird zurückreproduziert, wo die Umkehrung der Digitalisierung stattfindet. Es ist also nicht so, wie wenn jemand eine Live-Erfahrung macht, wenn in der Metropolitan Opera die Leute auf der Bühne singen, das wir digital aufnehmen, und dann überall in der Welt simultan projiziert. Nein, der Liveperformer versucht in einer Art Karaoke, das aufgefangene Event nachzuproduzieren. Es gehen Leute in Milwaukee oder Indien zeitgleich mit der Aufführung in der Met Opera in ein Kino und schauen sich die Met Opera an. Das ist die Umkehrung davon, jemand reproduziert diese „recorded performance" und inkarniert im wahrsten Sinne des Wortes das nochmals. Es ist keine Reinkarnation, aber es geht wirklich um die Person, es geht letztendlich um den Besucher, weil der Besucher als lebende Person hier auch in den Ausstellungsraum kommt.

HUO Genau, und deshalb muss an dieser Stelle die Wichtigkeit der Handlungsanweisungen für diese Ausstellung hervorgehoben werden. Der Leser, die Leserin des Kataloges hat ein Manual mit einer Gebrauchsanweisung für den Ausstellungsbesuch, die Darsteller haben ihrerseits Anweisungen, wie sie die einzelnen Werke umzusetzen haben. Liegen diese Anweisungen vor, kann die gleiche Ausstellung in Zukunft immer wieder realisiert werden, genau wie bei Theaterstücken oder Opern. Zwei der Teilnehmer der Ausstellung, Yoko Ono und Bruce Nauman, bauen ihre Werke auf solche Handlungsanweisungen und die entsprechende Teilnahme der Betrachter auf. Yoko Ono hat bereits in ihrer Kindheit in Japan Instruktionen geschrieben und als junge Künstlerin ihr visionäres Buch Grapefruit geschaffen. Grapefruit war eine ganz große Inspiration für Do It und wiederum auch für 11 Rooms. Auch bei Bruce Nauman tauchen diese Handlungsanweisungen, die loopartig wiederholt werden können, auf. Wall-Floor Positions, eine Videoarbeit von 1968, zeigt den Künstler in seinem Studio. Für eine knappe Stunde führt Nauman eine Sequenz von Bewegungen durch, die sich im Dialog mit Wand und Boden abspielen. Für 14 Rooms fordert er von den Performern eine Wiederholung seiner Bewegungen. Wenn die Auswahl von 28 Positionen durchgespielt ist, verlässt der Performer den Raum und der nächste kommt rein, um den gleichen Loop zu wiederholen. Genau dieses Konzept des Loops war uns von Anfang an sehr wichtig. Insofern geht mit der Teilnahme von Bruce Nauman ein Traum in Erfüllung!

Wenn man von Handlungsanweisungen spricht, kommt man automatisch auf den partizipatorischen Aspekt eines Werkes zu sprechen. Dominique Gonzalez-Foerster sagt immer, der Betrachter / die Betrachterin macht mindestens die Hälfte der Arbeit aus. Dies ist auf jeden Fall für ihre Arbeit wahr. Nur dürfen wir hier nicht sagen, was Dominique Gonzalez-Foersters Werk für 14 Rooms ist, da der Besucher/die Besucherin beim Betrachten herausfinden muss, was die Handlungsanweisung sein könnte.

KB Wenn eine Handlungsanweisung geheim bleiben muss, der Besucher aber mindestens die eine Hälfte der Arbeit ausmacht, dann ist die Frage interessant, wer dann die andere Hälfte der Arbeit ist. Yoko Ono installiert ihre Arbeit Touch in einen komplett abgedunkelten Raum. Die Handlungsanweisung „Touch" besagt, dass sich die Besucher anfassen sollen. Damit begeht Yoko Ono den letzten Tabubruch in unserer Gesellschaft, nämlich, dass man sich nicht nur nicht mehr direkt anschauen darf, sondern: Touch geht aber noch weiter: Man soll sich sogar anfassen. Es wird mit der physischen Distanz, der Integrität, der Unberührbarkeit zwischen Fremden gebrochen. Yoko Ono spielt mit der Interaktion eines Besuchers mit dem andern und es fragt sich, was in diesem dunklen Raum tatsächlich stattfinden wird. Was passiert, wenn er voll ist? Was passiert, wenn er fast leer ist? Wenn er fast leer ist, dann ist eine fremde Berührung die intimere Überschreitung, als wenn er voll ist, und der ungewollte Körperkontakt durch die vielen Menschen, wie er zum Beispiel im öffentlichen Verkehr gegeben ist, passiert.

HUO Das erinnert mich an Yves Kleins Le Vide und Armans Le Plein. Arman hat auf Yves Kleins leere Ausstellung Le Vide von 1958 bei der Galerie Iris Clert in Paris mit seiner Ausstellung Le Plein von 1960 geantwortet: Er stopfte dazu die gleiche Galerie mit Abfall voll.

Normalerweise haben Ausstellungen eine sehr limitierte Lebensdauer. Sie kommen, sie gehen, es gibt eine Tour, die ist logistisch und pragmatisch determiniert, sie geht in zwei, drei Städte, dadurch werden Kosten gesenkt. Normalerweise werden Ausstellungen aufgelöst, und es wäre hochkompliziert und sehr aufwendig, diese zu einem späteren Zeitpunkt zu rekonstruieren. Es wäre wahrscheinlich unmöglich, etwa die erste Berlin Biennale wieder zusammenzustellen. Man würde gewisse Werke nicht mehr bekommen, weil es sie gar nicht mehr gibt.

Unsere Ausstellung funktioniert aber nach einer ganz anderen Logik. Genau wie Do It ist diese Ausstellung eine Art von Loop in der Zeit. Sie wird niemals absterben, weil sie in Form von Handlungsanweisungen weiter existiert. Es kann durchaus sein, dass ein Kuratorenstudent oder eine Museumsdirektorin in hundert Jahren diese Ausstellung wieder zum Leben erweckt. Deshalb ist es wichtig, dass wir durch dieses Gespräch und den Katalog ganz viele Informationen weitergeben. Pierre Boulez hat einmal zu Philippe Parreno und mir, als wir an Il Tempo del Postino arbeiteten, gesagt: "That's the score of the score!" – das sind die zusätzlichen Informationen, die über die Noten hinaus dafür da sind, dass man in der Zukunft weiß, wie ein musikalisches Stück von Xenakis, Pierre Boulez oder Stockhausen gespielt werden soll.

Nach drei Jahren 11 Rooms bis 14 Rooms, kann man abschätzen, ob es langsam zu einem Ende kommt oder nicht. In der Vorbereitung für diese Ausstellung hatten Klaus und ich viele Ideen, wer hier in Basel den 14. Raum bespielen könnte. Wir hätten gerne zehn bis zwanzig Künstler eingeladen, aber die Fondation Beyeler und Art Basel haben uns gesagt, dass vierzig Räume ein bisschen zu viel wären … Es war schmerzlich, aber wir mussten uns beschränken. Wir haben aber wie schon in Sydney die Gewissheit, dass wir unser Projekt noch Jahre, wenn nicht Jahrzehnte fortführen könnten. Das sind optimistische Aussichten!

DIE KÜNSTLER

MARINA ABRAMOVIĆ

Die Performerin sitzt exponiert, nackt und mit ausgestreckten Armen auf einem Fahrradsitz hoch oben an der Wand. Sie ist in gleißendes Licht getaucht. Regungslos und mit starrem Blick scheint sie zu schweben.

Seit dem Beginn ihrer Karriere, Anfang der 1970er-Jahre in Belgrad, gilt Marina Abramović als Wegbereiterin von Performance als Gattung der bildenden Kunst. Der Körper war stets sowohl ihr Thema als auch ihr Medium. Indem sie ihre körperlichen und mentalen Grenzen in Arbeiten erforschte, die einfache Handlungen ritualisieren, hat Abramović auf ihrer Suche nach emotionaler und spiritueller Transformation Schmerzen, Erschöpfung und Gefahren standgehalten.

Als Studentin der Akademie der bildenden Künste, Belgrad, schuf Abramović Texte, Zeichnungen und konzeptuelle Arbeiten. Anfang der 1970er-Jahre begann sie ihre Arbeit mit Performance, setzte dabei ihren Körper als Medium ein und erkundete die Interaktion zwischen Künstler und Publikum. In der frühen Serie Rhythm (1973–1975) führte sie schwierige, bisweilen gewaltsame Aktionen aus, die die Möglichkeiten und Grenzen des Publikums als Zeugen austesteten.

Zwischen 1975 und 1988 arbeitete Abramović mit dem deutschen Künstler Ulay zusammen. Ihre gemeinsamen Arbeiten aus dieser Zeit handeln von Dualität und Zusammengehörigkeit, geschlechtsspezifischen Rollen und der Polarität männlicher und weiblicher Körper.

Nach der Rückkehr zu ihrer Solokarriere im Jahr 1989 setzte Abramović ihre Erforschungen neuen Terrains fort mit Performances, die sich unter anderem mit ihrer Biografie befassten – darunter auch die Geschichte und Mythologie ihrer Heimat, des Balkans. Sie reiste weiterhin um die Welt, nach Brasilien, Indien und Japan und lernte dabei von verschiedensten kulturellen Praktiken.

2005 führte sie im New Yorker Guggenheim Museum eine revolutionäre Serie mit dem Titel Seven Easy Pieces aus. Dabei handelte es sich um Neuinszenierungen bahnbrechender früher Performancewerke der 1960er- und 1970er-Jahre von Joseph Beuys, Bruce Nauman, Vito Acconci, Valie Export, Gina Pane und Abramović selbst. Ihre große Retrospektive im Museum of Modern Art in New York beinhaltete The Artist is Present, ein neues Stück, in dem Abramović 736 Stunden und 30 Minuten im Museum verbrachte, still an einem Tisch sitzend, während auf einem gegenüberstehenden leeren Stuhl mehr als tausend Besucher nacheinander Platz nahmen.

In Luminosity, einer erstmals 1997 von Abramović ausgeführten Performance, saß die Künstlerin – in helles Licht getaucht – auf einem Fahrradsitz, der hoch oben an der Wand befestigt war. Sie schien in völliger Starre vor dem Betrachter zu schweben. Diese sowohl körperlich als auch geistig außerordentlich fordernde Arbeit, in der die Performerin sich für dreißig Minuten in unsicherer Position befindet, verlangt ihr äußerste Konzentration und Disziplin ab. Abramovićs hell ausgeleuchtete Nacktheit vermittelt dem Publikum das Gefühl von Voyeurismus, die Performerin erscheint jedoch zugleich ebenso verletzlich wie stark.

Abramović performte Luminosity nur dreimal – in Amsterdam (1997) für siebenunddreißig Minuten, dann später in der New Yorker Sean Kelly Gallery (1997) und in der Großen Halle der Reitschule Bern (1998), jeweils für neunzig Minuten. Für 14 Rooms wird das Stück wieder performt.[1] Wie Abramović

erklärt: „In dieser Arbeit geht es tatsächlich um Einsamkeit, um Schmerzen und um spirituelle Erhöhung. Um Luminosität und um die transzendentalen Eigenschaften des Menschen im Allgemeinen."[2]

[1] Dieses Projekt wurde zuvor bereits im Rahmen von 11 Rooms während des Manchester International Festival in der Manchester Art Gallery, von 12 Rooms bei dem Festival der Künste an der RUHRTRIENNALE im Museum Folkwang und im Rahmen von 13 Rooms während der 27. Kaldor Public Art Projects in 2013 in Sydney gezeigt.
[2] Audiostatement der Künstlerin, www.moma.org/explore/multimedia/audios/190/1994 (eingesehen im Mai 2014).

ALLORA & CALZADILLA
REVOLVING DOOR, 2011

Eine Gruppe von Tänzern bildet eine Reihe quer durch den Raum und versperrt den Besuchern den Weg. Die Choreografie basiert unter anderem auf Protestbewegungen, Militärmärschen und Tanzformationen. Die Reihe dreht sich im Raum langsam im Kreis und zwingt das Publikum, sich wie in einer Drehtür zu bewegen.

Jennifer Allora und Guillermo Calzadilla arbeiten als Künstlerduo seit fünfzehn Jahren zusammen. Durch ihre experimentelle Kombination von Performance, Skulptur, Video und Sound erkunden sie die in die Kultur eingebetteten Geschichten und Inhalte und konfigurieren und kontextualisieren zahlreiche Elemente neu – von Architektur und Objekten zu Musik und Körperbewegung – um ihre poetischen Kunstwerke zu erschaffen.

Eine ihrer berühmtesten Arbeiten, Stop, Repair, Prepare: Variations on "Ode to Joy" for a Prepared Piano, wurde erstmals 2008 im Haus der Kunst in München performt, ehe sie 2010 im Museum of Modern Art, New York, und 2012 beim Kaldor Public Art Project 26 in der State Library of Victoria, Melbourne, gefeiert wurde. Um diese Arbeit durchzuführen, schnitten die Künstler ein großes Loch in die Mitte eines Bechstein-Flügels und passten die Pedale an, um es dem Performer zu ermöglichen, in das Klavier zu steigen und es von innen heraus zu spielen – quasi verkehrt herum und rückwärts.

Die wiedergegebene Komposition ist der vierte Satz von Beethovens Neunter Symphonie, bekannt als „Ode an die Freude", die gemeinhin als Dokument menschlicher Brüderlichkeit gilt. Das Loch im Flügel macht zwei ganze Oktaven funktionsunfähig und erzeugt, während die unverkennbare Melodie gespielt wird, Abweichungen sowohl in den physischen als auch in den akustischen Dimensionen der Spieler-Instrumenten-Dynamik und in den bereits vorab festgelegten Konnotationen.

Allora & Calzadilla vertraten die Vereinigten Staaten bei der Biennale von Venedig 2011 mit ihrer Ausstellung Gloria. Teil dieser Schau war auch Track and Field, ein umgedrehter Militärpanzer, der zu einem Laufband für eine Reihe sportlicher Darbietungen des amerikanischen olympischen Leichtathletikteams wurde. Mit den Worten des Duos: „Als Künstler sind wir an Praktiken interessiert, die die materielle Natur von Wahrnehmung in den Vordergrund stellen und die den Körper ins Zentrum öffentlicher Formen von Subjektivität stellen, die mit der Organisation von Macht zu tun haben."[1]

In ihrer aktuellen Arbeit für die documenta 13, Raptor's Rapture (2012), spielt ein Performer das älteste bis heute bekannte Musikinstrument – eine Flöte, die der Homo Sapiens vor 35 000 Jahren aus dem Flügelknochen eines Gänsegeiers geschnitzt hat – in Anwesenheit eines lebendigen Gänsegeiers, ein evolutionärer Abkömmling einer der ältesten Kreaturen, die die Erde bevölkert haben, und der vom Aussterben bedroht ist.

In Revolving Door (2011), ihrer Arbeit für 14 Rooms,[2] bildet eine Gruppe von Tänzern spontan eine Reihe oder menschliche Barrikade, die sich von einer Wand zur anderen erstreckt. Die Reihe dreht sich langsam in einer Kreisbewegung, die es dem Publikum ermöglicht, sich wie durch eine Drehtür von einer Seite des Raumes auf die andere zu bewegen, was die Barrikadenformation paradoxerweise durchlässig macht. Die Tänzer drehen sich im Raum in Formation und zeigen dabei choreografierte Bewegungen, die unter anderem politischen Protestbewegungen, Militärmärschen und Tanzformationen entnommen sind. Als poetische Betrachtung der zahlreichen verschiedenen Handlungen, die wir im Einklang hervorbringen, erzeugt Revolving Door eine komplexe Dynamik zwischen der Gruppe und dem Individuum.

[1] Calzadilla, zit. n.: Carlos Motta, „Allora & Calzadilla", in: BOMB Magazine, 109, Herbst 2009 (Interview mit den Künstlern).
[2] Dieses Projekt wurde zuvor bereits im Rahmen von 11 Rooms während des Manchester International Festival in der Manchester Art Gallery, von 12 Rooms bei dem Festival der Künste an der RUHRTRIENNALE im Museum Folkwang und im Rahmen von 13 Rooms während der 27. Kaldor Public Art Projects in 2013 in Sydney gezeigt.

ED ATKINS
NO-ONE IS MORE "WORK" THAN ME, 2014

Auf einem riesigen Flachbildschirm bemüht sich ein kahl geschorener, tätowierter 3-D-Kopf im Maßstab 1:1 um Lebensechtheit. Gleichzeitig ist ein Mensch anwesend, der der Anweisung folgt, die sechsstündige Tirade des Avatars darüber, wie man eine richtige Person wird, zu bezeugen.

Ed Atkins Werk handelt vom Prozess der Vermittlung des Lebens durch zeitgenössische digitale Technologien: Wo und wie Körper und Wesen dargestellt werden, einander selbst und anderen gegenüber, und auf welche Art und Weise unsere Erfahrungen mehr oder weniger nachweisbar sind, lässt sich auf ein gestaltgewordenes und immanentes Selbst zurückführen. Durch den Einsatz von CGI, HD-Video und Audio erforscht er diese Möglichkeiten, indem er eine lebensähnliche Bildsprache und Effekte explizit erschafft, um die sterblichen und nicht wiederverwertbaren Aspekte von Erfahrung zu unterstreichen, wobei er den materiellen Verschiebungen widersteht, die der digitalen Technik innewohnen. Atkins arbeitet alleine und entwickelt viele der Elemente im Bereich Animation, Schreiben, Sound und Performance selbst. Die exakten digitalen Arrangements seiner Videos simulieren eine dermaßen präzise Kritik des menschlich Scheinenden, dass dessen Verlockungen und Widerwärtigkeiten häufig simultane Erwiderungen sind, während Mitgefühl billig in Verkennung und Entfremdung übergeht. Eine der extremsten Ausprägungen, in denen das Internet unser Leben verändert hat, liegt in der Art und Weise, wie wir zueinander in Beziehung stehen und wie wir uns einander annähern, vertraut miteinander werden.

No-one is more "work" than me (2014), eine ganz neue Arbeit, die Atkins für 14 Rooms entwickelte, entspringt dem engen, paradoxen Spiel von Anonymität und extremer Intimität, die in Onlinebeziehungen so omnipräsent geworden ist, so fundamental in der Bewegung digitalisierter Abbilder und Emotionen. Diese sechsstündige Ersatzperformance durch einen stereotypen, abgetrennten, kahlgeschorenen männlichen Avatar erkundet dessen im Wesentlichen andernorts befindliche Körperlichkeit – die Erschwernisse seiner Menschlichkeit oder das Fehlen derselben – Gefühle, ein verletzlicher Körper, strömende Begierden – und die ambivalenten Strategien im Zentrum des Subjektes selbst. Gleichzeitig ist ein Mensch anwesend, der der Anweisung folgt, die sechsstündige Tirade des Avatars darüber, wie man eine richtige Person wird, zu bezeugen.

DOMINIQUE GONZALEZ-FOERSTER
R.145, 2014

Die Besucher werden hier hinsichtlich der Wahrnehmung des Raumes wie ihrer eigenen Gefühle auf die Probe gestellt, und zwar durch einen subtilen und überzeugenden Minimalismus, der nur durch das Zutun der Besucher aktiviert wird. Was genau geschieht, bleibt geheim.

Seit Ende der 1980er-Jahre hat Dominique Gonzalez-Foerster ein wunderbar subtiles und doch komplexes Œuvre geschaffen, das Filme, Installationen und Performances umfasst, die oftmals die Dimensionen von Raum und Zeit infrage stellen. Sie konzentriert sich dabei auf urbane Strukturen, die Welt von Architektur und Theater, und mit dem Blick einer Szenografin kreiert sie mise-en-scène-artige Installationen, die multidimensionale Narrative wiedergeben. Für die Künstlerin ist „der stärkste Moment in der Kunst jener der Heterogenität. Er ist nicht durch einen Stil gekennzeichnet, eine Signatur oder eine Idee".[1]

2007 nahm Gonzalez-Foerster an der großen Gruppenausstellung Il Tempo del Postino teil. Ziel der Ausstellung war es, zu definieren, wie bildende Künste unterschiedlich erfahren werden können durch die Bestimmung der „angemessenen" Zeit, die ein Publikum mit einem bestimmten Stück verbringen muss, um dieses zu erfassen. Aus diesem Grund fand die Reihe von Performances in einem klassischen Theater mit einem Auditorium statt, wo ein Stück dem anderen folgte. Gonzalez-Foerster stellte Sol is going Home vor, das aus einem ganzen Orchester bestand, welches einen Abschnitt aus Beethovens Sechster Symphonie spielte. Nach nur wenigen Takten verließ der erste Musiker den Orchestergraben. Einer nach dem anderen folgte, bis nur mehr ein einziger übrig war, der das Stück alleine beendete. Um eine sehr natürliche Atmosphäre zu erzeugen, sorgte die Künstlerin, was die Inszenierung betraf, nur für einige wenige Elemente, wie Musik, Licht und Ausstattung und überließ es den Musikern, den Raum nach Belieben zu verlassen. Zwischen 2008 und 2012 inszenierte Dominique Gonzalez-Foerster eine Reihe von Performances in Zusammenarbeit mit Ari Benjamin Meyers, darunter Arbeiten wie NY.2022 im Solomon R. Guggenheim Museum in New York, K.62/K85 bei Performa in New York und T.451 im Tensta Konstall in Stockholm. Im Bestreben, eine publikumsbasierte Erfahrung nachzubilden, verschmelzen die beiden Künstler Partitur und architektonische Struktur, um eine szenografische Erzählung zu schaffen. Inspiriert durch bestimmte Filme zu Musik und Literatur, wird der Betrachter in eine geteilte Erfahrung von Zerstreuung gezogen. Gonzalez-Foerster fand Gefallen am Prozess der Fragmentierung und setzte ihre Zusammenarbeit mit Tristan Bera fort. Zusammen entwickelten sie das Stück M.2062, eine Oper, die aus verschiedenen Lecture-Performances besteht. Darin erscheinen fiktive und real existierende Charaktere, unter anderem Ludwig II., Scarlett O'Hara, Edgar Alan Poe und Lola Montez, sie streifen umher, tippen Worte in Maschinen und tauschen Vorstellungen von Poesie und Fantasie aus. Das Konzept von Gonzalez-Foersters Präsentation für 14 Rooms bleibt ein Geheimnis. Die vorgegebene Struktur des fünf mal fünf Meter großen Raumes und die zu erwartende Erfahrung wird im Zentrum von Gonzalez-Foersters Arbeit stehen. Die Wahrnehmung des Besuchers/der Besucherin des Raumes und seiner/ihres Gefühlszustandes wird mit der Methode des ausserordentlich überzeugenden, jedoch subtilen Minimalismus, der für Dominique Gonzalez-Foersters Arbeit so typisch ist, auf die Probe gestellt.

1 Kommentar der Künstlerin, aus einem Interview mit Hans Ulrich Obrist, http://www.dgf5.com/info/t3/Texts (eingesehen im Mai 2014).

DAMIEN HIRST
HOLLY, GRETEL, 1992

In dieser Installation sitzen eineiige Zwillinge vor einem Paar Spot Paintings, angebracht an der Wand direkt hinter ihnen. Der Titel der Arbeit ändert sich mit den Namen der teilnehmenden Zwillinge. Als die Arbeit 1992 das erste Mal präsentiert wurde, hieß sie abwechselnd Marianne, Hildegard und Ingo, Torsten.

Seit seinem Abschluss 1989 am Goldsmiths College in London hat Damien Hirst einen großen und anspruchsvollen Werkkorpus geschaffen, der sich ganz allgemein mit den Themen Leben, Tod und Verfall befasst – oder auch parodiert – und sich des Kunstsystems als kapitalistischem Markt bedient. Er ist für Werke wie diamantenbesetzte Schädel, in Formaldehyd schwebende Haie, simulierte Autopsien und lebende Maden bekannt.

The Physical Impossibility of Death in the Mind of Someone Living (1991) ist zweifellos eine Ikone der Gegenwartskunst des 20. Jahrhunderts und eine von Hirsts berühmtesten Arbeiten. Sie besteht aus einem vier Meter langen Tigerhai, eingelegt in einem langen, mit Formaldehyd gefüllten Behältnis, und erregte ein enormes Presseecho, als sie 1992 bei der Präsentation Young British Art in der Saatchi Gallery gezeigt wurde. Ein weiteres legendäres Stück, For the Love of God (2007), besteht aus dem Abguss eines menschlichen Schädels aus dem 18. Jahrhundert, der mit 8601 Diamanten besetzt ist. Diese gewagte Arbeit wurde ursprünglich in der White Cube Gallery, London, ausgestellt und verbindet dekorative aztekisch und mexikanisch inspirierte Muster auf dem klassischen Memento-mori-Symbol des Schädels, das Künstler seit Jahrhunderten einsetzen, um auf die Vergänglichkeit menschlicher Existenz hinzuweisen.

Hirsts Arbeit für <u>14 Rooms</u>,[1] die 1992 bei Jay Joplings Stand auf der <u>Unfair</u> in Köln erstmals gezeigt wurde, besteht aus einer wechselnden Besetzung eineiiger Zwillinge, die vor zwei der legendären Spot Paintings platziert sind, die direkt auf die dahinter befindliche Wand aufgebracht wurden. Anstatt eine feste Form aufzuweisen, ändert sich die Arbeit im Laufe der Ausstellung kontinuierlich mit dem Einsatz verschiedener Zwillingspaare, und auch der Titel ändert sich mit den Namen der Teilnehmer. 2009 wurde die Arbeit im Rahmen der Gruppenausstellung <u>Pop Life: Art in a Material World</u> in der Tate Modern unter Mitwirkung von mehr als vierzig Zwillingspaaren erneut ausgestellt.

Hirst begann 1986 mit der Herstellung seiner Spot Paintings in der Absicht, eine endlose Serie mit unbegrenzten Farbkombinationen zu schaffen. Die Arbeiten sind von einer maschinell gefertigten Qualität und – sehr ähnlich den Prinzipien der Factory Andy Warhols – stellen auch sie die Vorstellung von Authentizität und Autorschaft infrage, ein zentrales Thema der Pop-Art, das zeitgenössische Künstler bis zum heutigen Tag beeinflusst. Die Vorstellung, zur selben Zeit gleich und doch andersartig zu sein, erstreckt sich auch auf die Zwillinge, die Hirst für seine Arbeit engagierte, und er erklärt: „Ich hatte diesen Traum – der erschreckend war – in dem ich mich selbst traf. Ich weiß, dass ich einzigartig bin. Aber ich sehe das wie Bücherstützen. Ich glaube, dass jeder zwei ist. Du schneidest dich selbst in der verdammten Mitte durch. Du bist zwei. Es untergräbt die Vorstellung der Einzigartigkeit. Daraus ziehe ich einen Trost, den ich liebe. Jeder Teil eines Paars hat sein eigenes Leben, unabhängig vom anderen, aber sie leben zusammen."[2]

[1] Dieses Projekt wurde zuvor bereits im Rahmen von <u>12 Rooms</u> bei dem Festival der Künste an der RUHRTRIENNALE im Museum Folkwang und im Rahmen von <u>13 Rooms</u> während der 27. Kaldor Public Art Projects in 2013 in Sydney gezeigt.
[2] Damien Hirst und Gordon Burn, <u>On the Way to Work</u>, London 2001, S. 131, zit. n. http://www.damienhirst.com/holly-gretel (eingesehen im Mai 2014).

JOAN JONAS
MIRROR CHECK, 1970

Die Performerin beobachtet und untersucht ihren eigenen nackten Körper mit einem kleinen runden Handspiegel. Der Spiegel dient als Symbol der Selbstporträtierung, aber auch als Mittel der Fragmentierung, das nur Teile, jedoch nie den gesamten Körper wiedergibt.

Joan Jonas ist eine anerkannte und einflussreiche Multimediakünstlerin, die mit den künstlerischen Mitteln von Performance, Video, Zeichnung sowie mit skulpturalen Installationen arbeitet. Nach dem Studium der Kunstgeschichte und der Bildhauerei setzte sie die Arbeit mit dem Medium Skulptur fort und erkundete Ende der 1960er-Jahre gleichzeitig performative Körperaktionen in Beziehung zu Film, Video und Raum. Jonas fand, dass Performance und Bewegung ihr eine größere Bandbreite boten, um Bild und Handlung zu verbinden. Ihre bahnbrechenden Arbeiten waren vom Film, von Literatur, bildender Kunst, zeitgenössischem Theater, Tanz und traditionellem japanischem Theater inspiriert.

In ihren frühen Performances setzte Jonas Spiegel als Requisiten ein und schuf so eine Distanz zwischen Performer und Betrachter, um so Themen wie die Rolle des Zuschauers, Geschlecht, Identität und das fragmentierte Bild der Frau zu erforschen. In ihrer Serie <u>Mirror Pieces</u> (1968–2004) wie auch in ihren Videoperformances (1972–2013) erkundete sie, wie sich die Wahrnehmung verändert, wenn ein Objekt oder der Körper aus einem anderen Blickwinkel betrachtet wird. Ebenso lenkt die Serie die Aufmerksamkeit auf den Unterschied zwischen Selbstbild und Wahrnehmung durch andere. In den Mirror Pieces spiegeln sich die Betrachter als Teil einer choreografierten Performance in lebensgroßen Spiegeln und sind gezwungen, ihrem Selbstbild in einem öffentlichen Umfeld entgegenzutreten.

Jonas' Mirror Check, ein Werk, das die Künstlerin 1970 erstmals performte, wird im Rahmen von 14 Rooms[1] präsentiert und ist vielleicht eine der intimsten und ergreifendsten Arbeiten dieser Serie. Wir beobachten, wie eine Frau ihren eigenen nackten Körper in einem kleinen, runden Handspiegel betrachtet. Sorgfältig und mit Bedacht beobachtet sie die Spiegelungen ihres ganzen Körpers und erforscht alle unterschiedlichen Blickwinkel und Perspektiven. Der Spiegel dient hier als Symbol der Selbstporträtierung aber auch als Mittel der Fragmentierung, der Teile, jedoch nicht den gesamten Körper wiedergibt. Es besteht eine Diskrepanz zwischen dem, was die Performerin sehen kann, und dem, was das Publikum sieht: Ein Spiegel gibt normalerweise ein Abbild wieder, doch was zeigt dieser Spiegel und was verbirgt er? Eine Spannung zwischen Illusion und Realität, Verführung und Distanz, Verhüllung und Nacktheit wird in dieser zehnminütigen Performance ausgelebt.

[1] Dieses Projekt wurde zuvor bereits im Rahmen von 11 Rooms während des Manchester International Festival in der Manchester Art Gallery, von 12 Rooms bei dem Festival der Künste an der RUHRTRIENNALE im Museum Folkwang und im Rahmen von 13 Rooms während der 27. Kaldor Public Art Projects in 2013 in Sydney gezeigt.

LAURA LIMA
MAN=FLESH/ WOMAN=FLESH – FLAT, 1997

In diesem Raum ist die Decke nur 45 Zentimeter hoch. Am Ende des Raumes liegt eine körperlich behinderte Person neben einer Lampe auf dem Boden. Der Betrachter muss kriechen oder sich hinlegen, um das Stück überhaupt sehen zu können.

Seit Anfang der 1990er-Jahre setzte Laura Lima unter der Gleichung Man=flesh/Woman=flesh Lebewesen in ihren zeitlich begrenzten Arbeiten ein, welche nur während der Öffnungszeiten der Galerie existieren. Die Künstlerin hat ein persönliches Glossar konstruiert, um die Natur ihrer Arbeiten zu erörtern, und vermeidet so Begriffe wie „Performance" oder „Performer". Sie erscheint nie selbst, sondern instruiert andere, um die Stücke zu präsentieren, die sie entwickelt hat. Sie hat bereits mit Kindern, alten Menschen, Männern, Frauen und Tieren gearbeitet, um sich ein Bild der Bedeutung ihrer Existenz zu machen und um dann die Grenzen von Autonomie und Abhängigkeit in menschlichem Handeln zu erforschen. Lima erklärt: „Mich interessieren die komplizierten sozialen Beziehungen, der Austausch von Verhaltensweisen, die im Laufe der Zeit unsere Wahrnehmung von Sprache und Leben verändern."[1]

Für ihre Arbeit Doped (1997) nimmt eine mit einem schleierähnlichen weißen Kleid bekleidete Frau ein Schlafmittel ein und liegt für Stunden schlafend auf dem Boden der Galerie, mit der Wand mittels eines langen, roten gewebten Netzes verbunden, das wie ein dickes Seil an ihrem Kopf befestigt ist. In To Age (2004) wurden Galeriemitarbeiter durch den Einsatz von Prothetik und Theater-Make-up mit ihren eigenen zukünftigen Gesichtern versehen, von der Zeit zerklüftet und faltig. In anderen Arbeiten kamen Tiere zum Einsatz, wie in <u>Gala Chickens</u> (2004), einer Arbeit für die Biennale von Lyon im Jahr 2011, in der Hennen mit festlich gefärbten Federn ausgestattet wurden, die normalerweise in brasilianischen Karnevalskostümen zum Einsatz kommen. Kostüme standen auch im Zentrum von Limas Arbeit <u>Costumes Store</u> (2003/06), in der den Besuchern blaue und durchsichtige Vinylkleidung zum Kauf angeboten wurde, die dann dazu ermutigt wurden, diese Kleider im alltäglichen Leben zu tragen.

In Limas Arbeiten <u>Man=flesh/Woman=flesh</u> (ab 1994) teilt die Künstlerin den Teilnehmern (die sie als „fleshperson" bezeichnet) eine Reihe von Aufgaben zu, für die speziell konstruierte Apparate oder Szenerien zum Einsatz kommen. Jeder Teilnehmer befolgt Limas Plan von Aktivitäten – gehen, saugen, schlafen, kämpfen und ziehen – kontinuierlich während der Dauer der Ausstellung. In Limas Arbeit für <u>14 Rooms</u>,[2] <u>Man=flesh/Woman=flesh – FLAT</u> (1997) ist menschliches Fleisch das grundlegende Arbeitsmaterial, das inmitten einer begrenzten architektonischen Umgebung positioniert ist. Unter einer Decke, die gerade einmal fünfundvierzig Zentimeter vom Boden entfernt ist, liegt eine Person ruhig da, nur mit einer Lampe ausgestattet, die den kleinen Raum beleuchtet. Der Betrachter muss kriechen oder sich hinlegen, um den Mitwirkenden zu sehen, der in diesem Fall eine körperliche Behinderung hat.

[1] Lima in der Korrespondenz mit Kaldor Art Projects, Februar 2001.

[2] Dieses Projekt wurde zuvor bereits im Rahmen von <u>11 Rooms</u> während des Manchester International Festival in der Manchester Art Gallery, von <u>12 Rooms</u> bei dem Festival der Künste an der RUHRTRIENNALE im Museum Folkwang und im Rahmen von <u>13 Rooms</u> während der 27. Kaldor Public Art Projects in 2013 in Sydney gezeigt.

BRUCE NAUMAN
WALL-FLOOR POSITIONS, 1968

Ein Performer vollzieht eine durch originales Videofilmmaterial des Künstlers vorgegebene Sequenz von 28 Positionen, die in Beziehung zu Wand und Boden stehen. Der Performer muss die ursprüngliche Choreografie des Videos studieren und die Bewegungen genau in der korrekten Abfolge wiedergeben.

Bruce Nauman ist einer der vielseitigsten und einflussreichsten Künstler, die seine Generation hervorgebracht hat. Er arbeitet mit einer Reihe von Medien, darunter Film, Video, Performance, interaktive Environments, Neon, Fotografie, Druck und Skulptur. Nach dem Studium der Mathematik und Physik an der University of Wisconsin in Madison von 1960 bis 1962 wählte er als Hauptfach schließlich Kunst und machte 1964 seinen Abschluss. Mit dem Master of Fine Arts der University of California, Davis, begann Nauman, ein Œuvre aufzubauen, das sich durch die Erforschung der Physikalität des Körpers, die psychologischen Aspekte des Ausdrucks und die ambivalente Kraft der Sprache auszeichnet. In seinen Arbeiten untersucht der Künstler unterschiedliche Formen und Materialien, die die Vorstellungen dessen, was Kunst und die Rolle des Künstlers ausmachen könnte, noch erweitern. In seiner ersten Einzelausstellung in Los Angeles (1966) schuf er eine Gruppe von Fiberglasskulpturen, die auf der Rückseite von Objekten basierten oder von Abdrücken seines eigenen Körpers angefertigt waren. Später im selben Jahr nahm er die Farbfotografie <u>Self-Portrait as a Fountain</u> auf, ein legendäres Bild, das die öffentlich vorherrschende Vorstellung eines Brunnens infrage stellte. Indem er einfach nur Wasser aus seinem Mund herausspritzen ließ, zitierte der Künstler nicht nur das berühmte Readymade von Marcel Duchamp von 1917 – der ein Ur-inal als Brunnen präsentierte –, sondern er wandelte den Akt auch in eine performative Handlung um. Dort, wo die physische und die psychologische Eigenschaft des Kunstwerkes sich vom Gegenstand zum Thema und wieder zurück verschob, fand ein konzeptueller Wandel statt.

Gegen Ende der 1960er-Jahre wandte der Künstler seine Aufmerksamkeit der Herstellung von Filmen und Videos zu. Mit rudimentärer Technologie nahm er sich in seinem Atelier beim Ausführen verschiedener Aufgaben selbst auf. Eine 16-Millimeter-Kamera wurde an einer Stelle platziert, von wo er bei der Ausführung einer Reihe von Bewegungen, Aktionen oder Happenings zu sehen war. Ein Beispiel für einen solchen Film ist <u>Bouncing Two Balls between the Floor and the Ceiling with Changing Rhythms</u>, in dem er mit weißem Malerkreppband ein Quadrat auf dem Boden seines Ateliers markierte und zwei Bälle so fest wie möglich auf den Boden prallen ließ, wobei er versuchte, einen bestimmten Rhythmus einzuhalten – was ihm immer wieder misslang.

Für <u>14 Rooms</u> hat Nauman einer Neuaufführung von <u>Wall-Floor Positions</u> von 1968 zugestimmt, einer Videoarbeit, die auf seiner Performance der Abfolge von Bewegungen an der University of California in Davis (1965) basierte. Er beschreibt die Arbeit folgendermaßen: „Mit dem Rücken zur Wand stehend für ungefähr fünfundvierzig Sekunden oder eine Minute, sich von der Wand weglehnen, dann in der Taille beugen, hocken, sitzen und schließlich hinlegen. Es gab sieben unterschiedliche Positionen in Bezug zu Wand und Boden. Dann führte ich die ganze Abfolge noch einmal durch, von der Wand wegstellen, die Wand anschauen, dann nach links und rechts schauen. Es gab achtundzwanzig Positionen und die ganze Präsentation dauerte in etwa eine halbe Stunde".[1] In <u>14 Rooms</u> führt ein Performer diese Abfolge von 28 Positionen in Bezug zu Wand und Boden streng nach den Vorgaben im Original-Filmmaterial durch. Der Performer muss die ursprüngliche Choreografie des Videos studieren und die Bewegungen genau in der korrekten Abfolge wiedergeben. Sobald er fertig ist, verlässt er den Raum und der nächste Performer kommt herein. Naumans Beitrag zu der diesjährigen Ausgabe von <u>14 Rooms</u> ist von höchster Bedeutung, nicht nur, weil er so in den Kontext der aktuellen Live-Art-Umgebung gesetzt werden kann, sondern auch wegen des Einflusses, den seine Arbeiten auf zeitgenössische Künstlerkollegen wie Marina Abramović und Tino Sehgal ausübten. Beide haben Naumans Arbeiten in frühen Stadien ihrer Karrieren neu interpretiert.

[1] Kommentar des Künstlers, http://www.eai.org/title.htm?id=4287 (eingesehen im Mai 2014).

OTOBONG NKANGA
DIASPORE, 2014

Die Performance wird von bis zu drei Frauen ausgeführt, die die Pflanze <u>Cestrum nocturnum</u>, die auch als Königin der Nacht bekannt ist, mit sich tragen. In ständigem Austausch mit der Pflanze navigieren die Frauen über eine topografische Karte auf dem Boden, die ihre Bewegungen durch verschiedene Territorien leitet.

Seit Beginn des Jahres 2000 arbeitet Otobong Nkanga mit einer Vielzahl von Medien, darunter Zeichnung, Fotografie, Installation und Performancekunst. Sie beobachtet soziale und topografische Veränderungen in ihrer Umgebung, die Komplexitäten, die in diese Erfahrungen eingebettet sind, und die Art und Weise, wie solche Dinge wie Rohstoffe, Boden, Erde und ihr potenzieller Wert regionaler und kultureller Auffassung unterworfen sind. „Ihre Arbeiten laden den Betrachter oftmals ein, sich in einen Dialog über die Nichtgreifbarkeit von Identität, Erinnerung, Wahrnehmung einzulassen und zu beobachten, wie sich diese verändern, wenn sie mittels spezifischer Arrangements und Erzählweisen präsentiert werden",[1] mithilfe von Sprache und ihres eigenen Körpers. Nkanga wurde in Nigeria geboren, wo sie auch ihr Studium der Kunst an der Obafemi Awolowo Universität in Ile-Ife begann, das sie dann an der École Nationale Supérieure des Beaux-Arts in Paris fortsetzte. 2008 schloss sie mit einem Master in Performing Arts von DasArts, Amsterdam, ab.

Bei der Biennale von Sharjah (2013) performte Nkanga Taste of a Stone: Itiat esa Ufok. Zwischen fünf und sieben Stunden täglich trug sie eine Pflanze auf dem Kopf und interagierte mit ihrem Publikum mittels tänzerischer Bewegungen, durch Singen und Sprechen, manchmal auch, indem sie die Pflanze einem Zuschauer übergab. Die Pflanze, Cestrum nocturnum (Königin der Nacht), die ursprünglich von den Karibischen Inseln stammt, sich jedoch in Südasien ansiedelte, zeugt vom Interesse der Künstlerin für Migration und das dichte Netz sozialer, politischer und wirtschaftlicher Spannungen, die auftreten können, wenn verschiedene Ressourcen von ihrem Ursprungsort ausgesiedelt, verdrängt oder entwurzelt werden. Interessanterweise wird die Pflanze zu einem weiteren Performer, jemand, mit dem Nkanga kommunizieren kann, mit dem sie sich bewegen und mit dem sie sein kann. Nkanga lässt sich gerne von ihren Gefühlen inspirieren, von ihrem Land, und in Beziehung zu diesem Land erforscht sie die Rolle von Kartierung, die Vorstellungen von Eigentum, die Geschichte des Kolonialismus und die wirtschaftliche Bedeutung, die damit verbunden wird.

Für 14 Rooms bearbeitete Nkanga ihre Choreografie und weist bis zu drei Frauen der Diaspora an, den Raum zu unterschiedlichen Zeitpunkten zu betreten, wobei jede von ihnen die Pflanze Cestrum nocturnum trägt. Eine topografische Karte auf dem Boden dient als Navigationspunkt und hilft den Frauen dabei, sich durch den Raum, durch verschiedene Territorien, zu bewegen. Die Künstlerin erforscht weiterhin die Sprache der Diaspora, des Verlassens des Ortes, der sich Heimat nennt, und der Vorwärtsbewegung in Richtung einer neuen Zukunft. Das Gleiche gilt für die Pflanzen, die zuerst aus ihrer Heimaterde entwurzelt werden, ihre Sporen an einem neuen Ort verteilen und so neue Identitäten erschaffen. Die Frauen kartieren den Boden, führen Gespräche, meditieren oder sitzen einfach mit ihren Pflanzen da, bewegen sich im Rhythmus, wenden sich ab, drehen sich herum, stehen still. Der Blick ist auf ihre Reise gerichtet, auf den Körper wie auch auf die Pflanze, auf die Möglichkeit einer Symbiose. Nkanga ist an der Verschiebung der Perspektive von Dingen interessiert, am Versuch, Zeit durch Erfahrung einzufangen, das Nichtgreifbare zu erfassen – und daran, diese Erfahrungen in permanenter Bewegung zu halten.

[1] www.berliner-kuenstlerprogramm.de/en/gast.php?id=1223 (eingesehen im Mai 2014).

ROMAN ONDÁK
SWAP, 2011

Ein Performer sitzt wie ein Verkäufer hinter einem Tisch, mit einem Gegenstand, den er mitbringt. Sobald der erste Besucher den Raum betritt, versucht der Performer, den Gegenstand gegen irgendein anderes Objekt zu tauschen, das der Besucher bei sich hat und das er bereit ist, gegen das Objekt des Performers einzutauschen. Dies setzt eine

endlose Kette von Tauschhandel und Naturalgeschäft in Gang, die bis zum Ende der Ausstellung anhält.

Roman Ondák zieht vertraute Elemente des alltäglichen Lebens heran und definiert sie neu, um unsere Erwartungen und Perspektiven zu überraschen. Er untersucht soziale Codes, Konventionen, Rituale und Formen des Austausches, indem er Objekte, Vorstellungen und Handlungen auf diskrete Art und Weise von ihrem üblichen Umfeld löst. Seine Installationen, Performances und Interventionen lassen sich bisweilen kaum von dem Kontext, in dem sie präsentiert werden, unterscheiden. Oft auf humorvolle Art und Weise veranlassen sie Betrachter dazu, zweimal hinzusehen und ihre vorgefassten Meinungen und Interaktionsweisen zu hinterfragen. In einer Reihe von Performances hat Ondák Teilnehmer gebeten, seinen Anweisungen zu folgen, sie jedoch gleichzeitig aufgefordert, ihre Kreativität einzusetzen. Die daraus resultierenden Arbeiten sind kontrollierte Studien kollektiver Vorstellungskraft. Für seine Arbeit Passage (2004) verteilte er Schokoriegel an fünfhundert Stahlarbeiter in Japan und bat sie, nachdem sie die Schokolade gegessen hätten, Skulpturen aus der Folienverpackung anzufertigen. Hunderte von winzigen Silberkonstruktionen wurden dann gemeinsam gezeigt und präsentierten – weit entfernt von Serienproduktion – eine Vision von Vielfältigkeit und Kreativität. Für Good Feelings in Good Times (2003) forderte er Menschen auf, eine Warteschlange vor einer Kunstgalerie zu bilden, die so eine künstliche Linie ohne Ziel erschufen, während für Teaching to Walk (2002) jeden Tag eine Mutter eingeladen wurde, die Galerie als Ort zu benutzen, an dem ihr Kind seine ersten Schritte üben konnte.

Für seine gefeierte Arbeit Measuring the Universe (2007) begann Ondák mit einem leeren Galerieraum und wies Mitarbeiter an, die Größe jedes Besuchers, seinen oder ihren Vornamen sowie das Datum des Besuches mittels eines schwarzen Filzstiftes an der weißen Wand festzuhalten. Als die Arbeit 2009 im Laufe von vier Monaten im Museum of Modern Art, New York, zu sehen war, wurden Tausende von Besuchern zu einem Teil der Arbeit und der Raum veränderte sich durch eine Vielzahl von Linien, Namen und Daten. Indem sie den Strom an Besuchern durch die Ausstellung festhielten, verschmolzen die schwarzen Striche zu einer dichten, dunklen Masse entlang der Wand und trafen bei der Durchschnittsgröße der Besucher zusammen, womit sie nur eine der vielen allgemeingültigen Aussagen enthüllten, die unsere sozialen Normen und Maße bestimmen.

Ondáks Arbeit für 14 Rooms[1] mit dem Titel Swap (2011) verbindet Kunst mit dem alltäglichen Leben. Der Künstler wählt einen Performer aus, der wie ein Verkäufer an einem Marktstand hinter einem Tisch wartet. Der Performer wird gebeten, ein Objekt zu wählen, das auf einem Tisch liegt, bis der erste Besucher den Raum betritt. Der Besucher erhält nun die Gelegenheit, das Objekt gegen irgendetwas zu tauschen, das er oder sie bereit ist einzutauschen – eine Münze oder eine Uhr, eine Feder oder ein Stück Papier. Der Performer bittet nun jeden weiteren Besucher, einen Gegenstand gegen ein Objekt auf dem Tisch zu tauschen, und setzt damit eine endlose Kette von Tauschhandel und Naturalgeschäft in Gang. Jeden Tag bleibt das letzte Objekt bis zum nächsten Morgen auf dem Tisch liegen. Zum Ende der Ausstellung nimmt der letzte Performer das letzte Objekt des Tages an sich.

[1] Dieses Projekt wurde zuvor bereits im Rahmen von 11 Rooms während des Manchester International Festival in der Manchester Art Gallery, von 12 Rooms bei dem Festival der Künste an der RUHRTRIENNALE im Museum Folkwang und im Rahmen von 13 Rooms während der 27. Kaldor Public Art Projects in 2013 in Sydney gezeigt.

YOKO ONO
TOUCH PIECE, 1963/2014

Besucher sind aufgefordert, einander im Dunkeln zu berühren. Einige haben vielleicht verbundene Augen, andere entdecken möglicherweise Stifte, mit denen sie Nachrichten an den Wänden hinterlassen können, was die Grenzen der Intimität und Privatsphäre eines jeden Besuchers herausfordert.

Seit mehr als fünf Jahrzehnten ist Yoko Ono als anspruchsvolle Künstlerin, Dichterin und Musikerin, aber auch als Video- und Performancekünstlerin bekannt. Indem sie die Komplexität der menschlichen Gefühle von Verlust und Konflikt bis hin zu Harmonie und Liebe erforscht, experimentiert sie mit der Auffassung ihres Publikums von Kunst und der Welt im Allgemeinen. In ihrer produktiven Karriere befasste sie sich mit einer Vielzahl von Medien und schuf permanent neue Formen künstlerischen Ausdrucks, womit sie die Beziehung zwischen Künstler und Betrachter infrage stellt. Sie zog Anfang der 1950er-Jahre nach New York und wurde – als Pionierin der Konzeptkunst – Teil der pulsierenden Avantgarde. Hier begann sie auch mit ihrer Instructions-Reihe. 1961 schuf sie Instruction Paintings, die ursprünglich aus Leinwänden mit verschiedenen Materialien und verbalen oder geschriebenen Instruktionen bestanden. Im darauffolgenden Jahr stellte sie lediglich die geschriebenen Instruktionen für die Gemälde aus, damit andere sie im Geist ausführen könnten. Ungefähr zur gleichen Zeit inszenierte sie eine Reihe bahnbrechender Performances, in denen es um Bewegung und Klänge ging, und 1964 performte sie Cut Piece in Kyoto und Tokio, ein wegweisendes Stück, das die Künstlerin bewegungslos auf dem Boden kniend zeigte. Das Publikum wurde dann eingeladen, auf die Bühne zu kommen, um Onos Kleidung mit Scheren abzuschneiden. Dieses Werk warf nicht nur Fragen nach Geschlecht und Identität auf, sondern symbolisierte auch das innere Leiden, dem Menschen alltäglich unterworfen sind.

Onos Engagement als Friedensaktivistin erschien regelmäßig und immer wieder als prominentes Leitmotiv in ihren Arbeiten. 1969 realisierte sie, zusammen mit John Lennon, sowohl Bed-In als auch War Is Over! (if you want it), eine weltweite Plakatkampagne für den Frieden. In den vergangenen Jahren schuf sie interaktive Arbeiten wie Wish Tree (1996), ein Werk, das Besucher dazu einlädt, persönliche Friedenswünsche an den Ästen zu befestigen. Über eine Million Wünsche sind so zusammengekommen. Der Imagine Peace Tower in Island ist eines der Ergebnisse der langfristigen Anstrengungen der Künstlerin zur Förderung von Frieden, aber auch von positivem Denken und Liebe auf der ganzen Welt. Ein ähnlich umfangreiches Projekt ist Smilefilms, wo ihr endgültiges Ziel darin besteht „einen Film zu machen, der von jedem Menschen auf der Welt einen Schnappschuss mit lächelndem Gesicht beinhaltet".[1] Das interaktive Werk ermutigt die Betrachter, ihr Lächeln auf eine Onlinedatenbank zu laden, die so permanent wächst.

Für 14 Rooms präsentiert Ono ihre Arbeit Touch Piece von 1963, die erstmals in ihrem Buch Grapefruit erschien, einer Sammlung von Instruction Pieces von 1964. Die Instruktion am Eingang des vollständig dunklen Raumes gibt nur eine Anweisung: „Touch". Besucher sind aufgefordert, einander im Dunkeln zu berühren. Sobald sie den Raum betreten, werden sie von Weihrauchduft willkommen geheißen und werden augenblicklich zu aktiven Mitwirkenden des Werkes. Einige haben vielleicht verbundene Augen, andere entdecken möglicherweise Stifte, mit denen sie Nachrichten an den Wänden hinterlassen können, was die Grenzen der Intimität und Privatsphäre eines jeden Besuchers herausfordert.

[1] Kommentar der Künstlerin, http://www.smilefilm.com (eingesehen im Mai 2014).

TINO SEHGAL
THIS IS COMPETITION, 2004

Tino Sehgals Arbeitsweise ist eine Inspiration für alle Rooms-Ausstellungen. Seit 2000 konstruiert er Situationen, die einzigartige Zusammentreffen von Menschen durch Bewegung, durch das gesprochene Wort und durch Lieder initiieren, und schafft damit pulsierende, lebendige Kunstwerke, die über die gesamte Öffnungszeit einer Ausstellung laufen. Sehgals Kunstwerke, die in dem Moment Form annehmen, in dem der Betrachter auf sie trifft, sind intim und einzigartig, geprägt von den Reaktionen und Blickwinkeln eines jeden Besuchers.

This is competition war ursprünglich bei der Art Basel 2004 zu sehen, wo es den Baloise Art Prize erhielt. Es handelt sich dabei um eine algorithmische Arbeit, die sich mit dem inneren Funktionsprozess von Märkten befasst. Darin versuchen zwei Interpreten, Werke mit einer bestimmten sprachlichen Einschränkung zu beschreiben: Keiner von beiden kann mehr als ein Wort hintereinander sagen. Diese Regelstruktur erzeugt ein kybernetisches Kontrollsystem, das die Handlungsfähigkeit beider Mitwirkenden begrenzt, während es die wechselnden Ergebnisse wiedergibt, die augenscheinlich Teil der Arbeit sind. Die Technologie hat also einen beträchtlichen Einfluss auf das Stück, obwohl spezifische technische Gerätschaften fehlen: Die Tatsache, dass Menschen einer algorithmischen Regelstruktur unterworfen sind, demonstriert das Ausmaß, in dem Maschinendenken die menschliche Kultur

beeinflusst. Gleichzeitig erweist sich diese Regelstruktur als fähig, Innovation und Vorstellungskraft Platz zu bieten und Vorstellungen von mechanischer Simplizität zu relativieren.

SANTIAGO SIERRA
VETERANS OF THE WARS OF ERITREA, KOSOVO AND TOGO FACING THE CORNER, 2014

Ein Kriegsveteran steht mit dem Gesicht zur Wand in einer Ecke des Raumes und reagiert weder auf das Publikum noch beachtet er es. Es handelt sich um eine tiefgreifende und beunruhigende Erfahrung für den Besucher, die Frage aufgeworfen wird, wie Veteranen innerhalb der Gesellschaft behandelt oder nicht behandelt werden sollten.

Der in Spanien geborene Künstler Santiago Sierra setzt in seinen poetischen und oftmals konfrontierenden Kunstwerken Arbeiter als Skulpturen ein. Er greift dabei auf die kunsthistorische Tradition des bezahlten Modells zurück, das oft von der Straße kam, und rekrutierte seine Modelle aus dem Kreis der Unerwünschten und Geächteten – Prostituierte, illegale Immigranten, Arbeitslose und Vertriebene. Arrangiert innerhalb festgelegter Parameter – wie minimalistische Erforschungen von Form – loten Sierras Performances individuelle und soziale Grenzen aus, um so soziale und kulturelle Ungleichheiten aufzuzeigen.

1999 tätowierte Sierra sechs arbeitslosen jungen Männern in Havanna, Kuba, eine permanente schwarze Linie auf den Rücken. Dafür zahlte er jedem Mann 30 US-Dollar. Für die Biennale in Venedig 2001 bezahlte er 133 illegale Straßenverkäufer – Einwanderer aus China, dem Senegal und Bangladesch –, dafür, dass sie ihre Haare blond färbten. 2009 erforschte er in seiner Arbeit

<u>Los Penetrados</u> sexuelle Varianten mittels verschiedener Paarungen von Rasse und Geschlecht. In vielen von Sierras Arbeiten sind die Gesichter der Mitwirkenden nicht erkennbar, indem sie verschwommen oder von der Kamera abgewandt gezeigt werden. So schützt er die Identität der Beteiligten und verleiht ihnen gleichzeitig einen überhöhten symbolischen Status. Anstatt isolierte Individuen zu sein, stehen sie sinnbildlich für eine bestimmte Klasse, ein bestimmtes Geschlecht oder eine bestimmte Kultur, und ihre Handlungen werden, wie auch die des Künstlers, zu politischen und sozialen Stellungnahmen.

Sierra schuf auch eine Reihe von Arbeiten, in denen Individuen und Gruppen in Rückenansicht, den Blick einer nackten Wand zugewandt, fotografiert werden. Die Mitwirkenden an solchen Arbeiten umfassten eine verschleierte weibliche Figur, Gruppen obdachloser Frauen, Wanderarbeiter und selbsternannte Anarchisten. Diese Arbeiten fordern uns dazu auf, über den Kampf all jener nachzudenken, die aus unseren wirtschaftlichen und politischen Systemen herausfallen, jene, die innerhalb existierender Machtstrukturen nicht vertreten sind.

In <u>14 Rooms</u> zeigt Sierra <u>Veterans of the Wars of ERITREA, KOSOVO and TOGO Facing the Corner</u> (2014),[1] eine Arbeit aus dem Bereich der Langzeit-Performance, in der eine Reihe von Kriegsveteranen aus verschiedensten Konflikten der Vergangenheit in den Ecken eines fünf mal fünf Meter großen Raumes mit dem Blick zur Wand stehen. Sie stehen lautlos und unbeweglich, wie im militärischen Einsatz, ohne in irgendeiner Art und Weise auf das Publikum zu reagieren. Von ihren Posten entfernen sie sich nur, wenn sie von einem anderen Veteranen ersetzt werden, der feierlich seinen Platz einnimmt, als handelte es sich um eine Wachablöse.
Die Erfahrung beim Betrachten dieser Arbeit ist tiefgreifend und bewusst beunruhigend. Wir können davon ausgehen, dass Kriegsveteranen aufgrund ihres selbstlosen, vielleicht sogar heldenhaften Einsatzes gewürdigt werden, doch Sierra präsentiert uns Figuren von weitaus größerer Komplexität. Er beschwört Trauma, Schuld und Angst, die inmitten von Mainstream und Militärkultur oft nicht anerkannt werden. Stehen die ehemaligen Soldaten strafweise mit dem Gesicht zur Wand? Warum können wir ihre Gesichter nicht sehen? Was geht in ihren Köpfen vor?

[1] Dieses Projekt wurde zuvor bereits im Rahmen von <u>11 Rooms</u> während des Manchester International Festival in der Manchester Art Gallery, von <u>12 Rooms</u> bei dem Festival der Künste an der RUHRTRIENNALE im Museum Folkwang und im Rahmen von <u>13 Rooms</u> während der 27. Kaldor Public Art Projects in 2013 in Sydney gezeigt.

XU ZHEN
IN JUST A BLINK OF AN EYE, 2005

Eine Person schwebt auf geheimnisvolle Art und Weise in der Luft, eingefroren in Raum und Zeit, den Gesetzen der Physik zum Trotz. Die Arbeit befasst sich mit der Vorstellung vom Körper als Material und mit der Materialität des Körpers und lotet beim Versuch zu verstehen, was wir sehen, die Grenzen physischer und kognitiver Möglichkeiten aus.

Die konzeptgesteuerte Arbeitsweise des produktiven und kontroversen Künstlers Xu Zhen umfasst eine große Bandbreite an Medien und setzt oft auf Humor, Ironie und den ausgeklügelten Einsatz von List. Für das im Rahmen von <u>14 Rooms</u> präsentierte <u>In Just a Blink of an Eye</u> (2005)[1] schwebt ein atmender Körper auf geheimnisvolle Art und Weise in der Luft, eingefroren in Raum und Zeit, den Gesetzen der Physik zum Trotz. Die Arbeit befasst sich mit der Vorstellung von Körper als

Material und mit der Materialität des Körpers und lotet beim Versuch, zu verstehen, was wir sehen, die Grenzen physischer und kognitiver Möglichkeiten aus. Wir warten auf Bewegung, darauf, dass der Performer aufsteht oder weiter fällt, doch stattdessen scheint sich die Zeit unerklärlich zu dehnen, und eine Lösung ist nicht absehbar. In vorhergehenden Wiederholungen der Arbeit, setzte Zhen Mitglieder marginalisierter Gemeinschaften, wie Arbeitsmigranten, ein, um die Performance auszuführen. In diesem Fall wurde das buchstäbliche Schweben zu einer Metapher für den schwebenden zivilrechtlichen Status.

Teil von Zhens Praxis ist die Beleuchtung der Mechaniken von Beobachtung und Wahrnehmung, im Besonderen die fremde Wahrnehmung seines Heimatlandes China. Eine seiner bekanntesten Arbeiten, 8848 – 1.86 (2005), ist ein fiktionaler Dokumentarfilm über die vorgebliche Mount-Everest-Besteigung des Künstlers, wobei sich der Titel auf die Höhe des Berges abzüglich der Größe Xu Zhens bezieht. In der Arbeit schneiden er und sein Team den Gipfel des höchsten Berges der Welt ab, um ihn wie eine Art Trophäe nach China zu bringen. Das ironische Werk wurde tatsächlich in einer Kulisse gefilmt, die sich auf dem Dach von Zhens Atelier in Schanghai befand, und die Installation beinhaltet sowohl die Kletterausrüstung der Expedition als auch den schneebedeckten Gipfel, der triumphierend in einer riesigen tiefgekühlten Vitrine präsentiert wird. Die Arbeit lotet die Grenzen der Leichtgläubigkeit so überzeugend aus, dass der dermaßen verkürzte Mount Everest es tatsächlich auf die Titelblätter schaffte. Durch und über seinen Humor spricht das Werk Chinas aktuelle Tibetpolitik an, die sich weigert, Tibets Kampf um Selbstbestimmung anzuerkennen. In einer nahezu imperialen Kampagne wird sein stolzer Gipfel mitleidslos gekappt.

Zhens Arbeiten werden oft als provozierend und kontrovers beschrieben, veranschaulicht durch das Stück The Starving of Sudan (2008), eine Installation im Long March Space in Peking, die die preisgekrönte Fotografie des Fotojournalisten Kevin Carter von 1993, in der ein Geier ein verhungerndes sudanesisches Kind belauert, neu inszenierte. In Zhens Version war der Geier animatronisch und das Kind (eine bezahlte, von ihrer Mutter beaufsichtigte Schauspielerin) war Teil einer Familie von Immigranten aus Guinea, die in Guanghzou lebte. Die Installation wurde durch die Reaktionen der Besucher komplettiert, von denen viele ihr Handy zückten, um Fotos zu machen. Durch die Miteinbeziehung des Publikums, das in Carters Rolle versetzt wurde, warf Zhens Arbeit komplexe ethische Fragen zur Thematik der Zeugenschaft auf.

[1] Dieses Projekt wurde zuvor bereits im Rahmen von 11 Rooms während des Manchester International Festival in der Manchester Art Gallery, von 12 Rooms bei dem Festival der Künste an der RUHRTRIENNALE im Museum Folkwang und im Rahmen von 13 Rooms während der 27. Kaldor Public Art Projects in 2013 in Sydney gezeigt.

EPILOG

JORDAN WOLFSON
(FEMALE FIGURE), 2014, 2014

Eine animatronische Tänzerin bewegt sich lasziv vor einem großen Spiegel. Sie versucht, Blickkontakt mit dem Betrachter herzustellen, während sie sich gleichzeitig selbst beobachtet, so wie auch das Publikum mit dem eigenen Spiegelbild konfrontiert ist.

Jordan Wolfson gehört zu jener jüngeren Generation von Künstlern, deren Arbeit unabhängig von einem spezifischen Medium anzusiedeln ist. So arbeitet der Künstler in Installationen ebenso wie in Video, Fotografie, Skulptur und Performance. Das Interesse des Amerikaners gilt der Debatte um das Menschsein (condition humaine) in der heutigen Welt und wie wir uns als Bewohner einer Umgebung, die in sich selbst kaum deutbar ist, selber definieren. Den Ursprung bildet bei Wolfson die Technologie, die weniger dazu genutzt wird, kalte, zu reinem Nutzen produzierte Maschinen zu generieren, vielmehr geht es ihm um die Schaffung neuer, „zeitgenössischer" Charaktere. Diese, entsprungen aus einer Welt, die dominiert wird von Kommunikation, Werbung und Marketing, entwickeln sich zu Narrativen, die uns die Sichtweise des Künstlers auf eindrückliche Weise aufzeigen und die uns und unsere Selbstdarstellung zum Thema machen.

Seit 2009 realisierte Wolfson eine Trilogie von Video-Arbeiten, <u>Con Leche</u> (2009), <u>Animation Masks</u> (2011) und <u>Raspberry Poser</u> (2012), die Animation nutzen, um jeweils unterschiedliche Handlungsabläufe wiederzugeben. Dabei bedient er sich nicht nur der Ästhetik von Animation, die an Disney-Zeichnungen erinnern, sondern generiert Erzählungen, die charakteristisch Dokumentationen ähneln. In <u>Con Leche</u> marschieren animierte Diet-Coke-Flaschen, gefüllt mit Milch, in einer Reihe durch die Straßen von Detroit. Die Ansicht der Stadt ist reales Material, während die Cola animiert ist. Produkt wie Szenerie sind aufgeladen durch Marketing und Medienpräsenz, zum einen als „das" Erfrischungsgetränk und zum anderen als die bankrotte Stadt, die zum Zeichen der Armut in den Vereinigten Staaten von Amerika wurde. Globales Produkt steht hier im Widerspruch zum Niedergang einer Stadt, die einst amerikanische Geschichte geprägt hat. Die Arbeit gehört zu jenen psychologisch komplexen Werken Wolfsons, in denen Bilder und Sprache traumgleiche Wiederholungen und Erprobungen erfahren.

Jordan Wolfson präsentiert im Rahmen von <u>14 Rooms</u> seine Installation (<u>female figure</u>) (2014), einen Animatronic Robot, die als letzter Raum wie ein Epilog des Projektes gesehen werden kann. Vor einem großformatigen Spiegel bewegt sich dieser weiblich anmutende Roboter lasziv hin und her, auf und ab. Der Roboter betrachtet sich selber, wie auch der Besucher mit seinem eigenen Spiegelbild konfrontiert wird. Auf diese Weise entsteht, zwar indirekt, eine Kommunikation zwischen den Individuen, den Besuchern, und dem Roboter. Basierend auf der Grundidee von <u>14 Rooms</u>, Performance Arbeiten real zu betrachten, sich tatsächlich visuell mit ihnen auseinanderzusetzen, kann Jordan Wolfsons Arbeit als ein Schritt in die Zukunft gedeutet werden. Wir sind isoliert in diesem Raum, mit uns selbst und mit der Maschine konfrontiert, die mittels Bewegungssensoren in ihren Augen unseren Blickkontakt sucht. Wir betrachten uns, während wir betrachtet werden. Die Arbeit geht in einem sehr expliziten Maße auf unsere Selbstdarstellung ein. Während wir mehr und mehr Bilder von uns selbst ins Internet stellen, nehmen wir nur mal all die „Selfies" von sozialen Netzwerken, repräsentiert der Roboter die technologische Zukunft, die, vom Menschlichen beeinflusst, sich selbst mustert, betrachtet und uns damit konfrontiert. Die Maschine wird zum immer funktionierenden, immer verfügbaren Subjekt einer Gesellschaft der kontinuierlichen Erreichbarkeit. Wolfson erschafft mit (<u>Female figure</u>) 2014 eine Maschine, die Narzissmus auf derart natürliche und körperliche Weise darstellt, dass sie zu einem Spiegel unserer selbst werden kann. Vielleicht genau aus diesem Grund fixiert uns Wolfsons Installation und zieht uns hinein in die Welt des maschinellen Unbewussten, hin zu unseren innersten Ängsten.

ARCHIV

JOHN BALDESSARI
UNREALIZED PROPOSAL FOR CADAVER PIECE, 1970/2011

1970 schlug der Künstler die Präsentation eines Leichnams im Kontext der Ausstellung Information im New Yorker MoMA vor, eine provozierende und herausfordernde Arbeit, die sich damit befasst, wie die Kunstwelt – und die Gesellschaft im Allgemeinen – mit dem Tod umgehen. Es handelt sich um ein nicht realisiertes Projekt, da ethische und juristische Bedenken der Umsetzung nach wie vor entgegenstehen.

John Baldessari ist einer der einflussreichsten Künstler seiner Generation. 1970 regte er eine provozierende und herausfordernde Arbeit an, die sich damit befasst, wie die Kunstwelt – und die Gesellschaft im Allgemeinen – mit dem Tod umgehen. Diese äußerst eindringliche Arbeit bezieht sich auf Andrea Mantegnas Gemälde der Beweinung Christi (um 1490) und auf Marcel Duchamps dreidimensionales Tableau Étant donnés, das dieser erst kurz vor seinem Tod 1968 fertigstellte. Baldessaris Vorschlag, einen Leichnam zu präsentieren, erinnert an Mantegnas realistische Darstellung Christi. Die Betrachter würden durch ein Guckloch eine liegende Figur aus dem gleichen Blickwinkel sehen, wie ihn auch die Arbeiten von Mantegna und Duchamp bieten – von den Füßen aufwärts. Dieser ungewöhnliche Einsatz von Perspektive bringt den Körper dem Betrachter so nahe, dass er eine starke emotionale Reaktion und ein tiefes Gefühl von Pathos hervorruft, da die Realität der eigenen Sterblichkeit in den Vordergrund rückt. Der Leichnam ist jedoch nicht das Thema der Arbeit. Das Werk befasst sich mit der Darstellung von Tod in der Kunst und damit, wie künstlerische Konventionen, so wie Beleuchtung und Inszenierung, eingesetzt werden können, um ästhetische Distanz zu schaffen. Erst durch Bemühungen des Manchester International Festival und der Manchester Art Gallery, konnte durch den Versuch, das Konzept endlich zu realisieren, das Projekt im Kontext von 11 Rooms weiter entwickelt werden. Bis dahin hatte keine Institution ernsthaft versucht, es zu präsentieren. Eine ganze Reihe internationaler Experten und Wissenschaftler im Bereich Pathologie, medizinische Ethik und Recht wurde hinsichtlich der juristischen und ethischen Fragen, die ein solches Werk aufwirft, konsultiert. Dennoch ist es bis jetzt nicht gelungen, die Zustimmung zur Präsentation einer Leiche im Rahmen einer Ausstellung zu erlangen. Es sind allerdings laufende Gespräche mit dem Künstler in Gange und es besteht ein ernsthaftes Bestreben durch das Manchester International Festival, die Manchester Art Gallery, die RUHRTRIENNALE und die Kuratoren, diese wichtige und tiefgründige Arbeit in Zukunft zu verwirklichen. Hunderte von E-Mails und Telefonaten zwischen Festival, Galerie, Ausstellungsmitarbeitern, Kuratoren, dem Atelier des Künstlers und den konsultierten Experten dokumentieren den Prozess bis dato. Diese Dokumentation, die im Zuge von 14 Rooms[1] gezeigt wird, dient als Beleg für die ernsthaften Anstrengungen, die getätigt wurden, um das Konzept auf sensible und respektvolle Art und Weise zu verwirklichen.

[1] Dieses Projekt wurde zuvor bereits im Rahmen von 11 Rooms während des Manchester International Festival in der Manchester Art Gallery, von 12 Rooms bei dem Festival der Künste an der RUHRTRIENNALE im Museum Folkwang gezeigt.

ARCHITEKTUR

HERZOG & DE MEURON

In der gleichen Messehalle wie 14 Rooms hatten wir schon vor ein paar Jahren, 2001, eine temporäre Architekturinstallation realisiert. Damals war es ein Musiksaal für den „Europäischen Musikmonat" – jetzt, 2014 geht es um 14 Räume, in denen 14 Künstler Liveperformances für kleine Gruppen aufführen. Dieses spektakuläre künstlerische Projekt hat schon in verschiedenen Städten stattgefunden und soll auch in den kommenden Jahren jeweils in einer anderen Stadt weitergeführt werden. 13 Räume waren es letztes Jahr, 14 Räume sind es dieses Jahr und 2015 werden es 15 Räume sein. Die temporäre Installation dieser Räume war stets etwas anderes, das Grundmodell, 5 mal 5 Meter Grundfläche, 3,5 Meter Raumhöhe, eine Türe, keine Fenster, stets das Gleiche. In den früheren Jahren waren die Räume jeweils wie eine Streusiedlung oder ein Haufendorf frei im Raum verteilt mit gässchen- oder platzartigen Zwischenräumen. Wir haben uns für eine strenge, lineare Anordnung entschieden mit zwei parallelen, weiß gestrichenen Fassaden mit jeweils sieben Türen. An die beiden Schmalseiten stellen wir je eine Spiegelwand, welche die weißen Fassaden mit den Türöffnungen optisch unendlich verlängert. Statt 14 Türen scheint es doppelt so viele zu geben oder dreimal oder viermal so viele. Die 14 ist eine zufällige Zahl, nächstes Jahr sind es bereits 15 und im Jahr 2100 sind es vielleicht 100.

Der Ort und die Stadt, in der die Ausstellung stattfindet, ist auch nicht relevant bei dieser temporären Installation, die weißen Wände und Türen könnten irgendwo stehen – im Gegensatz des HIER und JETZT der Begegnung von Kunstwerk und Besuchern. Die temporäre Installation ist deshalb sehr abstrahiert, beinahe wie eine typologische Skulptur – eine breite, platzartige Gasse wie in einer südamerikanischen, chinesischen oder europäischen Kleinstadt. Nur der hölzerne Türgriff, mittels dessen der Besucher den Raum betritt, ist von Tür zu Tür leicht verschieden. Es sind 14 verschiedene, hölzerne, digital gefräste Türklinken, die sich auf den ersten Blick wenig unterscheiden, aber etwas anders anfühlen.

Der einzige Hinweis zu einem konkreten Ort, ergibt sich aus dem Blick nach oben, wo sich statt des Himmels die archaisch anmutende Trägerkonstruktion der ältesten, erhaltenen Messehalle in Basel auftut.

ESSAY
PASSING SHOW

DAVID MALOUF

In einem seiner letzten und großartigsten Gedichte thematisiert John Keats die griechische Urne, die sein Leitbild für transzendente Kunst ist:

Thou, silent form, dost tease us out of thought,
As doth eternity: Cold Pastoral!
When old age shall this generation waste,
Thou shalt remain ...

Du Stille, die uns aus dem Denken schreckt
Wie Ewigkeit: Du kaltes Hirtenspiel!
Wenn uns das Alter fortrafft eines Tags,
Sollst du bestehn, ...[1]

Die besondere Eigenschaft, die er dem Kunstwerk zuschreibt, ist seine Konstanz im

Verlauf der Zeiten und der Handlungen und Generationen von Menschen, und dieses Beharren auf „Beständigkeit" geht zurück auf die Anfänge des ästhetischen Denkens. Shakespeare stellt die Behauptung auf, dass das, was bloß geschrieben (gedruckt) wäre, die Dauerhaftigkeit von Metall oder Stein aufwiese:

Not marble, not the gilden monuments
Of princes shall outlast my powerful rhyme, . . .

Kein Marmorbild, kein fürstlich Monument,
Soll diese mächtigen Reime überleben, . . .[2]

und geht damit auf einen Dichter zurück, der 1500 Jahre früher lebte, nämlich Horaz, der in Ode 30, Buch III schreibt:

Exigi monumentum aere perennius
Regalique situ pyramidum altius

Errichtet habe ich ein Monument, das Erz überdauert
Das den majestätischen Bau der Pyramiden überragt[3]

Die Behauptung – im Übrigen eine andauernde – ist die, dass das Kunstwerk, also das in Marmor gehauene, in Bronze gegossene, in Stein errichtete, das gemalte oder als Mosaik auf eine Wand aufgebrachte Objekt, nicht der Zeit und der „Gelegenheit" angehört, sondern dem, was Yeats in <u>Sailing to Byzantinum</u> als „the artifice of eternity", also das Kunstwerk oder den Kunstgriff der Ewigkeit bezeichnete.

Natürlich gab es von Beginn an auch eine andere Form künstlerischer Tätigkeit, die keinen solchen Anspruch stellte. Im Gegensatz zu Objekten, die fest im Raum existieren, in einer ewig währenden Präsenz, die der Zeit widersteht, gibt es auch darstellende oder performative Kunstwerke, die ausschließlich der Zeit und einer, wenn auch unendlich wiederholbaren Gelegenheit angehören. Sie sind abhängig von der unmittelbaren Energie und Interaktion von Schauspielern, Sängern, Tänzern, Musikern, die diese produzieren, aber auch von der Chemie des jeweiligen, ganz speziellen Publikums, wie auch von räumlichen und sonstigen Gegebenheiten des Ortes (etwa drinnen oder draußen). Keine Darstellung ist feststehend oder perfekt – was einen großen Teil ihrer Anziehungskraft ausmacht – oder gefeit vor Zufällen oder Risiken, und da man nicht – wie zum Objekt im Raum – erneut auf sie zurückkommen kann, bleibt sie – und das macht ihre ganz besondere Eindringlichkeit aus – nur als Spur in der Erinnerung (oder den Lebenserinnerungen) jener bestehen, die vor Ort waren, um sie zu erfahren.

Später, im 16. Jahrhundert, wurden solche Spuren von Darstellung auch in einigen Werken der anderen, nicht-performativen Art, ausfindig gemacht, zum Beispiel als Pinselstriche, als Zeichen des Handelns und der Präsenz, in venezianischen Gemälden sowie bei Velázquez und Rubens, später auch in der Pleinairmalerei der Impressionisten. Grundsätzlich galt jedoch die Unterscheidung von hergestellten oder dargestellten Werken bis ins frühe 20. Jahrhundert als Orthodoxie. Hergestellte Werke galten stets als das einzig Wahre und genossen eindeutig das höhere Ansehen.

Tatsächlich waren Maler, Bildhauer und Architekten jedoch oft in Genres tätig, die „zufällig" und ephemer waren: mittelalterliche Festwagen und Prozessionen, die bürgerliche oder religiöse Feierlichkeiten zelebrierten, die Triumphbögen und Tableaux, die Renaissancefürsten willkommen hießen, später auch Bühnenbilder, wie jene, die Inigo Jones für höfische Maskenspiele oder Ballettaufführungen schuf, aber auch die Verwandlungsszenen der Barockoper. Bernini schuf im Jahr 1638 die außergewöhnliche Inszenierung der Überflutung Roms, mit der Enthüllung zweier Gruppen von Publikum, zweier

„Theater", die einander wie in einem Spiegel gegenüberstanden, und Jacques-Louis David organisierte auf dem Höhepunkt der Terrorherrschaft, zur Feier der Tage des Revolutionskalenders gewaltige Festivitäten im Freien. Künstler unterschieden jedoch weiterhin zwischen Gelegenheitskunst und Kunst, die überdauern sollte. Berninis Cornaro-Kapelle, die theatralisch sein mag und deren Effekt von Augenblick und Illusion abhängt, nimmt ihren Platz in einem Theater der Ewigkeit ein – das ist ihr einziger Zweck. Die verschiedenen Generationen der Familie Cornaro, die als Beobachter der <u>Verzückung der heiligen Theresa</u> die Logen an beiden Seiten des Altars bevölkern, bestehen aus Marmor und sind in einem einzigen Augenblick der Gegenwart eingefroren. Sie sind stets zu betrachten wie auch das Schauspiel der Heiligen selbst, das gewissermaßen „fixiert" ist, da die heilige Theresa und die Engel in einem Moment der Ewigkeit vor ihnen schweben. Sogar Pozzos enormes Deckengemälde in der Kirche Il Gesù, das insofern zufällig ist, als es sich erst völlig erschließt, wenn ein einzelner Betrachter sich an einem bestimmten Punkt auf dem Kirchenboden befindet, wurde eigentlich geschaffen, um zu überdauern.

Die Herausforderung dieser Orthodoxie und der Hierarchie, auf der sie basiert, beginnt eigentlich erst 1916 mit den dadaistischen Inszenierungen im Cabaret Voltaire und später im Odeon, zunächst in Zürich, später dann in Paris, Berlin und andernorts. Die riesigen Spektakel, die Albert Speer in den 1930er-Jahren für die Nationalsozialisten arrangierte, fanden ihren Höhepunkt 1934 in Nürnberg und wurden von Leni Riefenstahl gewissermaßen auf Film „konserviert". In den 1960er-Jahren kamen die zahlreichen Installationen und Happenings dazu, dann zunehmend auch Arbeiten wie Christos Verhüllungen von Orten und öffentlichen Gebäuden, die Galerie-Performances von Gilbert & George, und – lokal begrenzt – von Mike Parr und Ken Unsworth, aber auch Deborah Warners <u>The Angel Project</u> beim Perth Festival 2000.

Ein großer Teil dessen, was die Kunst der Gegenwart aktuell ausmacht, läuft vorhergegangenen Orthodoxien zuwider. In Einklang mit einem Ausblick und einer Empfindsamkeit, die in Unmittelbarkeit und Präsenz etwas erkennen, das wesentlicher für die Kunst ist als das, was feststehend und permanent ist – „das Unvollkommene", um Wallace Stevens zu zitieren, das „so heiß in uns ist" – haben zeitgenössische Künstler Zufälligkeit, Performance, Schauspiel, aber auch Witz, Humor, Qual, Provokation, Affront und das Pathos von Vergänglichkeit und Irrtum aufgegriffen, um der Welt gegenüber wahrhaftiger zu sein, als dies in älteren Wahrheiten der Fall war. Sie laden uns ein – wie sie uns auch in die vierzehn Räume einladen, die die jüngste Zusammenarbeit zwischen Fondation Beyeler, Art Basel und dem Theater Basel ausmachen –, die Räume, die sie schaffen, in Besitz zu nehmen und zu Spielern und Betrachtern zu werden – bisweilen auch zu beidem –, die mit ihrer Anwesenheit die gebotenen Gelegenheiten erweitern und zu einem lebendigen Theater machen.

[1] Übersetzung Mirko Bonné.
[2] Übersetzung Friedrich Bodenstedt, 1866.
[3] Übersetzung Frieder von Ammon.

BIOGRAFIEN

MARINA ABRAMOVIĆ
**GEBOREN 1946 IN BELGRAD.
LEBT IN NEW YORK.**

Im Jahr 2014 hat Abramović Ausstellungen im CAC Malaga, Kistefos Museet, Oslo, und in der Serpentine Gallery in London geplant. Gleichzeitig plant sie die Eröffnung des Institute for the Preservation of Performance Art (MAI) in New York im Jahr 2015. Im Jahr 2012 wurde der Dokumentarfilm, Marina Abramović: <u>The Artist ist Present</u>, auf dem Sundance Film Festival uraufgeführt und hat seither große Aufmerksamkeit und Anerkennung erhalten. 2011 war Abramović Thema einer großen Retrospektive im Garage Center for Contemporary Culture in Russland und nahm an <u>The Life and Death of Marina Abramović</u>, der bejubelten Re-Imagination von Abramovićs Biografie durch den visionären Regisseur Robert Wilson teil. Sie war das Thema von <u>The Artist is Present</u>, einer großen Retrospektive im Museum of Modern Art in New York, 2010. Für ihre außergewöhnliche Videoinstallation und Performance <u>Balkan Baroque</u> erhielt Abramović bei der Biennale von Venedig 1997 den Goldenen Löwen. Ihre Werke waren in zahlreichen internationalen Großausstellungen wie der Biennale von Venedig 1997 und 1976 sowie der documenta in Kassel 1992, 1982 und 1977 zu sehen.

ALLORA & CALZADILLA

JENNIFER ALLORA: GEBOREN 1974 IN PENNSYLVANIA. LEBT IN SAN JUAN.
GUILLERMO CALZADILLA: GEBOREN 1971 IN HAVANNA. LEBT IN SAN JUAN.

Allora & Calzadilla haben an zahlreichen Ausstellungen, Biennalen und Events in Museen auf der ganzen Welt teilgenommen, wie zum Beispiel an der documenta 13 in 2012. Im Jahr 2011 haben sie die Vereinigten Staaten auf der Venedig Biennale repräsentiert. Eine Auswahl an Einzelausstellungen umfasst die Präsentationen in 2013 in der Fondazione Nicola Trussardi, Mailand und 2012 im Indianapolis Museum of Art. Weitere Stationen waren 2011 im Museum of Modern Art, New York, 2009 im National Museum of Art, Oslo, und in der Temporären Kunsthalle, Berlin; 2008 im Haus der Kunst, München, und im Stedelijk Museum, Amsterdam; 2007

im San Francisco Art Institute, in der Kunsthalle Zürich, in der Renaissance Society der University of Chicago, in der Serpentine Gallery, London, in der Whitechapel Gallery, London, sowie im Center for Contemporary Art Kitakyushu; 2006 im Palais de Tokyo, Paris, und im Dallas Museum of Art; 2004 im Institute of Contemporary Art, Boston.

ED ATKINS

GEBOREN 1982 IN OXFORD. LEBT IN LONDON.

2014 finden Einzelausstellungen seiner Werke im Palais de Tokyo, Paris, in der Kunsthalle Mainz – mit Bruce Nauman – und in der Serpentine Gallery, London, statt. Zu Atkins jüngsten Einzelausstellungen gehörten Präsentationen in der Chisenhale Gallery, London, im MoMA PS1, New York, in der Julia Stoscheck Collection, Düsseldorf und in der Kunsthalle Zürich. Er nahm an der Biennale von Venedig wie auch an der Biennale von Lyon teil, ebenso an den Gruppenausstellungen <u>Teen Paranormal Romance</u>, The Renaissance Society, Chicago (2014); <u>Speculations on Anonymous Materials</u>, Fridericianum, Kassel (2013–2014); und <u>Frozen Lakes</u>, Artist Space, New York (2013).

DOMINIQUE GONZALEZ-FOERSTER

GEBOREN 1965 IN STRASSBURG. LEBT IN PARIS UND RIO DE JANEIRO.

Dominique Gonzalez-Foerster bereitet augenblicklich eine bevorstehende Ausstellung im Centre Pompidou in Paris vor. Zuvor hatte sie ihre Arbeiten bereits in größeren Präsentationen gezeigt, wie in <u>SPLENDIDE – HOTEL</u>, Palacio de Christal, Parque del Retiro, organisiert vom Museo Nacional Centro de Arte Reina Sofia, Madrid (14. März bis 31. August 2014), <u>Cloud Illusions I Recall</u> (eine

Zusammenarbeit mit Cerith Wyn Evans), Irish Museum of Modern Art, Dublin (2013), M.2062 (Scarlett), Museum of Kyoto, Japan (2013), T.451, in der Tensta Konsthall und der Asplund Bibliothek, Stockholm (2012), chronotopes & dioramas, Dia Art Foundation, New York (2009) und TH.2058 im Rahmen der Unilever Series, in der Turbine Hall der Tate Modern in London (2008), Expodrome, Musée d'Art Moderne de la Ville de Paris/ARC, Paris (2007), Multiverse, Kunsthalle Zürich (2004).

DAMIEN HIRST

GEBOREN 1965 IN BRISTOL.
LEBT IN LONDON, DEVON UND GLOUCESTERSHIRE.

Seit 1987 war Damien Hirst in mehr als achtzig Einzelausstellungen und zweihundertfünfzig Gruppenausstellungen auf der ganzen Welt vertreten und Gegenstand von mehr als fünfundzwanzig Monografien. 1995 wurde er mit dem begehrten Turner Prize ausgezeichnet. 2012 zeigte die Tate Modern mit Damien Hirst eine bedeutende Retrospektive, die fünfundzwanzig Jahre seiner Karriere umspannte.

JOAN JONAS

GEBOREN 1936 IN NEW YORK.
LEBT IN NEW YORK.

Für den amerikanischen Pavillon der Biennale von Venedig (2015) wird Jonas eine neue Arbeit entwickeln und eine Retrospektive ihrer Arbeiten wird 2014 im Hangar Bicocca, Mailand stattfinden. 2009 erhielt Jonas in New York den Lifetime Achievement Award des Guggenheim Museums. Sie präsentierte zahlreiche Arbeiten und Performances in Museen und Galerien in der ganzen Welt, etwa im Museum of Modern Art, New York, im Museu d'Art Contemporani de Barcelona, im Centre d'Art Contemporain, Genf, im Castello di Rivoli, Turin, im Museo Nacional Centro de Arte Reina Sofia, Madrid, im Witte de With, Rotterdam, im Whitney Museum of American Art, New York, und in der Tate Modern, London. Bedeutende Retrospektiven von Jonas' Arbeiten fanden 2003 im Queens Museum, New York, 2000 in der Galerie der Stadt Stuttgart und 1994 im Stedelijk Museum, Amsterdam, statt. Sie nahm an der Biennale von Venedig 2009 teil sowie an sechs der prestigeträchtigen documenta-Ausstellungen in Kassel.

LAURA LIMA

GEBOREN 1971 IN MINAS GERAIS.
LEBT IN RIO DE JANEIRO.

Einzelausstellungen von Limas Arbeiten fanden im Museu de Arte da Pampulha, Belo Horizonte, Brasilien, in der Galeria Luisa Strina, São Paulo, im Hardcore Art Contemporary Space, Miami, in der Casa França Brasil, Rio de Janeiro, im Museo Universitario Arte Contemporáneo (MuAC), Mexico City, im Chapter Arts Centre, Cardiff und im Migros Museum für Gegenwartskunst, Zürich statt. Sie bereitet Einzelausstellungen vor für das Bonnefanten Museum, Maastricht, die Bonniers Konsthall, Stockholm und das Lilith Performance Studio, Malmö. Ihre Arbeiten wurden in Gruppenausstellungen und Festivals weltweit gezeigt, darunter 2011 die 11. Biennale von Lyon, 2009 die 7. Biennale von Mercosul, in Porto Alegre, und die Biennale von São Paulo 2006 und 1998. Gewinnerin des BACA Laureate, Niederlande, 2014.

BRUCE NAUMAN

GEBOREN 1941 IN FORT WAYNE, INDIANA.
LEBT IN NEW MEXICO.

Nauman vertrat die Vereinigten Staaten bei der Biennale von Venedig (2009) und die Ausstellung erhielt den Goldenen Löwen für den Besten Pavillon. Zu seinen Einzel- und

Gruppenausstellungen gehören: <u>A Rose Has No Teeth</u>, Berkeley Art Museum, Castello di Rivoli und Menil Collection (2007/08), <u>Raw Materials</u>, Turbine Hall der Tate Modern (2004), <u>Bruce Nauman</u> – eine bedeutende Retrospektive, organisiert vom Walker Art Center und dem Hirshhorn Museum, die auch ins Museo Nacional Centro de Arte Reina Sofia, Madrid, ins Museum of Contemporary Art, Los Angeles, ins Museum of Modern Art, New York, und ins Kunsthaus Zürich reiste (1993–1995) –, <u>Bruce Nauman 1972–1981</u>, Rijksmuseum Kröller-Müller, Otterlo, und Staatliche Kunsthalle Baden-Baden (1981), <u>Bruce Nauman: Work from 1965 to 1972</u>, organisiert vom Los Angeles County Museum of Art und vom Whitney Museum of American Art, New York (1972/73), sowie die documenta in Kassel (1968).

OTOBONG NKANGA
**GEBOREN 1974 IN KANO, NIGERIA.
LEBT UND ARBEITET IN ANTWERPEN.**

Nkanga hat an zahlreichen internationalen Ausstellungen teilgenommen und ihre jüngsten Präsentationen und Performances umfassen: <u>In Pursuit of Bling</u>, 8. Berlin Biennale (2014), <u>Glimmer Fragments in Symposium: Landing and Confessions</u>, Stedelijk Museum, Amsterdam (2014), <u>Foreign Exchange (or the stories you wouldn't tell a stranger)</u>, Weltkulturen Museum, Frankfurt am Main (2014), <u>Taste of a Stone: Itiat Esa Ufok</u>, 11. Biennale von Sharjah, Vereinigte Arabische Emirate (2013), <u>Contained Measures of Shifting States in Across the Board: Politics of Representation</u>, The Tanks in der Tate Modern, London (2012), <u>Contained Measures of a Kolanut in Tropicomania: The Social Life of Plants</u>, Bétonsalon, Paris (2012), <u>Contained Measures of Tangible Memories: Indigo Regina</u>, L'Appartement 22, Rabat, Marokko (2012), <u>Inventing the World: The Artist as Citizen</u>, Biennale von Benin, Co-

tonou, Benin (2012), ARS 11, Kiasma Museum of Contemporary Art, Helsinki (2011).

ROMAN ONDÁK
**GEBOREN 1966 IN ŽILINA.
LEBT IN BRATISLAVA.**

Einzelausstellungen von Ondáks Arbeiten waren zu sehen in der Common Guild, Glasgow und im Museo Nacional Centro de Arte Reina Sofía, Madrid (2013), im Deutschen Guggenheim, Berlin, im K21, Düsseldorf, sowie im Musée d'Art Moderne de la Ville de Paris (2012), im Kunsthaus Zürich (2011) und im Museum of Modern Art, New York (2009). Er nahm an Gruppenausstellungen an folgenden Orten teil: Palais de Tokyo, Paris, und Fundación Jumex, Mexico City (2013), Centre Pompidou, Paris (2014 und 2010) und documenta 13, Kassel (2012), an der Biennale von Venedig (2003, 2009 und 2011), der Berlin Biennale (2010), dem Hamburger Bahnhof, Berlin (2009) und der Tate Modern, London (2007).

YOKO ONO
**GEBOREN 1933 IN TOKIO.
LEBT IN NEW YORK.**

Yoko Ono war mit zahlreichen Ausstellungen in Museen vertreten, darunter Wanderausstellungen, die vom Museum of Modern Art, Oxford und der Japan Society, New York, organisiert wurden. Erst kürzlich wurde <u>Yoko Ono: Half-A-Wind Show: A Retrospective</u> in der Schirn Kunsthalle, Frankfurt am Main, im Louisiana Museum of Modern Art, Humlebæk, Dänemark, in der Kunsthalle Krems, Österreich, und im Guggenheim Museum, Bilbao, gezeigt (2013–2014). 2009 erhielt Yoko Ono bei der Biennale von Venedig einen Goldenen Löwen für ihr Lebenswerk, eine Anerkennung ihres lebenslangen Strebens nach der Freiheit zu handeln, zu erschaffen und zu lieben.

TINO SEHGAL
**GEBOREN 1976 IN LONDON.
LEBT IN BERLIN.**

Einzelausstellungen von Sehgals Arbeiten fanden bereits auf der ganzen Welt statt. 2014 hatte er seine erste große Schau in Brasilien im Centro Cultural Banco do Brasil in Rio de Janeiro. 2013 gewann Sehgal den Goldenen Löwen als Auszeichnung für den Besten Künstler bei der 55. Biennale von Venedig. Seine bisher größte Arbeit, These associations, wurde für die Turbine Hall der Tate Modern als abschließendes Kapitel der Unilever Series (2012) konstruiert. Für die documenta 13 präsentierte er This variation (2012). Das New Yorker Guggenheim Museum widmete Sehgal eine umfassende Einzelausstellung (2010), die sowohl vom Publikum als auch von der Kritik gefeiert wurde. 2005 vertrat er Deutschland bei der Biennale von Venedig.

SANTIAGO SIERRA
**GEBOREN 1966 IN MADRID.
LEBT IN MADRID.**

2013 fand seine erste große Retrospektive in der Kunsthalle Tübingen und in den Deichtorhallen Hamburg – Sammlung Falckenberg statt. 2010 führte Sierra das Kaldor Public Art Project 22 in der Queensland Art Gallery | Gallery of Modern Art in Brisbane aus. Er entwickelte eine Reihe unverwechselbarer Projekte im öffentlichen Raum und erhielt 2008 den Auftrag für eine Installation in der Turbine Hall der Tate Modern. Sierras Arbeiten wurden in zahlreichen Einzel- und Gruppenausstellungen auf der ganzen Welt gezeigt, darunter im MoMA PS1 in New York, dem KW Institute for Contemporary Art in Berlin, der Ikon Gallery in Birmingham und der Kunsthalle Wien. Er nahm an der Moscow Biennale von 2007 und der Sharjah Biennial von 2005 teil. Sierra schuf anlässlich der Biennale von Venedig 2005 eine neue Arbeit für das Arsenal und vertrat Spanien bei der Biennale 2003.

XU ZHEN
**GEBOREN 1977 IN SCHANGHAI.
LEBT IN SCHANGHAI.**

Zhens Arbeiten waren in zahlreichen internationalen Ausstellungen vertreten, darunter: Tate Liverpool (2007), MoMA PS1, New York (2006), das Mori Art Museum, Tokio (2005) und die Biennale von Venedig (2001 und 2005). 2004 gewann er die Auszeichnung für den Besten Künstler bei den China Contemporary Art Awards. Auch bei der Guangzhou Triennial, The Real Thing: Contemporary Art from China (2005) stellte er aus. 2012 fanden Einzelausstellungen von Zhens Werken in der Contemporary Art Gallery, Vancouver, und im Muzeum Montanelli, Prag, statt. 1998 war er Mitbegründer des einflussreichen, von Künstlern geführten Raumes BizArt Art Center in Shanghai und 2009 gründete er die MadeIn Company (eine Anspielung auf das allgegenwärtige „Made in China") mit einer Gruppe von Experten, die die Begriffe von Autorschaft, Ethik und Handel, in erster Linie das Kunstsystem betreffend, erforschen.

JORDAN WOLFSON
**GEBOREN 1980 IN NEW YORK.
LEBT IN NEW YORK UND LOS ANGELES.**

Seine Arbeit wurde international ausgestellt, unter anderem im Centre Pompidou (2010), in der Contemporary Art Gallery, Vancouver (2010), im CCA Wattis Institute, San Francisco (2009), auf der Torino Triennale, Turin (2008), im Swiss Institute Contemporary Art, New York (2008), in der Tate Modern, London (2007), auf der Moscow Biennale (2007), in der Serpentine Gallery, London (2006) und in der Kunsthalle Zürich (2004).

JOHN BALDESSARI
GEBOREN 1931 IN NATIONAL CITY.
LEBT IN SANTA MONICA.

Im Jahr 2013 hatte Baldessari seine erste Solo-Show in Russland im Garage Museum of Contemporary Art in Moskau. Zwischen 2012 und 2011 stellte er unter anderem im Museum Mönchehaus, Goslar, Van Abbemuseum, Eindhoven, Stedelijk Museum, Amsterdam und MCASD, La Jolla aus. Baldessari schuf auch Kaldor Public Art Project 23, Your Name in Lights (2011), in dem 100.000 Teilnehmer fünfzehn Sekunden Ruhm aus glänzenden Lichtern über dem Australian Museum in Sydney erhielten. Eine große Retrospektive seines Werks, Pure Beauty, war in der Tate Modern in London zu sehen (2009/10), ehe sie weiter ins Museu d'Art Contemporani de Barcelona (2010), in das Los Angeles County Museum of Art (2010) und das Metropolitan Museum of Art, New York (2010/11) zog. Ältere Ausstellungen umfassten eine Präsentation in den Kunstmuseen Krefeld: Museum Haus Lange, Krefeld (2009). 2005 fand eine zweiteilige Retrospektive von Baldessaris Werken im Museum Moderner Kunst Stiftung Ludwig in Wien (Works 1962–1984) und im Kunsthaus Graz (Works 1984–2005) statt. Seine Arbeiten wurden bei der Biennale von Venedig (1997 und 2009) gezeigt, bei der Carnegie International, Pittsburgh (1985/86), der Whitney Biennial, New York (1983), sowie bei der documenta, Kassel (1972 und 1982).

KLAUS BIESENBACH
GEBOREN 1966 IN KÜRTEN.
LEBT IN NEW YORK.

Klaus Biesenbach ist Direktor des MoMA PS1 und Chief Curator at Large des Museum of Modern Art, New York, wo er bahnbrechende Retrospektiven wie Kraftwerk (2012) und Marina Abramović (2010) kuratierte. Davor gründete er das Kunst-Werke (KW) Institute for Contemporary Art in Berlin (1991) und die Berlin Biennale (1996). 2006 wurde er zum gründenden Chief Curator des neuen Department of Media des MoMA ernannt und 2009 wurde er gründender Chief des Department of Media and Performance Art. Unter den zahlreichen Ausstellungen, die Biesenbach international organisierte oder mitorganisierte, waren: Korakrit Arunanondchai, MoMA PS1 und MoMA (2014), Christoph Schlingensief, Berlin und New York (2013 und 2014), EXPO1, New York und Rio de Janeiro (2013 und 2014), Cyprien Gaillard (2013), Antony and the Johnsons (2012), Rania Stephan (2011), Ryan Trecartin (2011), Francis Alÿs (2011), Laurel Nakadate (2011), 100 Years of Performance im Garage Center for Contemporary Culture, Moskau (2010), Andy Warhol: Motion Pictures (2010), Performance 9: Allora & Calzadilla (2010), Greater New York (2010, 2005 und 2000), Performance 4: Roman Ondák (2009), Performance 1: Tehching Hsieh (2009), Jonathan Horowitz und 100 Years (version 2) (2009), Pipilotti Rist (2008), Doug Aitken (Auftrag zusammen mit Creative Time; 2007), Fassbinder: Berlin Alexanderplatz (2007), Douglas Gordon und Into Me/Out of Me (2006), Regarding Terror: The Red Army Faction Exhibition (2005), die Shanghai Biennale (2002), Mexico City: An Exhibition about the Exchange Rate of Bodies and Values (2002), Disasters of War (2000), Hybrid Workspace bei der documenta (1997), Projected Images bei der Biennale von Venedig (1995) und 37 Rooms (1992), in Berlin.

HANS ULRICH OBRIST
GEBOREN 1968 IN ZÜRICH.
LEBT IN LONDON.

Hans Ulrich Obrist ist Co-Direktor der Serpentine Galleries, London. Davor war er Kurator des Musée d'Art Moderne de la Ville de Paris. Seit seiner ersten Schau <u>World Soup (The Kitchen Show)</u> im Jahr 1991 hat er mehr als zweihundertfünfzig Ausstellungen kuratiert. Gegenwärtig ist Obrist der Gastkurator der Ausstellung Gerhard Richters an der Fondation Beyeler, Riehen. 2013 war er Mitkurator der folgenden Ausstellungen der Serpentine Galleries: <u>Sturtevant: Leaps Jumps and Bumps</u>, <u>Adrián Villar Rojas: Today We Reboot the Planet</u>, <u>Marisa Merz</u>, <u>Wael Shawky</u> und <u>Jake and Dinos Chapman: Come and See</u>. Zudem war gemeinsam mit Klaus Biesenbach und den Kaldor Public Art Projects Mitkurator von <u>13 Rooms</u>, von <u>Do It 20th Anniversary Show</u> im ICI New York, zusammen mit dem laufenden Projekt <u>Art of Handwriting</u>, das auf Instagram und Twitter stattfindet.

Außerdem ist Obrist Mitbegründer von <u>89+</u>, einem langfristigen internationalen Forschungsprojekt, das mehrere Plattformen mit einschließt und als Abbildung der vor 1989 oder danach geborenen Generation ist. 2009 wurde Obrist zum Honorary Fellow des Royal Institute of British Architects (RIBA) ernannt und 2011 erhielt er den CCS Bard Award for Curatorial Excellence. Obrist hat an akademischen Einrichtungen und Kunstinstitutionen weltweit gelehrt und ist beitragender Herausgeber zahlreicher Magazine und Zeitschriften. Zu Obrists jüngsten Publikationen gehören: <u>A Brief History of Curating</u>, <u>Project Japan: Metabolism Talks with Rem Koolhaas</u>, <u>Everything You Always Wanted to Know About Curating But Were Afraid to Ask</u>, <u>Do It: The Compendium</u>, <u>Think Like Clouds</u>, <u>Ai Weiwei Speaks</u>, <u>Sharp Tongues – Loose Lips – Open Eyes – Ears to the Ground</u>, sowie aktuelle Bände seiner <u>Conversation Series</u>.

HERZOG & DE MEURON

Herzog & de Meuron ist eine Partnerschaft, die von fünf Seniorpartnern geführt wird – Jacques Herzog, Pierre de Meuron, Christine Binswanger, Ascan Mergenthaler und Stefan Marbach.

1978 gründeten Jacques Herzog und Pierre de Meuron ihr gemeinsames Büro in Basel. Die Partnerschaft ist über die Jahre gewachsen. Christine Binswanger ist seit 1994 Partnerin, es folgten Robert Hösl und Ascan Mergenthaler (2004), Stefan Marbach (2006), David Koch und Markus Widmer (2008), Esther Zumsteg (2009), Andreas Fries (2011), Vladimir Pajkic (2012), Jason Frantzen und Wim Walschap (2014). Ein internationales Team von 38 Associates und rund 360 Mitarbeitern arbeitet an Projekten in Europa, Nord- und Südamerika. Herzog & de Meuron hat Büros in Basel, Hamburg, London, Madrid, New York und Hongkong. Das Spektrum an Gebäuden, welche Herzog & de Meuron entworfen haben, reicht vom kleinmaßstäblichen Privathaus bis zur großmaßstäblichen städtebaulichen Studie. Viele ihrer Projekte sind renommierte öffentliche Einrichtungen, wie Tate Modern in London (2000) und deren Weiterentwicklung (2016) sowie das Nationalstadion in Peking, China (2008). Herzog & de Meuron haben aber auch bedeutende private Projekte, wie Fabrik-, Büro- und Wohngebäude, realisiert. In zahlreichen Projekten haben Herzog & de Meuron mit Künstlern zusammengearbeitet, herausragende Beispiele dieser Praxis sind die Zusammenarbeit mit Rémy Zaugg und Thomas Ruff sowie jüngst mit dem chinesischen Künstler Ai Weiwei. Mit ihm haben Herzog & de Meuron bereits für einen Beitrag zur Architekturbiennale Venedig 2008 und 2012 beim Serpentine Gallery Pavilion in den Londoner Kensington Gardens zusammengearbeitet.

Dem Büro wurden zahlreiche Auszeichnungen verliehen, darunter 2001 der Pritzker Architecture Prize sowie 2007 die RIBA Royal Gold Medal und der Praemium Imperiale.

Jacques Herzog und Pierre de Meuron sind seit 1994 (und 1989) Gastprofessoren an der Graduate School of Design (GSD), Harvard University, USA. Sie sind seit 1999 Professoren an der Eidgenössischen Technischen Hochschule Zürich (ETH) – Fakultät für Architektur, Netzwerk Stadt und Landschaft, und Mitbegründer des ETH Studio Basel / Institut Stadt der Gegenwart.

14 ROOMS

PATRONS

CO-CURATORS
Klaus Biesenbach
Hans Ulrich Obrist

DIRECTORS
Sam Keller – Fondation Beyeler
Marc Spiegler – Art Basel
Georges Delnon – Theater Basel

EXECUTIVE PRODUCER
Andreas Bicker

PRODUCERS
Marc Bättig
Ann-Christin Rommen

ASSOCIATE CURATOR
Samuel Leuenberger

ARCHITECTURE
Jacques Herzog
Pierre de Meuron
Andreas Fries
Maria Ángeles Lerín Ruesca
Liliana Filipa Amorim Rocha
Francisca Moura

PRODUCTION TEAM
Xenia Fünfschilling
Michael Gass
Gregor Hausmann
Thomas Puggl
Todd Uzel

GRAPHIC DESIGN
Christian Boros
Stefan Becker
Helen Dengler

PUBLICATIONS MANAGER
Renata Catambas

PROJECT TEAM FONDATION BEYELER
Mirjam Baitsch
Angelika Bühler
Martin J.-M. Burkhardt
Elena DelCarlo

PROJECT TEAM ART BASEL
Gerda van den Bergh
Laura Blagho
Magdalena Dysli
Dorothee Dines
Camilla Hall
Myrta Holinger
Nicola Hüll
Lucy Knight
David Meier
Roman Schlager
Thomas Schmidiger

PROJECT TEAM THEATER BASEL
Michael Bellgardt
Danièle Gross
Tina Keller

EDUCATIONAL PROGRAMME FONDATION BEYELER
Regine Bungartz
Sibilla Caflisch
Kaye Kirst
Annelie Knust
Marcel Leeman
Joshua Monten
Janine Schmutz
Patricia Wolfensberger

CHOREOGRAPHER
Rebecca Davis,
with the assistance of Michael Iles

The private patrons supporting the project represent the upper echelon of major international collectors and philanthropists:

Cristina Bechtler
Denise and Rolando Benedick
Joop van Caldenborgh
Ulla Dreyfus-Best
Nicoletta Fiorucci
Wendy Fisher
Francesca von Habsburg
Maja Hoffmann
Guillaume Houzé
Pierre de Labouchere
Michael Ringier
Tony Salamé
Gerd Schepers
Franz Wassmer
Dasha Zhukova

With the generous support of:

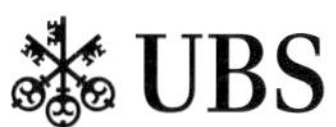
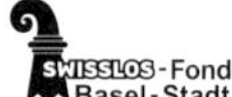
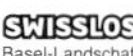

FONDATION **BEYELER** **Art|Basel** **THEATER BASEL**

PERFORMERS

Marina Abramovic and Joan Jonas:
Glynis Ackermann, Andrea Boller,
Linda Elsner, Naima Ferré, Janne
Gregor, Micaela Kühn, Ina Sladic,
Mirjam Spoodler, Anna Tenta
Allora & Calzadilla: Sandra Amato,
Marie Alexis, Bilonda Bukasa,
Alexander Carillo, Julia Diendorf,
Magnhild Fossum, Nikos Frakou,
Ursina Natalia Früh, Angela Pina
Ganzoni, Diane Gemsch, Myriam Gurini,
Elisabeth Marika Henry, Caroline
Jüngst, Roxane Kalt, Raisa Kröger,
Kathrin Knöpfle, Marketa Kuttnerova,
Laura Lienhard, Lindi Mlaba,
Marcella Moret, Muhammed Kaltuk,
Reut Nahum, Paola Napolitano,
Gabriela Pereira, Camille Queval,
Romana Ramer, Lady Luz Diaz de
Riedo, Lisa Rykena, Oliver Schmid,
Ingrid Schorscher, Simon Walti
Ed Atkins: Ralph Engelmann, Stephan
Grossenbacher
Damien Hirst: Melanie/Stephanie
Hausberger, Leonard/Raphael Kadid,
Luce/Anouk Pieters, Lina/Nadja Samira
Laura Lima: Lisa Simpson, Fabienne
Meier
Bruce Nauman: Jean-Nicolas Dafflon,
Guillaume Guilherme, Jeremy Nedd,
Oliver Pfulg, William Sanchez
Otobong Nkanga: Nathalie Bikoro,
Stéphanie Büchler, Hedat
Habtemariam, Donna Hastings, Aleta
Hayes, Bona König, Keishera James
Roman Ondák: Samuel Moor, Joel von
Mutzenbecher, Tony Osborne, Benedikt
Wyss
Santiago Sierra: Thomas Häsle,
Carsten Herrmann, Marcel
Houndjadan, Shaun Knight, Estifanos
Tesfagergisch
Xu Zhen: Patricia Flores, Anna
Regenass, Regina Flavia Schweizer,
Laura Schläpfer, Thomas Stocker
(May 2014)

ACKNOWLEDGMENTS

14 Rooms, Fondation Beyeler, Art Basel
and Theater Basel would like to thank:

The Artists and all Performers;

The Manchester International
Festival, the Manchester Art Gallery,
the international Arts Festival
RUHRTRIENNALE 2012–14, Kaldor
Public Art Projects and their
remarkable teams, whom greatly
assisted us to present this project in
Basel and to develop this book;

John Kaldor, Bettina Kaldor, Sophie
Forbat and Emma Pike, for their
extremely generous contribution of
documentation and content for this
book;

MoMA PS1, New York and The
Serpentine Galleries, London;

David Zwirner Gallery for their
extraordinary support for Jordan
Wolfson's project;

Afrikanischer Verein Region Basel;

and also Giuliano Argenziano, Katrina
Ashour, Rita Barracha, Molly Berman,
Rahel Blättler, Katrin Boskamp-
Priever, Eva Bottega, Branwen Jones,
Allison Brainard, L. M. Catambas,
Alienor de Chambrier, Freddie
Checkettts, Paul Clay, Polyanna
Clayton-Stamm, Rebecca Cleman,
Tricia Coleman, Sarah Degen, Alexia
Dehaene, David Dempewolf, Camille
Desprez, Constance Dominique, Anna
Drozda, Kessler Elisabeth, Oman Erika,
David Freilach, Rashel George, John
Glass, Heiner Goebbels, Lukas Haller,
Louise Hojer, Mundy Janina, Eileen
Jeng, Julia Joern, Amy Klement, Birte
Kreft, Bettina Kubli, Julia Lammer,
Debbie Lamming, Laurel Lange,
Carolyn Lazard, Nick Lesley, Mark
Linga, Sibylle Luig, Shayna McClelland,
Rachael McNabb, Maria Mitsch, Connor
Monahan, Clare Morris, Reuben Moss,
Juliet Myers, Dorothea Neweling,
Irene Perrin, Marietta Piekenbrock,
Alex Poots, Renate Pöppel, Karin
Prätorius, Sidney Russel, Amanda
Sachs-Mangold, Andre Schallenberg,
Laura Schleussner, Jason Schmidt,
Fabian Schöneich, Max Shackleton,
Michael Sirianni, Tas Skorupa, Gian
Enzo Sperone, Vajra Spook, Christine
Stäcker, Cristina Steingräber,
Stephanie Stockbridge, Leah Talatinian,
Alexandra Titze-Grabec, Lorraine Two,
Katie Vine, Meredith Walker, Angela
Westwater, Anja Wolsfeld, Xenia Wörle,
David Zwirner.

PARTNERS

HISTORY

FONDATION BEYELER, ART BASEL, AND THEATER BASEL
An intense collaboration between three of the most prominent cultural entities in Basel allows the city to present the exhibition 14 Rooms. In 2009 the same three partners already produced Il Tempo del Postino, co-curated by Hans Ulrich Obrist and Philippe Parreno.

Fondation Beyeler in Riehen is the most visited art museum in Switzerland and home to an outstanding collection of works by internationally recognized artists from classic modern and contemporary art.
fondationbeyeler.ch

Art Basel stages the art world's three premier modern and contemporary art shows, held annually in Basel, Miami Beach, and Hong Kong. Since its inception in 1970, it has been a driving force in supporting the development of great galleries and their artists, by promoting the ever-expanding patronage of the visual arts worldwide.
artbasel.com

Theater Basel is the city's municipal theater, with a mixed program of dance, music, and theater encompassing classics and contemporary productions.
theater-basel.ch

14 ROOMS is co-curated by Klaus Biesenbach and Hans Ulrich Obrist. First presented as 11 Rooms in July 2011 as part of the Manchester International Festival, the exhibition was commissioned by the Manchester International Festival, the International Arts Festival RUHRTRIENNALE 2012–14, and the Manchester Art Gallery. It was later presented at the International Arts Festival RUHRTRIENNALE in 2012 as 12 Rooms and then in 2013 by Kaldor Public Art Projects at Pier 2/3 in Sydney's Walsh Bay as 13 Rooms, the 27th Kaldor Public Art Project.
14rooms.net

MANCHESTER INTERNATIONAL FESTIVAL is the world's first festival of original, new work and special events and takes place biennially, in Manchester, UK. The Festival launched in 2007 as an artist-led, commissioning festival presenting new works from across the spectrum of performing arts, visual arts, and popular culture, and works with co-commissioning partners around the world to present new productions internationally.
mif.co.uk

MANCHESTER ART GALLERY is one of northwest England's most popular cultural venues. Located in the heart of the city, it hosts a world-renowned collection of fine and decorative art and, in addition to outstanding collection displays, delivers an ambitious program of temporary exhibitions that bring world-class historic, modern, and contemporary art to the city.
manchestergalleries.org

RUHRTRIENNALE is the international arts festival hosted by the Ruhr metropolitan area. The venues are the region's outstanding industrial monuments, transformed each year into spectacular sites for music, fine art, theater, dance, and performance.

At the events center, contemporary artists seek a dialogue with industrial spaces and across disciplines.
ruhrtriennale.de

MUSEUM FOLKWANG, founded in 1902, soon developed into one of the most important museums of modern and contemporary art in the world with an outstanding collection of nineteenth-century art and classic modernism, painting after 1945, photography, and posters. A distinctive feature is also its collection of ancient and non-European art. The collection activity and exhibition program of the Museum Folkwang includes all artistic media, bringing their most important exponents to Essen, Germany.
A new building by David Chipperfield Architects opened in 2010.
museum-folkwang.de

KALDOR PUBLIC ART PROJECTS has now for forty-five years created groundbreaking projects with international artists in public spaces, changing the landscape of contemporary art in Australia with projects that resonate around the world. In 2013, Kaldor Public Art Projects presented 13 Rooms in Australia as the 27th project in the series. Ambitious new architecture transformed a historic pier in Sydney and an innovative suite of talks, programs, and events was presented alongside the exhibition. 13 Rooms included twelve international artists and Australian participants Clark Beaumont. It was a landmark event for Sydney and received both critical acclaim and record attendance.
kaldorartprojects.org.au

CREDITS

TEXTS CREDITS
Curators in Conversation (Sydney, 2013) and Curators in Conversation (Basel, 2014), © Klaus Biesenbach, Hans Ulrich Obrist. Marina Abramović, Damien Hirst, Xu Zhen, © Talia Linz (TL), 27th Kaldor Public Art Project. Allora & Calzadilla, Joan Jonas, Laura Lima, Roman Ondák, Santiago Sierra, © Sophie Forbat (SF), 27th Kaldor Public Art Project. Ed Atkins, © Ed Atkins (ED). Dominique Gonzalez-Foerster, Bruce Nauman, Otobong Nkanga, Yoko Ono, © Samuel Leuenberger (SL). Tino Sehgal ,© Tino Sehgal (TS). Jordan Wolfson, © Fabian Schöneich (FS). John Baldessari, © Fiona Corridan (FC) and Mary Beth Whittingstall (MBW) at Manchester International Festival and Manchester Art Gallery, Marietta Piekenbrock (MP) and Dorothea Neweling (DN) at the International Arts Festival RUHRTRIENNALE 2012–14, and Renata Catambas (RC). Herzog & de Meuron, © Herzog & de Meuron (H&dM). Passing Show, © David Malouf.

IMAGE CREDITS & COURTESIES
All images from 11 Rooms are courtesy Manchester City Galleries. All images from 12 Rooms are courtesy of RUHRTRIENNALE 2012-14. All images from 13 Rooms are courtesy Kaldor Public Art Projects.

Pp. 27, 31, 33 (bottom), 49, 63, 65 (top right), 65 (below), 73, 79: Photo Jamie North. © Jamie North / Kaldor Public Art Projects; pp. 29, 51, 53, 89 (bottom): Photo Jörg Baumann. © Jörg Baumann / RUHRTRIENNALE 2012–2014; p. 33 (top), 47, 75 (both), 89 (top): Photo Alan Seabright. © Alan Seabright / Manchester City Galleries; pp. 35–37: Courtesy of Ed Atkins; pp. 39, 41: Courtesy of Dominique Gonzalez-Foerster; pp. 43, 45 (top): Photo Jamie North; pp. 45 (bottom): Photo Jens Nober; pp. 55, 57: Courtesy of Bruce Nauman, Sperone Westwater Gallery and Electronic Arts Intermix (EAI), New York; pp. 59, 61: Courtesy of Otobong Nkanga; pp. 67, 69: Courtesy of Yoko Ono; p. 69: Photo David Behl; © David Behl and Yoko Ono. Courtesy of Yoko Ono; p. 77: Courtesy of Xu Zhen; p. 79: Photo Howard Barlow. © Howard Barlow / Manchester City Galleries; pp. 83–85: Courtesy of Jordan Wolfson and David Zwirner, New York / London; p. 87: Courtesy of John Baldessari; pp. 93–95: Courtesy of Herzog & de Meuron.

PORTRAITS CREDITS & COURTESIES
Marina Abramović: Photo Marco Anelli. Courtesy the artist; Allora & Calzadilla: Photo Marion Vogel. Courtesy the Artists; Ed Atkins: Photo by Ed Atkins. Courtesy the Artist; Dominique Gonzalez-Foerster: M.2062 (Edgar Allan Poe), Le Palais de Tokyo, Paris 2013. Photo by Giasco Bertoli. Courtesy the Artist; Damien Hirst: Photo Anton Corbijn. Courtesy the Artist; Joan Jonas: Photo L. Barry Hetherington. Courtesy the Artist; Laura Lima: Photo Bernardo Ortiz. Courtesy the Artist; Bruce Nauman: Photo Jason Schmidt. Courtesy the Artist and Sperone Westwater, New York; Otobong Nkanga: Photo Wim van Dongen. Courtesy the Artist; Roman Ondák: Photo Adam Ondák. Courtesy the Artist; Yoko Ono: Photo Matthu Placek. Courtesy the Artist; Tino Sehgal: Courtesy the Artist; Santiago Sierra: Courtesy Estudio Santiago Sierra; Xu Zhen: Photo by Thomas Fuesser. Courtesy the Artist; Jordan Wolfson: Photo Andreas Laszlo Konrath. Courtesy David Zwirner, New York / London; John Baldessari: Photo Hedi Slimane. Courtesy the Artist; Klaus Biesenbach: Photo Casey Kelbaugh. Courtesy Art Basel; Hans Ulrich Obrist: Photo Casey Kelbaugh. Courtesy Art Basel; Herzog & de Meuron: (left to right) Senior Partners Christine Binswanger, Ascan Mergenthaler and Stefan Marbach, with Pierre de Meuron and Jacques Herzog. Photo Tobias Madörin. Courtesy Herzog & de Meuron.

IMAGE CREDITS
© 2014 for the reproduced works of Marina Abramović, Bruce Nauman, and Santiago Sierra: ProLitteris, Zurich © 2014 for the reproduced works of Damien Hirst: Damien Hirst and Science Ltd. All rights reserved. ProLitteris, Zurich © 2014 for the reproduced works of Allora & Calzadilla, Ed Atkins, John Baldessari, Dominique Gonzalez-Foerster, Joan Jonas, Laura Lima, Otobong Nkanga, Roman Ondák, Yoko Ono, Jordan Wolfson, and Xu Zhen: the artists.

COLOPHON

This book was published on the occasion of the exhibition 14 Rooms, curated by Klaus Biesenbach and Hans Ulrich Obrist, presented by Fondation Beyeler, Art Basel, and Theater Basel at Hall 3 of Messe Basel, Basel, 14–22 June 2014

EDITORS
Renata Catambas
Samuel Leuenberger

CONTRIBUTORS
Ed Atkins, Klaus Biesenbach, Renata Catambas, Sophie Forbat, Greta Granderath, Herzog & de Meuron, Samuel Leuenberger, Talia Linz, David Malouf, Dorothea Neweling, Hans Ulrich Obrist, Marietta Piekenbrock, Fabian Schöneich, Tino Sehgal, Marc Spiegler

COPYEDITING/PROOFREADING
Vajra Spook, Xenia Fünfschilling

TRANSLATIONS
Amy Klement, Alexandra Titze, Catherine Schelbert (for Herzog & de Meuron)

GRAPHIC DESIGN
BOROS
Stefan Becker, Helen Dengler

PAPER
Profibulk, 150 g/m²

PRODUCTION
Christine Stäcker, Hatje Cantz

REPRODUCTIONS
Weyhing digital, Ostfildern

PRINTING
Offsetdruckerei Karl Grammlich GmbH, Pliezhausen

BINDING
Gert Schallenmüller GmbH & Co. KG, Stuttgart

PUBLISHED BY
Hatje Cantz Verlag
Zeppelinstrasse 32
73760 Ostfildern
Germany
www.hatjecantz.com
A Ganske Publishing Group company

Fondation Beyeler
Baselstrasse 101
4125 Riehen / Basel
Switzerland
www.fondationbeyeler.ch

Art | Basel
MCH Swiss Exhibition (Basel) Ltd.
Messeplatz 10
4005 Basel
Switzerland
www.artbasel.com

Theater Basel
Elisabethenstrasse 16
4051 Basel
Switzerland
www.theater-basel.ch

ISBN 978-3-7757-3915-3

Printed in Germany